AMONG
Australia's
PIONEERS

AMONG
Australia's
PIONEERS

Chinese Indentured Pastoral Workers on
the Northern Frontier 1848 to c.1880

Margaret Slocomb

BALBOA.
PRESS
A DIVISION OF HAY HOUSE

Balboa Press books may be ordered through booksellers or by contacting:

Balboa Press
A Division of Hay House
1663 Liberty Drive
Bloomington, IN 47403
www.balboapress.com.au
1 (877) 407-4847

Printed in the United States of America.

ISBN: 978-1-4525-2480-1 (sc)
ISBN: 978-1-4525-2481-8 (e)

Balboa Press rev. date: 07/17/2014

The Green Leaf's Attachment to the Root

Don't ask me where to go,
my heart is attached to you.
Don't ask me where to go,
my passions go with you.
I am one of your green leaves,
My root is deep in your soil.
Waving farewell in spring breeze,
I leave here and go far away.
Whichever cloud I dwell upon,
my gaze is always on you.
If I sing in the wind,
the song is also for you.
So don't ask me where to go,
My road is full of memory.
Please bless me and I'll bless you.
This is the green leaf's attachment
to the root.

Wang Jian

(Inscription on Memorial Stone, Overseas Chinese Museum, Xiamen.)

Contents

Part I
Supply and Demand

Part II
Among the Pioneers

Part III
Love and Fortune

Tables, Figures and Illustrations

Tables

Figures

Illustrations

List of Abbreviations

BA	*Burnett Argus*
J. P.	Justice of the Peace
JRAHS	*Journal of the Royal Australian Historical Society*
MBC	*Moreton Bay Courier*
MBFP	*Moreton Bay Free Press*
MC	*Maryborough Chronicle*
MLC	Member of the Legislative Council
MPM	*Mount Perry Mail*
P. M.	Police Magistrate
SMH	*Sydney Morning Herald*

Preface

This book aims to add to the body of academic knowledge concerning post-slavery indentured labour that was recruited mainly in Asia and the South Pacific for employment in the colonies of Western imperialist powers as recently as the end of the Second World War. The focus is a narrow one and deals with the experiences of around two hundred Chinese labourers (out of a total number of a little more than three thousand men spread throughout eastern Australia) who were imported by European, mainly British, squatters to provide cheap, reliable labour on the pastoral runs of two northern frontier districts of colonial New South Wales between 1848 and 1853. It examines their working conditions during the five-year indenture period and also traces the lives of several of the men who, at the end of their contract, chose to remain in those districts which had become familiar to them and in which, perhaps, they regarded themselves as pioneer immigrants.

The preliminary archival research concerning the recruitment, arrival and deployment in Australia of the Chinese indentured labourers had already been conducted for two doctoral theses: Wang Singwu's *The Organization of Chinese Emigration 1848-1888: With Special Reference to Chinese Emigration to Australia* (San Francisco: Chinese Materials Center, Inc., 1978) and Maxine Darnell's thesis of 1997 entitled "The Chinese Labour Trade to New South Wales 1783-1853: an exposition of motives and outcomes" (unpublished, University of New England). The latter study which concerns the Northern Districts of the colony of New South Wales provided invaluable appendices that gave some of the indentured workers' names, their employers, and locations of contract. Without either of these foundation studies, the present work would have taken many more years of detailed research and expense. My gratitude and respect for these historians' work is sincerely felt.

Although there have been other studies of Chinese immigration and adaptation in Australian colonial history, particularly those by Cathie May, Shirley Fitzgerald, Eric Rolls, and Barry McGowan, to my knowledge, apart from the two theses already mentioned, there are none that deal specifically with Chinese immigration that was unrelated to the gold discoveries. The immigration experience of the Chinese indentured pastoral workers was so different from that of the Chinese diggers that they demand a history of their own.

The contiguous districts of Wide Bay and Burnett in what is now Queensland developed from the co-dependency of port and productive hinterland, and even today that alliance is recognized by the familiar reference to the hyphenated Wide Bay-Burnett region. The Wide Bay district had a more diversified economy and a more transient population than the Burnett which was solidly pastoral. There were Chinese indentured labourers in the Wide Bay but the local press, the *Chronicle*, took little interest in them individually. In the Burnett, on the other hand, the editor of the *Argus* delighted in reporting the crimes and escapades of the Chinese shepherds regularly and at length. Both newspapers, along with the leading metropolitan papers, also assumed responsibility through their editorials and reporting styles for shaping local attitudes towards the relatively large number of young, single, Chinese males in these remote districts. Colonial newspapers were an invaluable source of information.

Of concern to me during the writing of this book was making use of terms that are regarded today as politically and culturally inappropriate: reference to "coloured" labour, in particular, could not be avoided. There were European indentured labourers on Burnett sheep runs, but, for the most part, the squatters sought cheap and submissive labour that could be reliably supplied and easily accessed. They also preferred labour from sources where its real value on the harsh and often dangerous Australian frontier was unknown, even unknowable, to the immigrant workers. Once a five-year contract was signed, their wage rates were incontestable and a master's authority was firmly backed by labour law. The near-perfect sources for this sort of labour were India, China and the South Sea Islands and this labour was officially referred to as "coloured". Other sensitive terms are those of "white" and "black" with reference to Europeans and indigenous Australians and the relationship between them. I have also used "Kanakas" and "Celestials" which may be regarded by some descendants of South Sea Islander and Chinese labourers as disrespectful.

Accusations of slavery and racism haunt this episode of early Queensland history when several experiments with indentured coloured labour were conducted, all of them occurring in the Wide Bay-Burnett. These indentured labourers were never slaves, even though some employers' behaviour and attitudes towards them belied this. An indenture was a legal contract with prescribed time and wage limits. The colonial justice system, for the most part, upheld the basic tenets of the laws that provided a small measure of protection to the worker under contract. Many abuses occurred, but justice was also served. The presence and practice of racism with regard to these imported labourers, however, is far more difficult to defend or even to demonstrate.

I argue that frontier Australian society in the years before, say, 1874 or 1875, was racist specifically with regard to indigenous Australians. The history of first contact has been thoroughly researched, explored and recorded by historians and there is no question that the most abhorrent violence, perhaps genocide, was perpetrated against indigenous Australians who stood in the way of European colonisation. The destruction of Aboriginal society in the Wide Bay-Burnett was as swift, thorough and painful as it was elsewhere on the rapidly moving frontier of colonial Australia. Some Burnett squatters had a reputation for openness, even kindness, towards the indigenous people of that district, but this was at best an occasional and paternalistic response to the ultimately futile efforts of Aboriginal resistance to white dominion. European behaviour towards the Indian Hill Coolies, the Chinese Celestials and the South Sea Islanders was essentially different from the treatment of indigenous Australians.

It is difficult to reconcile the abusive treatment of Chinese labourers during the indenture period, abuse that was not less than torture in some instances, with the genuine support and general accommodation that was accorded them in the post-indenture period. There is no evidence, for instance, that the Chinese pastoral labourer, once he was free of his bond, was paid less than any other labourer hired on Burnett runs. There were cases of malpractice that were heard in the courts, but one imagines that the same employer tactics applied to all itinerant workers, not only towards Chinese workers. It can be said with confidence that no Chinese worker ever knowingly and willingly accepted less pay than was awarded to a European with equal skill in the same job. Furthermore, there are recorded instances of townspeople coming together to petition authorities or to submit character references to the court when it was felt that Chinese residents in their town were being treated unfairly. For example, Chinese seeking naturalisation during a difficult period after 1858 when legislators attempted to bring down discriminatory laws were given written support by the leading citizens of the Burnett to secure their certificates. Some former Chinese indentured labourers married European women, ran successful businesses, bought and sold property, and acquired personal wealth and status as local officials.

During the period under study, despite the general observance of British law and its institutions, it is safe to say that the colonial societies of the Wide Bay and Burnett districts were ruled by and for the interests of class; status and property took precedence even over race where social ranking was concerned. An indentured Chinese labourer, however, failed the test of social inclusion with relation to all points of difference from the dominant group and was left exposed to abuse and exploitation.

The presence of unfairly paid and physically abused coloured labourers in their frontier communities where justice was dispensed by local magistrates who were themselves employers of this sort of labour made liberal commentators in the colony uneasy. These educated men were highly conscious of the fact that only the law separated employment of this sort of cheap labour from slavery. Even on the frontier, the white population was familiar with the anti-slavery debate and with the issues of the American Civil War. In the Northern Districts, there was also the recent memory of the cruel system that had operated at the Moreton Bay penal settlement. It was the consciousness of both slavery and transportation that protected the Chinese from even worse abuse. What all the coloured indentured servants suffered, however, was scorn, from which there was no protection.

Scorn for the underpaid is not synonymous with racism but it is easily confused with racism when the underpaid belong to a visible "other" group. That the Chinese indentured labourers (as the Indians before them and the South Sea Islanders later) were forced to accept wages far below the standard rate was hardly their fault and like most assertive immigrants throughout history, they forcibly resisted this abuse, and were then punished for their resistance. Once free of the unfair conditions of contract, however, they were allowed to be as competitive as any other members of the community and were entitled to the same rewards that were as important socially as they were financially.

This does not mean that all Wide Bay and Burnett district residents warmly welcomed the Chinese and other non-Europeans who lived among them. Xenophobia was as rife in colonial Australia as it was elsewhere, but it was kept in check by British colonial policy and the law which offered naturalisation to aliens and free movement to peoples of the Empire and those from friendly states. After the mid-1850s, along with calls for self-government, however, came demands for the exclusion of immigrants who were not white. The arguments were typically shallow and prejudiced, but while temporary restrictions were placed on the immigration of Chinese by each of the three self-governing colonies of eastern mainland Australia, their force of implementation was moderated by the disapproval of the British Colonial Office. After 1874, with the formation of the first shearers' association and the first stirrings of nationalism, the call for a White Australia became a loud and sustained demand. The excuse for this shameless policy of racial discrimination is best remembered today as the need to protect workingmen's wages from the competition of cheap labour represented by Chinese immigration. The experiment with Chinese indentured labour in the Wide Bay and Burnett districts that commenced in 1848 had already proved this argument to be false. Their labour was cheaply bought only through deception and force on the part of the employers, not by any willingness on their own part to value their labour less than others. Reason and example, however, were superfluous to the debate as populist politicians and sensationalist print media, then as now, shaped the national identity.

Many people contributed to the writing of this book. The works of all historians cited in the bibliography and the careful selection and collection of these and specific district histories in regional and state libraries, along with easy public access to colonial newspapers and official records allow independent historians like myself to investigate those corners of the past that have a bearing on the big picture. The Wide Bay-Burnett constitutes only a small part of the Australian continent, but in the mid-nineteenth century it staged dramatic events that may be regarded as formative of the Australian character. I am grateful to all the librarians who gave me professional, courteous assistance. Local amateur historians also gave me access to their considerable knowledge and resources. Pat Smith of Mount Perry Shire Family History provided constant support and encouragement throughout this project; I also owe a debt of thanks to Cynthia Berthelsen of the Gayndah Historical Society, Trevor Power of the Banana Shire Historical Society, Buddy and Lynne Thomson of Boondooma Homestead, and Ada Simpson of the Ration Shed Museum at Cherbourg. Ray Poon, chairman of the Chinese-Australian Historical Association, generously shared his own research and reference materials with me. Carole Channer, another descendant of an Amoy shepherd, gave me the initial impetus to investigate the topic and to write the history.

PART I

Supply and Demand

Nothing obscures our social vision as effectively as the economistic prejudice. So persistently has exploitation been put into the forefront of the colonial problem that the point deserves special attention... Yet, it is precisely this emphasis put on exploitation which tends to hide from our view the even greater issue of cultural degeneration. If exploitation is defined in strictly economic terms as a permanent inadequacy of ratios of exchange, it is doubtful whether, as a matter of fact there was exploitation. The catastrophe of the native community is a direct result of the rapid and violent disruption of the basic institutions of the victim (whether force is used in the process or not does not seem altogether relevant). These institutions are disrupted by the very fact that a market economy is foisted upon an entirely differently organized community; labor and land are made into commodities, which, again, is only a short formula for the liquidation of every and any cultural institution in an organic society.

Karl Polanyi[1]

CHAPTER 1

Indentured Labour Migration in the Nineteenth Century

On May 14, 1833, when the British colonial secretary, Edward Stanley, rose to present to parliament the ministerial proposals to end slavery, more than eight hundred thousand African slaves still laboured on the sugar plantations of the West Indies and other possessions of the British Empire.[2] From 1788 until the abolition of the trade in 1807, British ships alone had transported thirty-eight thousand slaves across the Atlantic each year as part of a sordid trafficking in persons that had persisted for more than two centuries. When the law came into force on August 1, 1834, this workforce was nominally free; however, under the new system of apprenticeship, a supposedly interim arrangement of bonded labour given as a sop to the planters who were demanding compensation for their loss of property, the former slaves were still subject to the strict regimen of the plantations. Despite the confidence the planters had in the political power they were able to wield, they realized that they had to look for a more permanent method of supplying their labour needs. A solution was found in the indenture system with workers sourced mainly from India but also from China and other parts of the world affected by the era of new imperialism. In the terminology of the time, they were Asiatic or "coloured" labourers.

The British law abolishing slavery that was followed by similar laws enacted throughout the French, Dutch, and Spanish empires did not initiate the use of indentured labour in the colonies. In fact, in the preceding two hundred years, the worst years of the trans-Atlantic African slave trade,

1

more than half of all European migrants to the New World colonies had been indentured servants.[3] Even in the plantations of the Caribbean, white indentured servitude had preceded slavery.[4] There can be no doubt, however, that the new indentured migrants of the nineteenth century were recruited, first of all, to replace the labour of the slaves who were liberated in the Americas throughout the 1830s. Others were employed in colonies such as New South Wales (eastern Australia) when the cessation of convict transportation to that British possession threatened the supply of cheap labour to the pastoral industry.[5] Later in the century, after most of the northern districts of that colony, including the Wide Bay and Burnett districts, had separated from New South Wales and created the new colony of Queensland, indentured Melanesian workers from various islands in the South Pacific constituted the labour force on new sugar plantations where neither slaves nor convicts had ever been engaged.

Indentured Labour Migration

"Indenture" eludes fine definition. It is an ancient institution, as is labour migration in general. Stanley Engerman describes this form of contract labour migration as

> One mode along a spectrum of forms of migration, permanent and temporary, whose purpose is to move populations from one area to another, and, possibly, to influence (or limit) the selection of occupations after arrival. It combines characteristics of free and involuntary migration, and the relative components of freedom and coercion have long been a subject of controversy.[6]

This rather broad definition may apply equally to indentured migration, both before and after the abolition of slavery. For the place and period under study, that is, a colony of the British Empire in the third quarter of the nineteenth century, an indentured worker is understood to have been a labourer, usually "coloured," who was recruited and bound to an overseas employer by a contract, presumed to have been voluntarily entered into before departure to the place of work, for a specified period of time, ranging between three and seven years, in return for stipulated remuneration and conditions that may or may not have included return travel to the point of recruitment on completion of the contract. It was the existence of this legal or quasi-legal contract that set the trade apart from other forms of labour migration in the period under review.

The so-called new indentured migrants who were employed in the outposts of the British and other European empires in the nineteenth century, post-slavery, differed from those of earlier centuries in several respects. The most obvious of these was their place of origin: they came mainly from India, and then China, and various Pacific Islands but after 1834, Africans, including former slaves, also indentured themselves, as did Japanese and Javanese.[7] Europeans and some North Americans continued to indenture themselves but their numbers were greatly reduced during this period as other forms of migration offered them greater opportunity. This new form of labour migration was also highly age and sex selective, being single, young, adult, and male, although some Indian labourers were accompanied by their wives, who were also indentured servants, and even their children. The system was also regulated, efficient, and cost-effective in terms of recruitment, transportation, and assignment. This was especially the case with regard to colonial Indian labour migration overseas, where the indentured labour trade amounted to a regular industry that was carefully supervised by the bureaucratic colonial administration there. In fact, Douglas Hay and Paul Craven refer to the indenture system as "industrial immigration."[8]

Despite the regular efficiency with which indentured labour flowed around the world between 1834 and the end of the Second World War, it remained a highly controversial business. Although the new labour trade was supposed to represent a modern and rational market for the buying and selling of free labour, in the older literature, according to Hay and Craven, an indenture had always been considered to be "a mark of unfreedom."[9] The implications of this, for the employer and the receiving society in general, must surely have carried over to the new system, despite the official terms of engagement and the imprimatur of the British Colonial Office or its European equivalent.

In spite of popularly held opinion, however, an indentured worker was not a slave, even though what the employers sought was not just cheap, reliable labour but a workforce that was also meek, docile, and submissive, terms that abound in the literature on the topic and that are surely more applicable to slave than to free labour. Despite the common perceptions, there were important distinct differences from slavery: at the end of the contract period, at least until restrictive immigration policies were introduced, the indentured worker was free to return home, settle or re-engage on his own terms of hire; children born during the contract period were certainly not the property of the employer; and, in case of coercion and abuse by his employer, he had, in theory at least, the same rights of appeal to British justice as other colonial residents.

Nevertheless, in practice, there were abuses at all stages in the process that were reminiscent of the slave trade. Recruitment, in some cases, was barely different from kidnapping; the sea voyages were cramped, hazardous, and not uncommonly undertaken in those same vessels latterly used to trans-ship African slaves; and in the often remote areas to which the indentured workers were assigned, recourse to justice or even some measure of protection under the law was rarely accessible. Despite the contract, the indentured worker did not choose his place of work or his occupation; those matters were non-negotiable and usually determined by the employer's manager or overseer to whom he was consigned and with whom he did not share a common language. An agreeable workplace was purely a matter of chance, and a contract was little guarantee of freedom of action because, as Hay and Craven point out, "Freedom of contract does not mean freedom to abandon the contract."[10] The only alternative to complete submission to a given situation, absconding, was deemed a criminal act under law, and penal sanctions applied. The law defined and prescribed the indentured worker's situation to the extent that these authors regard indenture as "an important and varied form of the socio-legal relation of master and servant," and one that had more to do with the unequal power relations between employer and employee than with the rational exchange of labour on a free market.[11]

A Socio-Legal Relationship

Master and Servant laws drafted and implemented in the British colonies were used as a powerful means of enforcement of the terms of contract and as an equally powerful deterrent to indentured workers' claims for fairer terms and conditions. The workers' market bargaining advantage should have been high. After all, following the abolition of slavery and the almost simultaneous cessation of convict transportation, demand for cheap, reliable labour was at a premium throughout the developing colonial world, and in some instances, most notably on the dangerous and violent northern frontier of white settlement in distant New South Wales, it was practically unobtainable. Given such high demand, workers of the same linguistic and ethnic background in any one location might have been expected to organize themselves and bargain collectively for higher wages and better conditions. However, although records of magistrates' benches were full of individual acts of disobedience, negligence, and even attempted suicide by these new indentured labourers, organized strikes or other forms of collective action taken by them were rare and short-lived. Hay and Craven argue that it was the severity of consecutive Master and Servant acts, in conjunction with other laws on vagrancy, public order, access to land, and so on that were "crucial in constructing masters' coercion" and eliminating resistance.[12] Master and Servant legislation was, they claim, "a catalogue of constraints and disincentives" that created firm boundaries around the exercise of workers' freedom of action.[13]

The laws, in fact, were used to fashion the kind of workforce that was preferred by the employers and the joint stock companies that owned or leased the plantations, the mines, and the vast pastoral properties that represented imperial wealth and power. In the British colonies, Master and Servant legislation applied to all workers, not only to those on indenture, but indentured labour was used to maintain the employer's advantage in any contest over wages and conditions. In Hay and Craven's opinion,

> Master and Servant law was carefully designed to create labour markets that were less costly, more highly disciplined, less "free" than markets in which the master's bargain was not assisted by such terms. Even where indentured labour coexisted with a more open labour market, employers were well aware that the effect of a bounded sector under more coercive sanctions was to depress wages in the wider labour market as well.[14]

Indentured labourers were therefore in the invidious position of wedge between capital and free labour. Even more than skin colour and language differences, this fact set them apart from the existing regular workforce and earned its further contempt, because, according to Peter Corris, "[T]he migrant labourer [is] without honour where he works, for his function is to do what the people there will not do."[15]

In some respects, from a socio-legal perspective at least, the experiences of all indentured immigrant workers were similar; in other ways, they differed significantly, not only from place to place, job to job, but also according to the degree of support they received from outside. In the colonial Australian context, the Indian workers were protected to a large extent by regulations imposed by the colonial administration in India that carried the weight of the British Colonial Office throughout the rest of the empire, while the South Sea Islanders had such strong advocates in the London Missionary Society that, as Peter Corris observes, "By the turn of the [twentieth] century the Queensland trade was governed by seven Acts of Parliament, eighteen schedules, fifty-four regulations and thirty-eight instructions."[16] Even if many of these rules and regulations went unobserved or were even unknown to those who were meant to police them, he adds, their mere existence was cautionary. The Chinese indentured workers, on the other hand, had no recourse to Exeter Hall.[17] The early emigrants not only risked permanent exile by leaving China illegally, but also bore the brunt of negative stereotypes fostered by hysterical media reports about Chinese resistance to British imperial ambitions on China's territory. Paradoxically, this lack of concern for their welfare and the absence of official oversight stood the more resourceful and resilient among them in good stead. Having completed their period of indenture, some of the Chinese shepherds from the 1848 to 1853 experiment became naturalized citizens, married European immigrant women, purchased property and conducted successful businesses or even stood as candidates and won places in local government. Not all had successful lives, but it can be said that the experience of the Chinese indentured workers of the 1848 to 1853 experiment was genuinely a migrant experience, not merely that of sojourning labourers.

Numbers

The crisis that struck the British and European financial markets in 1837 caused widespread socio-economic distress that continued throughout the Hungry Forties and triggered a massive flow of out-migration, principally to other temperate climate areas, especially those in North America where the opening of new lands beyond the Mississippi River offered opportunities previously undreamt of by Europe's poor. Following the discovery of substantial gold deposits in California and Alaska in 1849, and two years later in the southeastern Australian colonies of New South Wales and Victoria, this flow became a veritable flood. Other factors, including great changes taking place in agriculture and the iron and steel industries, as well as the rapid extension of rail and oceanic transportation, facilitated the voluntary emigration of around 46.5 million people from Europe mainly to the Americas, but also to Australia, New Zealand and South Africa, in the century from 1821 to 1920. According to the figures quoted by Stanley Engerman, the vast majority of these emigrants (slightly over forty-five million) left Europe after 1846.[18]

These were aspirational migrants bent on creating a better life for themselves and their children than the one they left behind. For the most part, too, they were urban people, or at least most recently residents of towns and cities. They did not emigrate in order to work, as perhaps their parents had, as little more than peasants for the local nobility in some rural colonial backwater, and the long campaign to end slavery would, in any case, have warned them away from engaging with the plantations. Moreover, the development of class consciousness that accompanied the wave of revolutionary fervour of the 1830s and 1840s, along with the social ferment mobilized by groups including the Chartists, Owenites, socialists, and communists made them unlikely candidates for the sort of labour that was in most demand in the colonies, namely mass labour for the plantations and the mines, or solitary labour as shepherds and hut-keepers on the vast pastoral runs. Consequently, because they were unable to obtain the white workers that suited their needs, the plantation owners and the big pastoralists looked first to India, then China, and elsewhere for a steady supply of labour.

In raw figures, the total number of indentured workers who joined this huge intercontinental flow of migrants was comparatively small. In fact, according to Engerman, the illegal slave trade to Cuba and Brazil between 1821 and 1867 accounted for nearly as many individuals as did all the trades in contract labour.[19] On the other hand, in the areas where they were consigned to work, they often accounted for a significant proportion of the local non-indigenous population. According to estimates given by Engerman, starting from 1838 (or 1826 in the case of Réunion) until 1918, around 1.6 million Indians were recruited for plantation labour in British colonies, principally Malaya, British Guiana (with approximately one-quarter of a million each), Natal and Trinidad (152,400 and 143,900 respectively), and on behalf of French planters in Mauritius (451,800) and Réunion (86,900).[20] British Guiana, Trinidad and other parts of the British West Indies also received Chinese indentured labourers, although far fewer than the number of Indians. Out of a total of approximately 330,000 Chinese workers contracted between 1849 and 1907, two-thirds of them went to Cuba and Peru. Altogether, including Japanese, Pacific Islanders, Javanese, Africans, and those from Portuguese possessions,

Engerman suggests that just over 2.4 million indentured labourers joined the intercontinental movement of people in the nineteenth and early twentieth century. Figures quoted by David Northrup for roughly the same period add up to slightly more than two million; the main differences being the inclusion of 57,869 European and North American indentured migrants to the Caribbean and Hawaii in his total figure, and the exclusion of Chinese indentured migrants to Malaya.[21] Therefore, according to both estimates, non-indentured European migration was more than twenty times greater than that of Asian, African and Pacific Islander contract labour migration to the colonies during that period. Approximately half of all these indentured workers were contracted during the quarter-century from 1851 to 1875.[22] According to their destinations, they laboured on plantations, down mines, and on railway construction sites but they were also sometimes engaged to work as domestic servants, agricultural labourers, deckhands, cooks, porters, and so on.

Indentured labour migration, at least in the British Empire, ended with the First World War. A little-known episode in its history involved the recruitment of approximately two hundred thousand Chinese workers, principally from impoverished peasant families in North China, by Britain, France and Russia between 1916 and 1920 for trench-digging, burying war dead, building aerodromes, transportation, making explosives, and so on.[23] The Chinese Labour Corps, as it was known, formed the largest contingent of foreign workers employed by Britain during the war; Indians, black South Africans, Egyptians, and West Indians were similarly employed.

If the number of Indian and Chinese indentured labour migrants was small in comparison to the number of European emigrants in the second half of the nineteenth century, it was infinitesimal when compared to population movements in their own countries. Northrup estimates that only one in ten of those Indians who left their native village in search of work opportunities during the last quarter of the century ventured abroad and of those who did, only a further one in ten numbered among the new indentured migrants.[24] Van Den Boogaart and Emmer note that labour migration from India to Ceylon alone (2,321,000 migrants) was more extensive than all the regulated emigration outside India.[25] They argue that "the regulated intercontinental contract migration falls into insignificance besides the much larger migration of workers within Asia and partly also inside Africa" and that "European penetration into nineteenth century India and China was, at best, responsible for an increase in a pre-colonial migration that had already been going on for a long time."[26]

Conditions in China throughout the period of contract labour migration were generally chaotic. Unlike India, where the British colonial administration regulated and counted human movements, in China, because external migration was prohibited by imperial decree until the Convention of Beijing that concluded the Second Opium War, 1856 to 1860, most of the migration from southern China to overseas destinations did not enter the public record. Northrup estimates that between 1847 and 1924, almost 7.5 million Chinese emigrated, either temporarily or permanently, as labourers to various destinations in Southeast Asia but also to the Americas, Australia, Hawaii, other Pacific islands, and various other parts of the world wherever their labour was in demand. Chinese researcher, Zhu Guohong, however, taking the much longer period, 1801 to 1925, suggests that only three million labourers left for overseas destinations, although he concedes that the majority of them emigrated between 1851 and 1875.[27]

Like their Indian counterparts, most Chinese engaged in regional labour migration, overwhelmingly to what is now Malaysia and Indonesia, and only a small proportion, or seven per cent of the total number, according to Northrup's reckoning, took part in the intercontinental indentured labour trade.[28] As mentioned previously, the intercontinental indentured Chinese were recruited mainly for Cuba and Peru, where conditions were among the worst in the whole history of the trade. These abuses were known in China, and in 1873, following a series of official investigations, the Qing administration put a stop to the trade. Most Chinese seeking opportunity abroad, however, had no need of the Western contract labour system. They had long relied on their own clan organizations and methods by which would-be emigrants could borrow money for their passage to a preferred destination against their future earnings in any number of fields including railroad construction, gold panning, fruit picking, and tin mining.

Experiments in the Australian Colonies

Compared to other would-be destinations, Australia was a minor importer of indentured labour but it must be remembered that especially during the peak period of the intercontinental contract labour trade, 1851 to 1875, the colonial population was very small, and the size of the potential employer population was very small indeed.

Until the early 1860s when the sugar plantations created a demand for mass labour, the needs of employers were chiefly related to the pastoral industry, especially for shepherds. The obvious source of supply, according to the newspaper editor in the far northern Moreton Bay district of the colony of New South Wales in 1848, was India where, it was argued, "the natives of Hindustan like ourselves live under the same Government and should be permitted to derive every beneficial consequence of such connection."[29]

There had been early, small experiments with Indian labour in the Australian colonies but abuses of the trade in Bengal and concern in England for the protection of coolies caused a temporary halt to the traffic.[30] A loophole in the ban permitting the emigration of sailors and menial servants, however, allowed some enterprising squatters to import small numbers of Indian indentured servants. Among them was Philip Friell of Tent Hill station in what is now southern Queensland who produced a pamphlet, reproduced at length in the colonial press, entitled "The Advantages of Indian Labour in the Australasian Colonies" setting out the terms and conditions of hire that included repatriation at the end of a five-year contract, unless the contract had been cancelled by magistrates for misconduct.[31] Within a relatively short space of time, however, Friell was deeply disappointed with his experiment. Rather than offering the coolies protection, he argued, the aim should have been to protect the colonists from "people notorious in their disregard of law." In particular, he blamed the women among them whom he considered to be the chief instigators of any discontent and "totally useless."[32]

Colonial regulations on the importation of Indian coolie labour proved too problematic for the Australian squatters, and in all no more than a few hundred were ever hired. The new colony of Queensland passed legislation in 1862 enabling the importation of Indian coolie labour but by the time official approval was received from India, that colony had discovered another source of non-European labour for its sugar plantations, namely the New Hebrides and other Pacific Islands.[33]

The neighbouring Pacific Islands had long represented a potential labour pool for the Australian pastoralists, hungry for cheap labour as the supply of convicts from Britain dried up. In 1847, adventurer and entrepreneur, Ben Boyd, had briefly and unsuccessfully attempted to employ the labour of around 190 islanders, including seven women, from the New Hebrides and the Loyalty Islands, on his vast and far-flung pastoral holdings in New South

Wales.[34] So immediately unpopular was this importation of islander labour
that the local Masters and Servants act was amended in the second half of
1847, excluding "any native of any savage or uncivilized tribe, inhabiting any
Island or Country in the Pacific Ocean, or elsewhere" from its legislation.[35]
By April the following year, according to Alan Dwight, about one-third of
them had been repatriated and others seem to have been "loose" in Sydney.[36]
"The general feeling in the colony," he notes, "was that they were failures as
shepherds."

The history of the Melanesian labour trade in Australia has generally
been tainted by suspicions of violence around recruitment and controversy
over repatriation but most researchers now agree that the majority of the
islander recruits volunteered for work in Queensland and that many of them
willingly hired on for further three-year terms after their initial repatriation,
thus putting stories of entrapment and forced labour in doubt. Deryck Scarr
explains,

> There is good evidence that in some areas recruits were first
> obtained by outright force. The activities of the Peruvian
> blackbirders in the Gilbert Islands in the 1860s are notorious
> and well-documented, and there is no reason to dispute the
> established view that in Melanesia, similarly, many recruits
> in the early years of the labour trade to Fiji, Queensland,
> Noumea, and Samoa were kidnapped.[37]

He continues, however, that during the later decades of the century,
the years when the trade in Queensland was at its peak, it was very much a
voluntary affair.

From 1863, until the First World War, thousands of young men and
some women from islands in the western Pacific Ocean joined the indentured
labour force. In general, their destinations were not as distant as the ones
for those who left from India or China. According to Peter Corris, about
one hundred thousand islanders went to Queensland, Fiji, Samoa and New
Caledonia to work mainly on sugar and copra plantations. Some of them were
briefly engaged, once again unsuccessfully, on pastoral runs in Queensland,
until a law restricted their employment to the coastal strip and to tropical
agriculture.[38]

The contribution of Melanesian labour to the development of the
Queensland sugar industry cannot be under-estimated. In 1871, the

Melanesians constituted a workforce of 2,326; that number rose to 11,745 by 1885 and then fell gradually to 8,795 by the end of the century as the sugar industry moved away from the plantation model to family farms and became less reliant on this so-called Kanaka labour.[39] After federation of the Australian colonies in 1901, and following legislation favouring a White Australia, a total of 7,068 islanders were repatriated.[40] When the deportation was officially complete on July 31, 1908, according to Peter Corris, there were 1,654 islanders remaining in Australia who had been granted exemptions. "A very small number of men evaded deportation by taking to the bush," he continues. "On the other hand, among those repatriated were many (chiefly old people who chose to return with their non-exempt friends, and the children of non-exempt parents) who were eligible to remain in Australia."[41]

In between the small Indian experiment and the relatively large-scale importation of Melanesian labour, there was an attempt to supply the needs of the rapidly expanding pastoral industry with Chinese shepherds from Amoy, now Xiamen, one of the five Chinese treaty ports that had been opened to Western trade by the First Opium War, 1839 to 1842.

The discovery of gold in New South Wales and Victoria in 1851 resulted in a huge influx of prospectors from all over the world, including China. The controversy and sporadic violence provoked by their large and highly visible presence on the gold fields from Ballarat in the south of the continent to the Palmer River in the far north have since served to obliterate from Australian history the economic contribution of a far smaller number of indentured Chinese who were already employed on the pastoral runs and in associated industries in nearby settlements when gold was first discovered. According to David Northrup, between 1848 and 1880, there were six thousand indentured and one hundred thousand "other" Chinese who took part in the intercontinental labour migration to Australia. The "other" presumably refers to the gold-miners, while among the six thousand "indentured" were roughly three thousand men who were shipped from Amoy between 1848 and 1853 to work in the pastoral industry, chiefly in the Northern Districts of New South Wales. Later in the century, other Chinese workers were recruited through Singapore to work on Queensland sugar plantations and others to labour in mines and construct railways in the Northern Territory.[42]

By 1875, the intercontinental indentured labour trade with China was finished. Abuses in the transfer of Chinese workers to Cuba and Peru and the slave-like conditions under which they worked there were brought to the notice not only of the Chinese commissioners sent to report on the situation but also to that of the general public and humanitarian action groups in England and the United States of America. At the same time, in the U.S.A. and parts of the British Empire including Australia, demands for exclusionary laws directed mainly at Chinese immigration were becoming an effective rallying-point among growing nationalist movements and labour unions all intent on power and privilege for white settlers only. Only three of the original 1,500 or so Amoy men who had arrived in the Northern Districts in the mid-nineteenth century were registered on the 1913 index of "Coloured Labour and Asiatic Aliens in Queensland".[43] All three of them, James Cooley (86 years old) and Charlie Cue (84 years old) of Banana Shire in the Rockhampton police district, and Joseph Sims (88 years old) of Yingerbay via Roma, still gave their occupation as "labourer". There were one or two other old men, likewise naturalized subjects of the Crown, who were married to European women, and protected from overt discrimination by Europeanized names, who managed to avoid the oppression and humiliation of the list.

Causes and Consequences

The new indentured labour trade, post-slavery and convict transportation, involved a comparatively small number (between two and two and a half million) of mainly Asian migrants, the majority of whom were recruited and employed in the peak period of 1850 to 1875. The question that arises is not so much why they chose to emigrate for work, but rather why this group chose to indenture themselves to foreign employers in distant lands, while so many more of their compatriots were migrating to regional destinations according to familiar schemes organized by local labour brokers.

Most of the literature on the topic repeats the argument that it was the push of domestic circumstances and the pull of overseas opportunities that motivated them to emigrate. Lord Olivier who had joined the British Colonial Office in 1882 argued,

> The compulsion that forced the "indentured" coolie to go from India or China... the real compulsion, the need that made him accept these quasi-servile conditions, surrendering his freedom of action for five, or very usually ten, years, was precisely the same as that which induces the English agricultural labourer to work his six or seven days a week

from morning till evening for the whole of his active life, at
subsistence wages—the alternative, to wit, of starvation.[44]

Neither Indians nor Chinese were strangers to famine and hunger. In
the nineteenth century, overpopulation, crop failure, and widespread social
and economic change assisted by European penetration of their countries
undoubtedly resulted in mass labour migration of all types: internal and
external, short- and long-term, regulated and unregulated. Engerman,
however, warns against this too obvious explanation. He notes that poverty
and frequency of famine may explain why overseas out-migration was
attractive both to individuals and their societies but he argues that there were
no obvious differences in these factors before and after the opening of the
contract labour trade that favoured increased migration.[45]

A second, popularly held explanation is that they were kidnapped or
tricked into the trade. Enough research has now been done, however, to allow
us to dismiss the notion of widespread and constant use of "blackbirding"
and fraud in relation to the trade in contract labour. In the early years of
the Melanesian labour trade, there were definitely instances involving force
and violence, and stories of kidnapping were rife in relation to the trade in
China. No doubt there were abuses in the system of using crimps and sub-
agents to recruit so-called volunteers in China, while in India where the trade
was regarded with acute suspicion by the British colonial authorities and
hence heavily regulated, there were doubts that volunteers for intercontinental
migration understood the nature of their contracts or the conditions they could
expect to find at their destinations. The analogy then was always with slavery,
as today it would be with human trafficking. As Engerman says, "Legally
[indentured labour] was quite different from slave labour, yet it attracted
a similar moral condemnation."[46] If we allow that some of the emigrants
were forced or tricked, we must also allow that many were free agents who
made decisions based on rational choice according to personal circumstances
ranging from the need to support family dependants, escaping from military
conscription, taking advantage of a potentially life-changing opportunity,
accompanying friends and brothers, or even satisfying curiosity and the spirit
of adventure. We should accept that the majority of the two million or so
migrants were volunteers and that the majority of these movements of people
were "contractual, legally accepted, regulated, and enforced in both areas of
outflow and inflow."[47] After all, the trade ended not because of a lack of supply
of labourers but for reasons that were purely political. The trade offended

nationalist sentiments in India, moral sensibilities in England and the U.S.A., and stirred racist hatred in colonies throughout the British Empire that were emerging into nationhood.

On the other hand, it was not a ready supply of hungry, eager volunteers that created the intercontinental labour trade in the mid-nineteenth century but the growing demand for physical, unskilled labour in the colonies for the kind of work that other migrants did not want to do. Engerman concurs with this argument, noting, "[T]he basic motive for contract labour was the desire for movement of labour into areas of 'labour shortage' on the part of European colonizers and planters."[48] He warns that "labour shortage" is an ambiguous term; certainly it occurred in the process of slave emancipation and during the early stages of settlement but mostly a "shortage" coincided with a desire to increase plantation or pastoral production for export markets. Recovery from the severe economic depression of the late 1830s and early 1840s, coinciding with important gold discoveries in North America, Australia and South Africa resulted in strong growth in world markets and an almost undiminished demand for agricultural commodities until the severe fall-off in the 1880s. Fluctuations in the indentured labour trade reflected these ebbs and flows.

Strange foreign destinations like Cuba and New South Wales were made to seem more attractive to the would-be emigrant labourers from India and China than regular, safer destinations in their home region. When mass labour migration from southern China commenced in the 1840s, a typical emigrant worker to Singapore, for instance, would have arrived through the credit ticket system. He was indebted twice, first to a labour broker or the junk master at the port of embarkation who would advance him the passage money, and then, on arrival, the employer would take over the debt that the worker eventually repaid through his labour. This was a well-worn system by the time Western merchants such as Messrs Tait, Syme and Muir entered the trade. They set up special facilities in Amoy for the recruitment and passage of labourers and hired Chinese brokers who sub-contracted their recruiting work to local "crimps". The system reflected the one in India, although the Indian trade was tightly regulated by the British colonial authorities. There were obvious risks in both systems, local and foreign, but the advantage of the latter lay in the offer of an advance, equivalent to two months' wages that was supposed to be paid to the recruits before they sailed. It would allow them to settle debts that their families invariably had and also to make provision for those they left behind until the promised remittances arrived.

In the early years of the trade, the recruits appear to have had no control over their fates once a contract was signed. A safe voyage and a destination somewhere in the British Empire where their contracts were recognized in law would seem to have been key factors in surviving their term of indenture; a prosperous employer was a better guarantee of fair conditions than one verging on bankruptcy; and an occupation that provided for the companionship of fellow nationals would have eased the loneliness of exile. Nevertheless, homesickness, unfamiliar illnesses, the severe imbalance of the sexes, and further alienation caused by unfamiliar surroundings, strange food, absence of reassuring religious rites and festivals, and separation from family and friends must have affected all of them from time to time. Suicide was not uncommon. Among the Chinese guano miners in Peru in the 1850s, it was a regular occurrence; one overseer reported more than sixty successful attempts in just one year.[49] Desertion was a much more common way of escaping from a bad situation but the penalties if the absconder was caught were severe; short-term absenteeism, gambling and opium-smoking provided safer releases from the stresses of their situation. There were protests and strikes among all groups and in most places, but according to Northrup, the absence of large-scale protest was more striking. "Most migrants," he says, "made the best of the difficult conditions they encountered, worked hard, lived frugally, and survived to the end of their indentures."[50] He concludes that those who had the good luck to survive their migration and their indenture were both physically and financially better off than they would have been had they stayed home, that they derived both material benefit and personal improvement from their experience. Whether the Indian and Chinese indentured labourers would have benefited more had they chosen to take the more popular route of regional labour migration is hard to say.

For the employers, the experiment with indentured coloured labour was a qualified success. As noted previously, employers sought out this labour in an effort to force down general wage rates. While wages paid to indentured workers were low compared to available free labour, the costs involved in acquiring them were substantial. In order to get a reasonable return on money outlaid before the labourer commenced his duties, productivity throughout the course of the indenture—three years in the case of the South Sea Islander, and five years for Indians and Chinese employed within the Empire—had to remain consistently high. Low productivity and high absenteeism, however, seem to have been prevalent in all areas right throughout the history of the trade. Northrup claims that to sustain productivity, employers relied more on "the stick of enforcement than the carrot of wages."[51] There is no doubt that harsh punishment was inflicted on these imported labourers. On the other hand, in colonial New South Wales, if a servant complained to the authorities about physical abuse by his employer, the matter was taken seriously. The difficulty, of course, was finding a way to make a valid complaint. Theoretically, as Lord Oliver remembers, the system itself was just:

> According to the traditions in which the generation to which I belong was brought up,... British Colonies were organic human communities having populations of various admixtures of race, but all of equal rights as British subjects... The policy of the Colonial Office in its administration of mixed communities was held very strictly to the principles of Victorian Liberalism... The experiences and lessons of the revolt against the slave-trade and slavery had not passed out of mind.[52]

This does not mean that oppression and ill-treatment of indentured workers in the Australian colonies of the British Empire did not occur but it is fair to say that abusive behaviour on the part of some employers was held in contempt by others and prosecuted in the courts. If not slavery, then the recent experiences and lessons of the convict era had not passed out of Australian minds either. At the same time, protection by the state of these imported indentured labourers was not, as Lord Olivier reminds us, a "democratic compulsion." It was rather "a paternal and humanitarian compulsion, imposed from without by the circumspection of the Indian and British governments."[53] He felt that without that protection, there would have been a great deal of cruelty and oppression towards them, just as there was in places like Cuba and Peru.

In hindsight, the era of indentured labour and the arguments and debates it triggered can be seen as part of the longer struggle for the great humanitarian principles of freedom and equality that so absorbed the nineteenth century, beginning with the abolitionists' campaign against slavery that argued that free labour was superior in both morality and productivity to unfree labour. The long anti-slavery campaign was conducted in tandem with workers' struggles to improve their status and conditions. The arguments of this grand debate, of course, would have been beyond the comprehension of the three thousand or so young Chinese men who landed on the shores of eastern Australia between 1848 and 1853. As time would tell, however, many of them entered into the spirit of the debate with gusto.

CHAPTER 2

The China Trade

The China trade in intercontinental indentured labour, that is, to destinations beyond East and Southeast Asia, began with a shipment of men to Cuba in 1847, although there had been some earlier, isolated experiments to plantations in the West Indies and Mauritius. These indentured labourers constituted one part of a great exodus of men from southern Chinese ports that accelerated as the century progressed. Between 1851 and 1875, there was a spike in the number of departures particularly from the coastal towns and villages of the southern provinces of Fujian and Guangdong to overseas destinations. According to Zhu Guohong's estimates, four times as many Chinese emigrated during that period as had emigrated in the preceding half-century.[1] About one-quarter of his perhaps modest figure of 1.28 million who left China during those twenty-five years can be classified as indentured labourers but apart from an unknown number of them who were deceived, kidnapped or otherwise forced to board the ships, these men undoubtedly shared similar motives with all the others who made the decision to leave at that time. For all of them, the "pull" factors were powerful inducements, especially the gold discoveries that occurred almost simultaneously in North America and Australia, as well as the insatiable demand for cheap labour in the Americas and the developing colonies of British and other European empires, along with the organized trade that facilitated their participation in it. The "push" factors were equally strong. Around the middle of the nineteenth century, conditions throughout China verged on the chaotic as the Qing dynasty began to crumble under the combined weight of internal rebellion and external aggression from the Western imperial powers.

Origins

It was men from the southeast coast of China, comprising the maritime provinces of southern Zhejiang, Fujian and east Guangdong, along with those from Lingnan, that is, Guangdong province, excluding those eastern prefectures bordering Fujian but inclusive of neighbouring Guangxi province, who constituted the Chinese diaspora of the nineteenth century. Westerners may recognize these people more by their dialect groupings: colloquially, they are Hokkien, Teochiu and Cantonese and, in fact, these terms are more native-place definitions than linguistic ones. The Hokkien emigrants were from those places in Fujian that shared the dialect that was spoken around port towns such as Amoy (Xiamen), Quanzhou and Zhangzhou. The Teochiu were identified with those eastern Guangdong prefectures in and near Chaozhou and Swatow (Shantou), while the Cantonese were principally from the Pearl River delta region, especially Siyi, the "four districts", as well as Sanyi, Zhongshan and outlying districts.

The following distinctions are inexact because, in fact, there were communities where all these groups, as well as Hakka, were represented throughout Southeast Asia and other overseas destinations where Chinese settled but, in general, emigrants from Guangdong—the Cantonese— went to the United States of America, typically in groups from the same village or county and on the credit-ticket scheme or with the financial support of family members who had gone before them.[2] They were attracted initially by the gold discoveries in California and many also laboured on railway construction right across America.[3] The Chinese who left for Australia in large numbers after 1851, similarly attracted by gold, were also typically Cantonese. The Teochiu from east Guangdong, in the coastal region bordering southern Fujian, went to Thailand and the countries that constituted the former French possessions of Indochina, while the natives of Fujian, the Hokkien people, generally set out as coolie labourers to neighbouring countries, especially the Philippines, North Borneo and the Straits Settlements (Singapore, Penang and Malacca), the Dutch East Indies (Indonesia), and Burma. Most of the indentured labourers, those on intercontinental contracts, including the three thousand or so who arrived in Australia between 1848 and 1853, and the majority of those who made the first perilous voyages to Cuba, Peru and parts of the Caribbean embarked at the port of Amoy until civil disorder there in 1853 shifted the hub of the emigrant labour trade to Canton, Macao and also Hong Kong where Western merchants set up agencies to conduct recruitment that occurred mainly in Guangdong and Guangxi provinces.[4]

As this study concerns chiefly those few thousand men who entered Australia between 1848 and 1853 on indentured contracts, the focus will be on Fujian and the conditions there, as well as in China generally in the nineteenth century, that forced or persuaded them to depart, and that greeted the few who returned from their sojourn overseas.

Fujian and Early Contact with the West

Its location, topography and history all combined to make Fujian the most likely of China's provinces to produce emigrants. Fujian is a narrow maritime province, looking out towards the South China Sea and the island of Taiwan that lies less than 150 kilometres offshore. To the west, it is bordered by mountains. Most of the province is highland, and the soils of the narrow coastal plain are not fertile. Population pressure in the province increased significantly in the first half of the nineteenth century; estimated at eleven million in 1776, the provincial population had almost doubled to twenty million by 1851, a rate of growth that was in line with that of the general population that rose from around 230 million in 1770 to 394 million in 1830, and by 1850 had probably increased to 430 million.[5] Famine was no stranger in Fujian, although the introduction of New World crops, especially root vegetables such as taro and sweet potato, had eased the frequency of famine over the preceding two centuries. The severe limitations of cultivated land area and soil quality meant that Fujian had long been an importer of the food staple, rice, another factor which tied it to maritime commerce.

The Fujianese were sailors and merchant seamen, famous up and down the coast of China and on the trade routes to Korea, Japan and Southeast Asian ports. The towns of Quanzhou and Fuzhou were renowned as thriving entrepôts from the heyday of China's maritime age that began during the Southern Song dynasty around the middle of the twelfth century and continued well into the Yuan dynasty when great fleets set out to challenge Japan and Java, and Chinese contacts with foreign lands were widened. Quanzhou, dating from the early eighth century, with its sheltered, deepwater harbour at the mouth of the Jin River, was one of the greatest ports in the world when Marco Polo described his visit to this "noble and handsome city":

It is indeed impossible to convey an idea of the concourse of merchants and the accumulation of goods, in this which is held to be one of the largest and most commodious ports in the world.[6]

Known from the Arabic and Persian transliteration as Zaytun or Zaitum, it was home to thousands of Indian, Arab and Persian traders who made their fortunes there when the ancient Silk Road through central Asia fell prey to bandits and warfare as a consequence of the An Shi rebellion (755-763AD) against the Tang dynasty, and the great trade route from East to West took to the sea. Throughout the Song and Yuan dynasties, Quanzhou enjoyed a cosmopolitan mix of cultures, as its archaeological remains of Muslim mosques and Christian tombs testify.

The subsequent Ming emperors (1368-1644), however, were ambivalent about maritime commerce. The first Ming emperor sought to restore order and security disturbed by dynastic change by clamping down on foreign trade, allowing it to function only through the state-sanctioned tribute system. His successor, the Yongle emperor, reversed this policy, and during his reign, with fleets commanded by the eunuch admiral Zheng He, between 1405 and 1433, Chinese merchant ships crossed the Indian Ocean to the Persian Gulf and the east coast of Africa. When Yongle shifted his capital northward to Dadu (modern Beijing), however, the Ming withdrew once again from the sea. The great port of Quanzhou declined and the formal structures and institutions serving foreign trade there also collapsed.

Subsequently, smuggling and piracy were rife all along the southern coast. Pirate groups that included Japanese as well as Chinese fugitives and even some escaped black slaves of the Portuguese harassed the southern coastal towns, looting and seizing people for ransom. The arrival of the Portuguese traders into the region was cause for imperial concern. In 1557, they had established a trading station at Macao in the Pearl River delta and made their mark and fortunes by taking advantage of the imperial ban on direct trade with a belligerent Japan to act as middlemen on behalf of the southern Chinese merchants.

The government's initial response to this foreign intrusion and anarchy on its seas was to ban overseas trade completely, thus making an outlaw of every Chinese who ventured abroad. The reality of rapid social and economic change that occurred during the long Ming reign, however, forced a change of policy and informal overseas trading was again legalized in 1567. Almost simultaneously with the lifting of the ban, in 1570, the Spanish established a colony at Manila. Silver from Mexico carried in the Spanish galleons en route for Europe was traded there for Chinese silks, porcelain, and other products. Both the goods and the silver were handled by thousands of Chinese traders, Hokkien merchants from Zhangzhou and Quanzhou, who flocked to what is now called the Philippines. By the beginning of the seventeenth century, there were twenty thousand Chinese residing there, mostly in the Manila area.[7]

Silver specie from the Manila trade flowed in ever-greater quantities into the homeland creating a commercial boom. The focus of maritime activity was again the southeast coast, especially Amoy, a port town one hundred kilometres or so south of Quanzhou that was founded at the beginning of the Ming dynasty. From there, the Zheng family, wealthy coastal traders and mandarin officials who owed their status to the Ming, commanded trading networks that stretched from Manila to Nagasaki. When the Ming dynasty ended in 1644, the family patriarch, Zheng Zhilong, gave his allegiance to the new Qing dynasty but his son, Zheng Chenggong, better known as Koxinga, remained loyal to the Ming. Under him, Amoy became a bastion of resistance to the new regime, while it remained a flourishing international trading port.

By the 1640s, the Dutch East India Company was well established in the South China Sea and commanded the carrying trade between Southeast Asia and Japan. The Ming government had refused the Dutch permission to establish a base on the mainland, so they worked first out of facilities on the Pescadores Islands in the Taiwan Strait, just offshore from Amoy, and then, after 1624, from a settlement on the island of Taiwan itself. In this, they were encouraged by the Zheng clan who also occasionally used the island as a haven for their vast commercial fleet.

For more than a decade after the fall of the dynasty, Koxinga and the Zheng clan defiantly ruled the southeast coast in the name of the Ming. Millions of people in the coastal belt from south of the Yangzi River to the Pearl River delta declared themselves ready to support Koxinga's crusade to return the Ming to power. An attempt by him to retake the iconic former royal capital, Nanjing, in the late 1650s, however, was heavily defeated. In 1660, the second Qing emperor, Shunzhi, effectively cut off the source of supplies to his navy when, in accordance with an imperial directive, the entire southeast coastline was forcibly evacuated; homes were destroyed and villages burned as the populace was forced inland to a distance of some fifteen kilometres from the shore.[8] All coastal shipping was outlawed. Fujian was the worst affected; around 8,500 farmers and fishermen were said to have died between 1661 and 1663 as the order was enforced.[9] According to John Keay, "[T]he coastal strip reportedly reverted to wilderness; all habitations were abandoned; 'even the swallows' nests were empty'."[10]

The ban on maritime trade was lifted in 1684, following the surrender of Koxinga's son who had held out against the Qing on the island of Taiwan. The Dutch, meanwhile, had pragmatically transferred their own allegiance to the Qing but they were then ousted from Taiwan in an epic battle with the Zheng armada and forced to sail away. The island was finally annexed and made a prefecture of Fujian, a status it maintained until 1885 when it became a province in its own right. Even after this definitive defeat of the Zheng clan, however, the Qing court remained uneasy, fearing that remnants of Koxinga's forces taking sanctuary in Southeast Asia might foment plots against the dynasty.

The loyalty of the southern provinces of Fujian and Guangdong could never be taken for granted. Their distance from the court in Beijing and the greater distance caused by the southern dialects which remained virtually unintelligible to the northerners set them further apart. The men of Fujian may have observed the Qing command on pain of death to shave the front of the head and at the back braid their hair into a queue in keeping with Manchu customary practice but they harboured a deep grievance against the Qing that was carefully nurtured right throughout the south until it burst out in popular revolt in the mid-nineteenth century.

Tea and Opium

From the beginning of the eighteenth century, ships of the English East India Company were making regular trips to Canton, and the cargo they loaded there was tea, for which there was a seemingly unquenchable demand in Europe, and especially in England. From the two hundred thousand pounds (ninety tonnes) sold in London in 1720, demand had risen to nine million pounds (four thousand tonnes) by 1770 and this demand would double and double again in the nineteenth century.[11] The tea came from the slopes of northern Fujian mountains such as Wuyi Shan, and when the Chinese word for the infusion made from the plant's leaves entered the English language, it did so in its native Fujian dialect form, *te*. Sweetened with sugar produced by slave labour on plantations in the British West Indies and consumed by all social classes, it was the commercial product par excellence of the eighteenth century. In spite of the heavy tariffs imposed on its importation into Britain, as the figures suggest, by 1770, tea and the China trade was outstripping the Company's trade with all other markets.

At the time, all European business with China was confined to Canton. On a narrow strip of land along the foreshore of the Pearl River, the trading companies— Spanish, Dutch, Danish, Swedish, English, Austrian, and American—built their agency houses or "factories" which they were permitted to use only in the trading season from October to March, while grudgingly observing the strict Chinese rules and regulations that governed the lives of foreign residents. Women were prohibited, so families had to live at Macao, a three-day sampan ride away, which the Qing had allowed the Portuguese to retain as their trading base after the coastal-withdrawal policy was lifted. The potential returns to state revenues from a properly regulated trade with foreigners eager to participate in the China market were obviously vast but, according to Jonathan Spence, "[B]eyond setting up four maritime customs offices (one in each of the coastal provinces south of the Yangzi) and trying to enforce an across-the-board tariff of twenty per cent on foreign imports, the Qing state failed to develop the necessary mechanisms, preferring instead to work through systems of kickbacks or purchased monopolies."[12] The Cantonese merchants formed a Cohong (*gonghang*), a monopolistic guild through which all European trade was channelled.

Therefore, China's preparedness for the inevitable European penetration of its markets was woefully inadequate. It soon became apparent that Chinese merchants had little interest in purchasing Western, and more specifically English, manufactured goods. The tea exports had to be paid for in silver bullion, and considering the ever-increasing demand for the product, the trade imbalance was substantial. The East India Company therefore sought a high-value cash crop as a countervailing form of exchange. The solution was opium, and by the end of the eighteenth century, the notorious opium drug trade with China was underway. The Company established a monopoly for opium grown in India and then sold licences to selected country traders, Western merchants with factories in Canton, who sold the product to the Cohong, who then sold it on to local merchants right up the coast as far as Tianjin.

Very soon, silver started to flow in the opposite direction. Figures provided by Spence suggest that from 1729, when two hundred chests of opium were sold to China, the quantity rose to a staggering forty thousand chests in 1838, each chest containing between 130 and 160 pounds (sixty to seventy kilos) of opium.[13] By that year, the opium trade was sustaining the habits of 12.5 million Chinese addicts and the profits of 156 private British merchants in Canton, their numbers having more than doubled in the previous five years.[14]

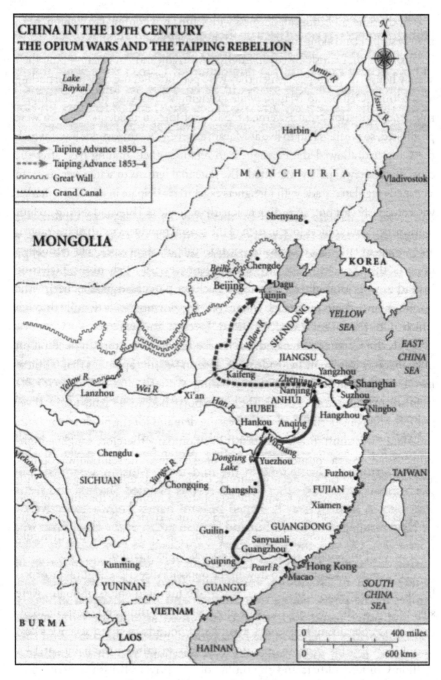

Figure 1 - China in the 19th Century.

Source: John Keay, *China: A History* (Hammersmith: HarperPress, 2008), p. 468

In 1834, the East India Company lost both its monopoly on Indian opium and the "out-and-back" China monopoly that had restricted shipments of trade goods to and from the East to Company ships. The East India Company's supervision of the China-London trade was replaced by that of the British government in the person of Lord Napier who arrived in Macao in 1834. The agency houses greeted these decisions of the British parliament with delight and the opium trade gained pace. The consequences for China, however, were disastrous. By the 1830s, silver was flowing out of China at the rate of nine million taels (at 37.6 grams per tael) per year. As all official taxes had to be paid in silver, hoarding was inevitable and increased demand for silver forced down the value of copper cash, the regular form of exchange among the peasantry. Effects were felt everywhere, but particularly in the south. Urban unrest, unemployment and social ills associated with the drug trade all grew alarmingly.

The state response to social disturbance was to ban the import of the drug. Early in 1839, Imperial High Commissioner Lin Zexu, a Fujian-born scholar-official renowned not only as an outstandingly capable statesman but especially for being singularly incorruptible and devoted to duty, was sent to Canton to enforce the ban. The traders were ordered to surrender all stocks and to sign an undertaking to forgo all future opium trading. Until they complied with the orders, they were detained at Canton. One of the detainees, Robert Forbes, an American merchant in Canton wrote about the experience in his "Personal Reminiscences":

> Without any warning, Lin made his appearance at Canton on the 10 March and on 19th he issued a proclamation demanding of the foreign community the instant delivery of every chest of opium within the waters of China! The Hong merchants through whom all legitimate foreign trade was conducted, were threatened with death if the imperial mandate was not immediately obeyed.
>
> All the servants, compradores, and cooks were ordered off; we were prisoners in our own factories or houses; all trade ceased. The second superintendent of British trade, Mr Johnson, proceeded to the fortified entrance of the river and delivered to Lin's officers 20,283 chests of opium of the then nominal value of $10 million.[15]

>   Early in May, the last chest having been delivered, and
> the whole 20,283 destroyed by dumping into trenches and
> admitting the river water, the treble cordon of guard-boats
> was removed, and trade was opened; servants came back,
> and all breathed freely again.[16]

The intervention by the Qing provided the British government with a pretext for war. Powerful merchants like Jardine and Matheson argued that they had delivered the opium to the Chinese authorities on the understanding that they would receive compensation. Rather than pay the merchants, the British government took the opportunity to retaliate against the Chinese, and an expedition of three thousand troops from India plus ships of the Royal Navy headed for the Pearl River.[17] The First Opium War, 1839-42, resulted in China's first humiliating defeat at the hands of the West. The Treaty of Nanjing that was signed in August 1842 forced a heavy payment on China for the opium that was destroyed, the cost of the war itself and even the outstanding debts of the Cohong which lost its monopoly of trade, although there was no mention of regulating the opium trade itself. Five coastal ports, including Amoy and Fuzhou in Fujian province, were declared open to Western trade and residence with consular representation. The Americans, French and a host of other nations followed with their own treaties that included the principle of extra-territoriality, the right to be tried by one's own national law for criminal offences committed in China, and other privileges. A most-favoured nation clause ensured that privileges granted to one nation applied to all, thus ensuring that China could not forge alliances with one against the other.

The Qing dynasty was already two hundred years old when the Treaty of Nanjing was signed and it displayed all the symptoms of decrepitude. The terrible consequences of the drug trade on the populace and the economy merely highlighted weak imperial authority, appalling corruption and China's total unpreparedness to deal with the challenges posed by a technologically advanced and commercially avaricious West. Peasant revolt was common at the end of all dynasties as it would be at the close of the Qing, but China had never experienced anything like the great Taiping rebellion that almost overthrew the Manchu government between 1851 and 1864 when it was finally put down in a terrible massacre.

Peasant Life in Nineteenth Century China

Long before the First Opium War and further Western aggression that forced the opening of China, and before the flood of Christian missionaries who, along with their religious tracts, introduced new concepts about the state and alternative forms of political governance, China had played host to foreign scholars and traders, including Europeans, whose aims were in no way revolutionary or exploitative. There had been exchanges with foreigners at a level higher than simply trade for centuries. The presence of foreigners in their land, however, would have been unimaginable to the vast majority of Chinese. At the turn of the nineteenth century, the Chinese Everyman was one of at least 340 million peasant villagers, out of a total population of around 360 million, who "stood bounded by circles of social control extending from family elders to the remote structure that he knew to be surmounted by the emperor."[18]

The villager's quotidian routine was circumscribed by nature and tradition. Typically, he or she cultivated the land that was owned or tenanted by their farming family, although rapid population growth by then was putting severe pressure on the size of individual holdings that, by one estimate, had shrunk to 2.36 mu (one mu is about 613 square metres) per capita by 1812.[19] In Fujian, circumstances would have been even more overcrowded than that average figure suggests; fishing would have been one means to supplement family income there but migration to the towns to seek wages was increasingly normal practice, especially for the second and later sons of large families. Throughout the countryside, many peasants who were forced off the land turned to vagabondage, whether by choice or by need, and they represented a potential political force.

Despite internal migration, family ties remained very strong and native place defined a person as much as his or her surname. "One was a Lin or a Wang," it is said, "but, almost as importantly, one was a Lin or a Wang from so and so county."[20] This strong native place identification was inherited by children and grandchildren born elsewhere. Above all, "home" was where one's body returned for burial, in ancestral soil, so that the soul could receive the propitiatory offerings of later generations. For the emigrants who did not return, this must have been their greatest regret.

At the level above the immediate family was the lineage group which traced its ancestry, whether real or fictive, through the male line to a common elder, the first ancestor to settle in a particular area. These lineage groups were more significant in the south of China than in the north. In rural Fujian, in particular, the epithet "fortress family" was applied to these family groups that were powerful both socially and economically. A "big surname" (*daxing*) commanded respect. When daxing merged, they formed clans, although use of the word "clan" is imprecise. It was used previously, for instance, to describe just one daxing from Fujian, the Zheng clan, although in fact the Zheng family did not need to form alliances to exhibit its power. The formation of these powerful clans could be disruptive of social order and competition among them led to armed feuding, vendettas and pitched battles that were common in southern Fujian in the eighteenth century and later endemic also in Guangdong. Homes of the rich Fujianese were heavily fortified. Further tension resulted from competition between poorer farmers and recent immigrants. "All in all," it is said, "southern Fujian was no place for the squeamish. So thoroughly ingrained was its unruliness that observers speak of the region as having a tradition of violence."[21] The Qing government identified the region as a potential trouble spot, Spence notes, and kept it heavily garrisoned.[22]

The family, the clan, and the village may have represented means of identification and social organization but, ultimately, as Chesneaux suggests, the Chinese peasant was subject to nature, the landlord, and especially the yamen, the office and residence of the bureaucrat or mandarin who administered government business at each level of the power pyramid.[23] China was a highly bureaucratized state, and power flowed from the emperor, through provincial governors, town prefects and sub-prefects, to county magistrates. At the county level, the yamen was also the court of law, the prison, barracks, arsenal and treasury, and tax granary. For the peasant, it represented state power, so it was this symbol that the peasants always sacked and burned when they rose in revolt.

The county magistrate was not just the delegate of the emperor's earthly powers, Eric Wolf notes, but also performed a ritual function:

> By ancient tradition the district magistrate was the magician of the people. In case of flood, he would go to the river or lake to demand the receding of the water by throwing his official belongings into the water. In case of drought he would issue an order to stop killing pigs and would organize a parade with all the paraphernalia suggesting rain, such as umbrellas and long boots.[24]

30

Jonathan Spence supports this argument with his depiction of the magistrate of Hua "who leads his county residents to the rhythm of the rituals dictated by the state."[25] Every village and neighbourhood had its spirits and deities and all had to be appeased and venerated at the prescribed times of the year. Solemn ceremonies were held and sacrifices offered in the local temple for the gods and spirits that had force for the whole community. On these occasions, the magistrate would also read aloud the emperor's "Sixteen Instructions" on virtuous behaviour, exhorting the people to show respect and obedience to the state and one's elders, and to practise harmony, thrift, industry, scholarship, good manners, prompt payment of taxes, and mutual security. Between the magistracy and the mass of the peasantry were the scholar officials who performed the work of a local bureaucracy. Repositories of traditional learning and drawn by the examination system from the elite class of the great clans, they were regarded as the mainstay of an orderly society.

Wellsprings of Violence

In the mid-nineteenth century, a massive assault on the authority of the Chinese state almost destroyed the Qing dynasty. Agrarian unrest had been stirring all over the country since the beginning of the century but between 1850 and 1870, there occurred waves of rebellions of exceptional size that involved millions of peasants and affected nearly all eighteen provinces. Angry peasants rose up under the various banners of the triads, the Muslim minorities, and especially the Taiping rebels. In those twenty years, more people were killed in China than on all the battlefields of Europe during the First and Second World Wars combined; survivors were left destitute and displaced, their fields ravaged, and their villages burnt. Floods, famine, and the agrarian crisis all played a part in the rebels' cause but ideology, both old and new, was also important. Each major outburst of revolt coincided with a further thrust of Western imperial aggression. The rebellions were eventually and successfully put down by the Qing military but at too great a cost for the dynasty to survive for long.

Secret societies, commonly referred to as triads, provided an element of continuity for peasant revolt in terms of both leadership and refuge. They were, Chesneaux observes, directly involved in all peasant rebellions in Chinese history.[26] In the north, the societies were connected with the White Lotus tradition and were predominantly folk-religious in origin and purpose while in the south, triads such as the Society of Heaven and Earth (*tiandihui*) were more political.[27] The tiandihui was founded in Zhangzhou prefecture, Fujian province, around 1761, at a time when many Qing government institutions were beginning to falter. Along with secret passwords and hand signals, their members were bonded by blood oaths and a pledge to overthrow the Qing and restore the Ming. Their strategies included the robbery of wealthy homes and storehouses to amass funds for this grand ambition but they also promised to provide protection and support, and in this way attracted peasant recruits.

In May 1853, some three thousand members of the Small (or Sheathed) Swords, as the society was popularly known, took control of Amoy. Since being captured by the British in August 1842 and then designated a treaty port, the town had resumed its reputation as a major trading centre, but most of the visiting ships were Asian-owned. According to Robert Nield, apart from tea and sugar, the thirty or so resident Europeans there traded mostly in opium.[28] The leading British firms in Amoy, Syme, Muir & Co. and Tait & Co., were also coolie traders. Government forces failed in two attempts to defeat the rebels who left of their own accord in November, although the Western press reported, "The leaders of this society are still, however, on the coast, receiving voluntary contributions from disaffected villagers."[29] Meanwhile, Taiwan was again in revolt, and Canton, too, was reportedly threatened by "large bodies of men assembled in arms."[30]

Qing forces were engaged in suppressing simultaneous uprisings over a vast area of Chinese territory. In 1851, the Nian Rebellion broke out in the northern region between the Huai and Yellow Rivers. Mismanagement of Yellow River dyke works and the silting up of stretches of the Grand Canal had caused agricultural distress and interrupted the important rice trade with the south. Barge workers banded together into their own secret associations, both to protect their jobs and to tyrannize the local farming communities. Jonathan Spence suggests that they had no clear-cut religious affiliation, political ideology, strategic goals or even unified leadership until 1852 when leaders of the eighteen separate Nian groups met and proclaimed as their joint head Zhang Luoxing, a northern Anhui landlord. With a relatively small combined force of between thirty thousand and fifty thousand troops, they harried the imperial forces right across northern China until 1868, employing a highly successful form of guerrilla strategy.

Two other rebellions, both led by Muslims erupted in the southwest and northwest of China in 1855. Known as the Red Turbans, the rebels in Yunnan

32

province rose up against heavy land taxes and extra levies that were imposed on their Muslim minority, while in the northwest provinces of Shaanxi and Gansu, the Muslim minorities were encouraged by both the Taiping generals and the Nian troop leaders to forge an anti-Qing alliance. Fortunately for the government, successful alliances among disparate rebel forces like these were rarely successful. Historically, peasant revolts were reactions to injustice, whether in the form of unfair taxation, excessive demands for bribes or corvée labour, or the brutality of landlords. They were not revolutionary in the sense of struggling to change the order of things; in fact, had they been asked, peasants who joined these rebellions might have argued that they were struggling to restore order and propriety to their society, not to change it.

In the middle of the nineteenth century, however, a strange confluence of events and ideas shook the very fundament of Chinese society and tradition. The waves of violent popular uprisings that rolled across China coincided with the main thrusts of Western imperialistic aggression, the First and Second Opium Wars.[31] The Treaty of Nanjing that ended the first war by forcing open four more trading ports in addition to Canton resulted in severe economic dislocation in the south, especially in the Pearl River area. Among the new treaty ports, only Shanghai grew and profited from Western access, the others, including Amoy, being either unable or unwilling to make the structural changes that were necessary to deal with Western trade. In Canton, as commerce shifted northwards to Shanghai, thousands of those already dependent on Western business—boatmen, porters, and so on—were left without a means of making a living. Effects of the economic downturn were felt inland from Canton, in the West River region, where embattled, dispossessed Hakka people had started to move into lowland areas, putting themselves directly in competition with the local Punti (*bendi*) people for scarce arable land. In the 1850s, there was fierce fighting between these ethnic groups. It was in this context of turmoil and strife that the Society of God Worshippers, the Taipings, evolved.

In 1851, a failed candidate for the Confucian state examinations, Hong Xiuquan, a Hakka from Guangxi Province, founded his own dynasty, the Celestial Kingdom of Great Peace (*taiping tianguo*). Believing himself to be God's second son, the brother of Jesus Christ, he led his army of disaffected and landless peasants, boatmen, porters, charcoal burners, vagabonds and brigands to the former Ming royal capital, Nanjing, where he ruled for eleven years in defiance of the Qing. This ragtag army represented a potent historical mix, "the power of ethnicity combined with religion, a power that almost ended the life of the dynasty."[32]

The apocalyptic and millenarian visions of the Taiping leaders followed a long tradition in China. The leading Western chronicler of the Taiping rebellion, Jonathan Spence contends that foreign religion, however inadvertently, reinforced and sanctioned these existing tendencies. He states unequivocally,

> It is my belief that Hong's visions were shaped in some fashion
> by the overlapping layers of change that the Westerners were
> bringing to China along with their Christianity.[33]

When quasi-religious visions had led to peasant revolts in the past, the state usually blamed followers of the White Lotus sect, adherents of the eclectic folk-Buddhism cult that venerated a female deity and was based on long-held millenarian views of catastrophe on earth. Millenarian beliefs, however, thrived also in the Western religious tradition, among the Puritan visionaries, for example, and Spence argues that these impulses were carried into China in the early nineteenth century, especially through American Baptist missionaries. "By the early 1830s," he notes, "these new forces were institutionally established in South China, ready to compete with indigenous Chinese elements for the loyalties of the youthful Hong Xiuquan."[34]

The Treaty of Nanjing had allowed the first foreign missionaries to work in the newly declared treaty ports, although one Protestant missionary, the Rev. Dr Morrison, had worked alone in Canton between 1808 and 1830. At the end of 1852, there were seventy-three Protestant missionaries, mostly Americans, in the five treaty ports and Hong Kong.[35] Despite their small number and government restrictions on their travel inland, the missionaries had been very conscientious. Bible translations were circulating widely by 1850, including special editions that were prepared for separate dialects, including those of Fujian and the Hakka regions of west Guangdong and Guangxi. The foreign missionaries acknowledged that their work had influenced the Taiping rebels, but they believed that the uprising would be good for both mission work and commerce. Late in 1853, the British Foreign Office published communications it had received from the British missionary representative in China, the Rev. Dr Medhurst, containing his explanation of the Protestant Christianity attributed to the insurgents.[36] It was clear, he said, that they had a considerable knowledge of Christianity and that there would be "a perfect toleration" for missionaries should the insurrection succeed. Moreover, he believed, "[the Taiping rebels] would doubtless admit of commercial intercourse." He reasoned that it was already too late for Europeans to clear themselves of all connection or at least sympathy with the rebels in the eyes of the Chinese government but he advised that the British government at least should refrain from contact with either party.

While its troops were already stretched to the limit battling insurrection on so many fronts, the Qing were forced into a second opium war by Western powers determined to have diplomatic representation in Beijing. The Treaty of Tianjin that concluded the so-called Arrow War—an allegedly illegal Chinese search of this British naval vessel had precipitated the war— from 1856 to 1860 met all Western demands, including the opening up of a further ten treaty ports, most importantly inland along the Yangzi, the open preaching of Christianity, and the freedom to travel inside China. When the Qing resisted the clause that would permit foreign ambassadors to live in Beijing, Lord Elgin, Britain's chief negotiator, ordered his troops to march on the capital. On the day the British sacked and burnt the Yuan Ming Yuan (the Garden of Perfection and Light), the beautiful summer palace on the outskirts of the capital that had been designed for the Qianlong emperor by Jesuit architects in the preceding century, the Qing succumbed to all their demands. This treaty and the supplementary Peking Convention of 1860 added a further harsh indemnity, opened Tianjin as a treaty port, and permitted emigration of Chinese labourers on board British ships. The trade in indentured labour that had been doing brisk business out of Amoy and Macao since 1847 was now legal.

In April 1864, the Taiping rebel leader, Hong Xiuquan, died. Three months later, Qing troops re-entered Nanjing and in a final terrible slaughter, the rebellion was crushed. Tens of millions of people were dead as a result of one man's vision of a world of Great Peace (*taiping*), equality and perfection, including perhaps seventy per cent of the population of Anhui province alone.[37] Hong, Jonathan Spence writes, was one of those people who believe it is their mission to make all things "new, for the surprise of the sky-children."[38] It is a central agony of history, he adds, that those who embark on such missions so rarely care to calculate the cost.

By 1873, most of China was pacified. Before the Qing dynasty finally collapsed in 1911, making way for a fragile republic, there would be more violence and further humiliating defeats at the hands of foreigners, including the Japanese, but by then, millions of Chinese had left their homeland, and most of them and their descendants would never return.

Migration

Flight is a natural response to the fear of both violence and the consequences of having engaged in it. The Taiping rebellion and all the other rebellions against the state in the third quarter of the nineteenth century left tens of millions dead or homeless. The roads teemed with wandering refugees and villagers displaced by seemingly endless warfare. Among these homeless masses, there were also defeated rebels fleeing justice. One sure route of escape for them was passage on a foreign ship with the promise of paid work on disembarkation. Genealogies found in Guangxi province where the Taiping rebellion had formed among the Hakka people tell of rebels fleeing to California, Vietnam and Singapore or being shipped off to Cuba and the Dutch East Indies following the defeat in 1864.[39] The fierce inter-ethnic battles for land between the Hakka people and the Punti, the established Cantonese, in Guangdong, similarly put many villagers from the Pearl River region to flight.

The lifting of the ban on emigration in 1860, a condition contained in the Peking Convention following the Second Opium War, formally recognized the trade in indentured labour and the regular flow of other migrants from the south that had been in progress since the late 1840s. In the 1860s, the government also recognized the right of emigrants to send remittances home to their families which was an important reform for all parties concerned and a further incentive for emigration. Until then, men from the south had left their country with little hope of being able to return. The ban specifically forbidding foreign travel from Fujian and Guangdong dating from the early eighteenth century had made emigration a capital offence, so those who left were criminal by definition, on par with rebels, traitors and deserters. Therefore, those who left before 1860, and that included all who took part in colonial Australia's experiment with Chinese indentured labour from 1848 to 1853, could not have expected to return. The right of Chinese to emigrate, to visit or return to their homeland at will was not formally recognized until 1893, far too late for most of those men who had survived their indentures in places like Cuba, Peru, the British West Indies and even the vast, empty pastoral runs of colonial Australia.

The China trade in indentured labour ended in 1874. When all the rebellions were quashed and the country was again reunited under Qing rule, China experienced a brief period of enlightenment known as the Tongzhi Restoration which was guided by an exceptional group of provincial officials whose aim was to re-establish the basic values of Confucian government. One of their first undertakings was to send commissions to Cuba and Peru to investigate and report upon the conditions of Chinese indentured workers in those countries. What they discovered so horrified the imperial court that the trade in indentured Chinese labour was stopped altogether. The commissioners' reports included stories of abduction and forced transportation, of slave-like working conditions and punishments including the use of stocks, leg chains, flogging, and even execution. Nevertheless, men from Fujian and Guangdong continued to emigrate, according to age-old chain migration patterns and their own local schemes that assisted their passage abroad. Increasingly, however, they would face discrimination and exclusionary laws from the same receiving countries that had once so eagerly sought their labour.

CHAPTER 3

The Australian Frontier

In 1847, as the indentured labour trade was getting underway in Amoy, the British colony of New South Wales was recovering strongly from the financial crisis that had temporarily halted the pell-mell development of pastoral runs that now occupied vast swathes of the country from Port Phillip District in the south to the former penal settlement of Moreton Bay in the north. With the decision to end the transportation of convicts to New South Wales after 1841, and the declaration of Moreton Bay as a free settlement in February 1842, the Northern Districts, those above the thirtieth parallel, had become very attractive to adventurous squatters eager to be first to take advantage of the rich potential of the sub-tropical savannah.[1] The Australian Waste Lands Bill that went before the British House of Commons in August 1846 proposed that lands beyond the boundaries, those ineffective limits on location that had tried to restrict European occupation to nineteen counties in the vicinity of the original settlement at Sydney, might be occupied in "runs" with pasturage for four thousand sheep under licence for eight to fourteen years at a cost to the squatter of ten pounds per annum.[2] The Waste Lands Act received royal assent and was complete by February the following year. The fine grazing land of the Darling Downs, the northern frontier of settlement at the time, had already been taken up, so newcomers continued farther north to the territory drained by the Boyne and the Dawson rivers, the latter named by the explorer Ludwig Leichhardt on a recent expedition.

Discovery for the white settlers of this so-called "Northern Country" was attributed to Henry Stuart Russel who crossed from Wide Bay to the Boyne River in 1842 and, noting its suitability for pastoral purposes, he established the first station in the area, Burrandowan, stocking it the following year. Others soon followed him and concurred with his estimate that the land drained by the Boyne, very open, well-grassed and with an abundance of fresh water, could depasture half a million sheep and a proportionate number of cattle. The best country, however, was declared to be some two hundred kilometres northwest of the earliest stations on the Boyne, where others soon found excellent pasture beside a "very fine river ... having the characteristics of a large English river, with low banks, of great breadth, and having large creeks with rocky beds running into it."[3]

In November 1846, Assistant Surveyor Burnett and his deputy, Captain Perry, attempted to trace the Boyne to its mouth, thought to be at Port Curtis. They were forced back by dense scrub at 24.53 degrees south latitude, but they had reached saltwater swamps and knew they were close to their goal. Their efforts were in aid of siting a proposed new colony at Port Curtis for some three thousand Pentonville exiles and convicts from Van Diemen's Land and this colony, it was hoped, would also act as a labour depot for the quickly developing pastoral industry in the area.[4] The Pentonville experiment at Port Curtis never eventuated but white settlement in the area continued to expand and prosper. Assistant Surveyor Burnett, meanwhile, in a further expedition in 1847, proved that the river he traced was not identical with the Boyne and his perseverance was rewarded by an official decree that "the river in question, in its whole course from the Darling Downs to its junction with the sea at Hervey's Bay, shall henceforth be designated as the River Burnett."[5] The finer details of its course from source to mouth remained inexact for the time being, but the river would give its name to the Burnett district that was proclaimed in the *Government Gazette* of November 7, 1848, along with the neighbouring districts of Wide Bay and Maranoa; the boundaries of the district were gazetted in April 1851. These boundaries, consisting of ranges and great rivers, formed an oval-shaped bowl encompassing 13,601 square miles (roughly thirty-five thousand square kilometres) of well-drained land that was divided almost in half laterally by the Burnett and Auburn rivers.[6] The defining boundaries of the Burnett district were the lines separating the Burnett from the Brisbane River and its tributaries in the south, the confluence of the Burnett and the Dawson rivers in the north, the Great Dividing Range on the west and the lesser coastal range dividing the Burnett from tributaries and other streams that drained into Wide Bay on the east.

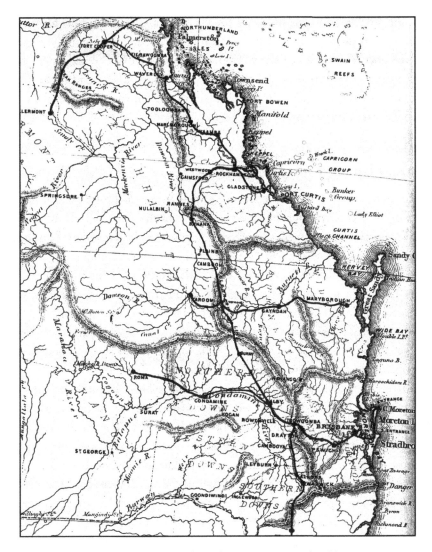

Figure 2 - Area of Pastoral Settlement in Queensland by 1859

Source: L. E. Skinner, *Police of the Pastoral Frontier* (St Lucia: University of Queensland Press, 1975).

At Separation in 1859, the colony of Queensland extended from Waverley station at Broad Sound to the border with New South Wales. The electric telegraph line shown in this map of 1868 did not exist then, nor did the townships of Mackay, Fort Cooper, Clermont, Springsure, Roma, or St George. The map clearly shows the Wide Bay and Burnett districts, bounded by Fraser (Great Sandy) Island and ranges to the north, south and west, with the townships of Gayndah and Maryborough centrally located.

The proclamation meant that occupiers could now legally tender for runs. Captain Maurice Charles O'Connell, son of the former lieutenant governor and member of the first Legislative Council, Sir Maurice O'Connell, grandson of the early governor of New South Wales, William Bligh, and godson of another, Lachlan Macquarie, was appointed first commissioner of crown lands for the Burnett district.[7]

Burnett Runs

In February 1849, Commissioner O'Connell accepted the first claim for a lease in the Burnett under the new regulations of the Waste Lands Act. This was for Rawbelle station that had been taken up by the Trevethan brothers. It was the largest of the runs in the upper Burnett, in a remote and, as time would tell, very dangerous location. Within a year, twenty-nine runs covering more than half a million acres had been claimed by tender in the district, payments made for the first year's rent and occupation of the runs authorised, pending preparation of the leases.[8] Grazing capacity was estimated to be four or five sheep per acre, or one head of cattle for every four acres, although, as elsewhere, most runs were stocked with sheep.

There was a steady movement of stock into the lower Burnett from about the middle of 1846 and the first wool teams from the new district arrived at North Brisbane in 1848 from John Borthwick's run, Tarong, after a ten-day journey via Limestone (now Ipswich).[9] Some of the lower Burnett runs, such as those on Barambah Creek, including Barambah and Mondure stations, and on the Boyne and Stuart rivers, especially Burrandowan, were typical "gentry" holdings. Mondure, of around 350 square miles, which was more or less average for a Burnett run, was first leased to Richard Jones, a wealthy Sydney merchant, pastoralist, a president of the Bank of New South Wales, and an original member of the New South Wales Legislative Council. Along with his brother-in-law, John Ferriter, he had already established nearby Barambah station. During the 1830s, the two were best known for their commerce with China, the East Indies and India, mainly in tea imports. In the mid-1850s, Jones' daughter, Mary Australia, married William Bligh O'Connell, younger brother of the commissioner of crown lands for the Burnett and the couple received Mondure as a wedding gift.

Burrandowan, the first of the Burnett runs and always the largest, was established by the already successful Darling Downs squatter, Henry Stuart

Russell. Well-watered and tucked into the lee of the Bunya Mountains, Burrandowan was a vast, rich squattage. After stocking the run, Stuart Russell sold Burrandowan in 1844 and it was sold again in June 1847 to Philip Friell, formerly of Tent Hill on the Stuart River where he had experimented with Indian labour. Friell died unexpectedly on board ship returning from England in 1854 and the station was then managed by Gordon Sandeman, during whose time in charge Burrandowan carried sixty-five thousand sheep. In 1870, the run was sold to Robert Towns, the leading importer of coloured labour to Queensland. In fact, Burrandowan was the major employer of Indian, Chinese and South Sea Islander pastoral labour throughout the whole period to 1880 when cattle began to replace sheep on Burnett runs and the demand for labour eased.

On the whole, the Burnett squatters were never quite as aristocratic in their bearing as those of the Darling Downs where, according to Duncan Waterson,

> The Pure Merinos soon created, or attempted to recreate, a society as similar as possible to that in the Old World they had left… Their model was eighteenth century English rural society.[10]

This is not to say, however, that there were not "gentlemen" by birth and education among the Burnett squatters, and several of them also had intimate connections with the bourgeoning Sydney-based colonial elite who more than made up in influence and wealth what they may have lacked in breeding. In 1853, an observer regarded the Burnett squatters as "all mostly a hard-working race, risen from the ranks you may say; that is, by their industry and perseverance, with little or no capital, they have risen to their present independent position."[11] Perhaps for those reasons, they tended to be more imperious, argumentative, demanding, driven, and more directly involved in the political affairs of the day than the older, quasi-aristocratic Downs squatters ever were. That observer did not care for these "squatter Boers" of the Burnett, describing them as

> … hospitable and generous to those bearing letters of introduction, correctly and properly authenticated by a Sydney merchant, with a balance at their bankers', and who probably require sheep, stock, or stations; whilst to those not

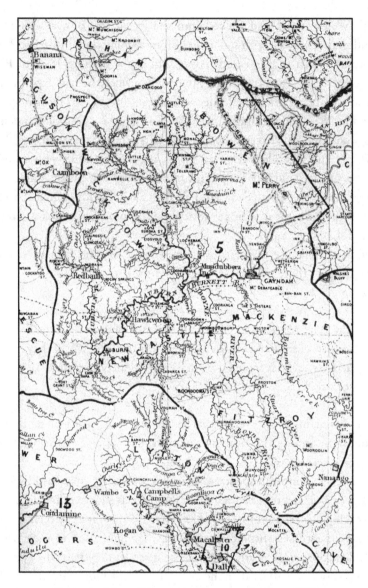

Figure 3 - Map of Queensland census districts, 1871:
Burnett District

Source: L. E. Skinner, *Police of the Pastoral Frontier* (St Lucia: University of Queensland Press, 1975).

The runs of Mondure and Boonara are recorded on this map as Proston Station and Hawkins Station respectively. Booubyjan is roughly halfway between Hawkins Station and Ban Ban Station. Durah and Jimbour stations which are mentioned in the text are shown near the southwest boundary of the district.

provided with this talismanic ring, a cold, rigid, reserved, and freezing suspicious hospitality is dispensed as a matter of necessity... For, of all narrow-minded men, the Burnett squatters, or rather the clique round about Gayndah, is certainly the most contracted.[12]

From as early as 1850, most of them were vociferously pro-separation from New South Wales but they were equally opposed to Brisbane being named capital of the new colony they demanded. Their stiff-necked obduracy came at a cost. When the New South Wales government finally acceded to their demands for protection during the Aboriginal War, they refused to accept the advice of the commandant of the Native Police, Frederick Walker, and then proceeded to call for and won his dismissal from the force, with serious repercussions not only for the integrity of this special police force, but for the lives of remote area squatters and indigenous people alike.

In 1859, when a large portion of the Northern Districts finally separated from New South Wales and formed the new British colony of Queensland, the first governor, Sir George Bowen made a tour of the colony and wrote generally of the squatters he met:

These gentlemen live in a patriarchal style among their immense flocks and herds, amusing themselves with hunting, shooting, fishing and the exercise of a plentiful hospitality. I have often thought ... that the Queensland gentlemen-squatters bear a similar relation to the other Australians that the Virginian planters of a hundred years back bore to the Americans.[13]

Like most generalisations, this description was no doubt true in part and on occasion, such as during a visit from the colonial governor. During the decade before the governor's tour, however, there was little time for relaxation on Burnett runs, and even an Eton education would have been sorely tested by the likes of young William Harvey Holt who, at age eighteen, found himself getting his colonial experience at Yenda station in 1851.[14]

Robert Wilkin and William Holt of Yenda were among that restless group of young squatters who continued to push the frontier northwards into the midwaters of Barambah Creek and eventually to the headwaters of the Burnett River itself. In the vanguard were the Archer brothers who settled Eidsvold and adjacent Coonambula and Culcraigie stations in the central upper reaches of the district. They were accompanied by others including James Blair Reid (Ideraway), Ned Hawkins (Boonara), the Lawless brothers (Booubyjan and Windera), the Lawson brothers (Boondooma), David Perrier and William Henry Walsh (Degilbo), and Henry Herbert and William Humphreys (Ban Ban and Wetheron). By 1870, almost all these squattages in the Burnett district had changed hands at least once. Among the first settlers, Charles Haly, lessee of Taabinga and the first elected member of the New South Wales parliament to represent the Burnett, stayed a little longer only to sell up in 1875, leaving Booubyjan station as the only one which still remains in the hands of the original settler family.

The reasons for selling up and leaving the district were probably as numerous as the squatters themselves. First among these reasons, however, was financial opportunity, speculation being rife at a time when it was said that those with access to funds worth £500 to £1,000 could be confident of a healthy return on their investment.[15] By 1847, according to various analyses, the colony was enjoying either a reprieve from the severe depression in the financial market which had put a brake on pastoral expansion and wool prices from the beginning of the decade, or it had already recovered from the downturn. It was, in any case, a year of optimism, one that encouraged already experienced squatters to drive their flocks north from Bathurst or, in the case of Gregory Blaxland and William Forster, from the Clarence District in search of new pastures.

The colony had already established its reputation as a supplier of fine wool to England's mills and, before the 1851 gold rush that changed the young economy in dramatic fashion, wool, as T. A. Coghlan reminds us, represented two-thirds of the total value of the exports of the colony, and tallow, the product of boiling down sheep that was sold for use mainly in the English armaments manufacturing industry, represented about one-quarter of the value of the remaining exports.[16] These facts, he says, explain the dominant position of the pastoralists and account for the favourable terms granted them for the occupation of crown lands; it was felt that the whole colony depended upon their prosperity. The squatters, among them the colony's leading officials and legislators, did indeed represent a powerful self-interested lobby. According to James Boyce,

> The fact that by 1849, some 1019 squatters occupied nearly
> 17.7 million hectares in eastern Australia did not reflect a

rational public-policy choice of Australian "reality", but the power of a vested interest.[17]

Speculation must surely have been the major reason for the steady handover of runs in the Burnett. It was, after all, a well-established tradition in the colony's pastoral industry to purchase a licence or lease, stock the run and then sell the disposable stock and improvements at a profit to a newcomer. For the squatters, the real profits came not from the export of their wool, but from the physical expansion of the industry itself. Speculation, in many ways, provided the dynamic for the spread of the industry and for the constant redefining of the colonial frontier. Risk-taking was part of the squatter's character. A case in point was that of the partnership of Humphreys and Herbert which ended in 1850, soon after they were granted leases for Wetheron and the three adjacent runs that were managed as one property. It is said that they tossed a coin to decide who would have which run; in the toss-up, Humphreys won Wetheron, and Herbert had to settle for Ban Ban.[18]

If risk-taking was part of the squatter's character, so too was restless ambition. For all its promise of high-spirited adventure, pioneer squatting life, according to Michael Roe, was "tedious, lonely, even brutal, set in a strange environment; it had little attraction save anarchic freedom and the promise of wealth."[19] Once a run was stocked and leased, the ambitious young squatter seemed impatient to escape the confines and responsibilities of the strange, small society that the run created. Three of the nine Archer brothers, David, Tom and John, highly experienced and superb bushmen, were typical of this mindset. They soon sold their splendid Eidsvold run and continued north until they eventually settled down on Gracemere station located almost exactly on the Tropic of Capricorn and not far from the present-day city of Rockhampton.

From his tour of the colony in 1859, the first Queensland governor may have taken away memories of an idyllic life on the squatters' runs, but the day-to-day reality of white society lived on the frontier was another matter altogether. These are the stark recollections of an early settler on the Darling Downs:

> If I could piece together the picture of that epoch ... the savage deeds, the crude life, the hatred between men and women and country, the homesickness, the loneliness, the despair of inescapable exile in the bush; the strange forms of madness and cruelty; the brooding, inturned characters;

and, joined with this, an almost fanatic idealism which repudiated the past and the tyranny of the past and looked to the future in a new country for a new heaven and earth, a new justice; on the one hand, the social outcasts, men broken by degradation and suffering, on the other, the adventurers: blackest pessimism balancing the most radiant optimism— if I could only see all this, then I would understand.[20]

In the early years, life on the Burnett runs involved all these facets of personality and character. Colonial frontier society brought together a strange mix of people from many different backgrounds of ethnicity, class, religion, education, and experience. In normal circumstances, they would never have crossed paths but on the frontier, as in war perhaps, they were intimately dependent on each other for their survival. The most obvious social division at the time, that between bond and free, was as rigorous as caste. In his seminal work on the colonial Australian character, Russel Ward notes that until 1850, in New South Wales as a whole, the ratio of "old" to "new" Australians, that is those of convict origin and their offspring to free immigrants, was approximately three to two, and the figure was higher "up the country" where in 1851, at the beginning of the gold rush, it was still nearly two to one.[21]

In the Burnett, however, the returns of the New South Wales census of the non-indigenous population, taken on March 1, 1851, suggest quite a different societal structure.[22] The total district population was recorded as 852, with a gender ratio, female to male, of one to seven. Three-quarters of the 740 males were aged twenty-one to forty-five, but there were only fifty-nine wives in the district, at least on the night of the census. All the women recorded in the district were "free", including two emancipists. The gender disparity was the highest in the whole colony, but the difference in "civil condition", one's ranking on the scale from bond to free, was surprisingly low. On the Darling Downs, among the male population, there were slightly more emancipists and ticket-of-leave holders than native-born or free immigrants. In the Burnett, on the other hand, there were only eighty-eight ticket-of-leave holders, and a further 180 emancipists in the total male population that was almost two-thirds native-born or "arrived free". In the adjacent district of Wide Bay, the ratio of native-born/free arrival to those of convict origin was even higher at almost three to one. It is safe to assume that these figures were false; on the frontier, where labour was always acutely short, it made no sense to query a man's background if he declared himself "free" on a census return. The

Five of the nine Archer brothers and a friend (centre back) in Brisbane, 1867. Tom is standing second from the left. (John Oxley Library, State Library of Queensland, Neg: 8875)

frontier presented a perfect opportunity for a man to re-invent himself. Half of the entire population of the Burnett gave their occupation as "shepherds and persons in the management of sheep." This was surely "civil condition" enough.

In the Burnett, however, the returns of the New South Wales census of the non-indigenous population, taken on March 1, 1851, suggest quite a different societal structure.[22] The total district population was recorded as 852, with a gender ratio, female to male, of one to seven. Three-quarters of the 740 males were aged twenty-one to forty-five, but there were only fifty-nine wives in the district, at least on the night of the census. All the women recorded in the district were "free", including two emancipists. The gender disparity was the highest in the whole colony, but the difference in "civil condition", one's ranking on the scale from bond to free, was surprisingly low. On the Darling Downs, among the male population, there were slightly more emancipists and ticket-of-leave holders than native-born or free immigrants. In the Burnett, on the other hand, there were only eighty-eight ticket-of-leave holders, and a further 180 emancipists in the total male population that was almost two-thirds native-born or "arrived free". In the adjacent district of Wide Bay, the ratio of native-born/free arrival to those of convict origin was even higher at almost three to one. It is safe to assume that these figures were false; on the frontier, where labour was always acutely short, it made no sense to query a man's background if he declared himself "free" on a census return. The frontier presented a perfect opportunity for a man to re-invent himself. Half of the entire population of the Burnett gave their occupation as "shepherds and persons in the management of sheep." This was surely "civil condition" enough.

All the same, whether gentleman squatter, freed or bond convict, ethnic English, Irish, Scottish, Chinese, or "other", the loneliness, that "despair of inescapable exile in the bush" must have afflicted all of the Burnett residents from time to time. Give or take one hundred or so residents who lived in closer quarters in the township of Gayndah, the lingering image left by results of the 1851 census is one of around 750 foreign souls scattered across more than 35,000 square kilometres of a still unknown, even hostile land, most of them occupied with the care of half a million sheep.

Burnett Urban Society

The small township of Gayndah offered some respite from the loneliness and tedium of the bush. Founded in 1849 on the site where the commissioner of

crown lands chose to locate his office, on the banks of the Burnett River near
James Blair Reid's run, Ideraway, it grew quickly to serve the needs of the
squatters, as a newspaper article written in September 1850 reported,

> This new township is already beginning to assume an air of
> activity which will be no doubt greatly increased as the wool
> season advances. There is an excellent hotel, where every
> accommodation and comfort is afforded to travellers, at
> reasonable charges. There are also a butcher, shoemaker, and
> two blacksmiths established here. There is every probability
> of this township becoming a general warehousing place
> for wool and rations, etc. for the west and north-west
> settlers. Several carriers are already fully employed in this
> business, and from the central position of Gayndah, it is not
> unlikely that settlers will generally make arrangements for
> warehousing wool here, to be forwarded by carriers to Wide
> Bay, and get their rations in the same manner.[23]

A *Sydney Morning Herald* reader was so taken by this "flourishing account"
that he made the journey overland to Gayndah to decide what prospect there
was for opening a store or an inn there. The date of his eyewitness report
would more or less have coincided with the taking of the 1851 census:

> Gayndah, situated on the banks of the Burnett River,
> contains at the present time a population (including servants
> and children) of one hundred inhabitants, scattered over
> a distance of five miles. There are four public-houses, ...
> two stores for the supply of the squatters and their men,
> one butcher, and a shoemaker. Three constables and a chief
> constable, with two doctors, complete the inhabitants.
> Gayndah is an extremely badly selected and unhealthy
> place for a township; a long sandy green, with a few bark huts
> scattered along it in would-be streets, surrounded so entirely
> by high ridges or thick scrub that hardly a breath of air can
> reach the perspiring inhabitants.[24]

He believed that Gayndah would never be a place of importance, including
in his argument the fact that "almost every station in the two districts of Wide

Bay and Burnett is supplied with Chinese or Coolie labourers, whose wages are so small they have nothing to lay out …". The township that had "sprung up like a mushroom" would "wither and fall to the ground", in his opinion. The colonial authorities believed otherwise and in June that year Gayndah, along with Maryborough, the central township for Wide Bay and the seaport for Burnett wool, was gazetted as a police district.[25] The township provided a social and commercial hub, especially for the squatters and their wives, the main event of the annual social calendar being the Gayndah races that commenced in June 1852.

Dreams and Disappointment

For some squatters, the difficulty of farming sheep on the frontier of white settlement proved too daunting. Early optimism was soon eroded by the daily grind of coping with diseases among the flocks such as scab and catarrh and combating introduced pests like speargrass, not to mention the native dogs that ravaged the flocks, recurrent droughts and floods, and distance from everything that represented civilization to them. The immediate and seemingly intractable problems, however, were the militant resistance from the indigenous peoples to white settlement, and the chronic shortage of affordable labour.

There could hardly have been a more optimistic pastoralist in the Burnett than B. J. Bertelsen, overseer for Ned Hawkins who had brought stock north from Bathurst in 1846 and marked out Boonara on a tributary of Barambah Creek. At the end of the following year, he wrote to the *Moreton Bay Courier* in praise of the district, giving what he termed "an account of the doings of our northern pioneers in the march of civilisation and subjugation of the wilderness to the purposes of man."[26] The runs on tributaries of the Burnett, he believed, were the best he had found since crossing the country from Bathurst, with the exception of some of the stations on the Darling Downs. He explained,

> The grass resembles that growing in Europe, being very
> thick, abounding with herbage, barley, and kangaroo grass,
> quite equal to the much lauded oaten-grass on the Downs.
> On my arrival, I was much pleased with the country; indeed,
> it exceeded my utmost expectations, for it resembles English

park scenery, with rich undulating ridges, large flats, and abundance of water... [T]he country in the immediate neighbourhood of the Burnett is sandy, scrubby, and good for nothing; but that on the tributaries is very open, with rich soil, and excellent pasturage for sheep. There is still a good deal of country unoccupied in this part of the district; I expect, however, it will soon be taken up by the Brisbane gentlemen whose runs cannot be compared with this country.

His drays, he said, were the first to travel the new road to Maryborough, the shipping port at Wide Bay, a journey of about sixty miles (one hundred kilometres), far shorter than the usual route to Brisbane through Limestone.

Soon after news of the 1849 California gold discoveries reached the Burnett, Ned Hawkins, Bertelsen's employer, paid a visit to Tom Archer on Eidsvold station. They discussed the matter and, as Tom Archer recalled, "I was getting tired of the monotony of settled bush life" so they formed a party of three squatters, three "black boys" and two "Chinamen" and sailed to America to join the rush, leaving Bertelsen in charge at Boonara.[27] In February 1850, Hawkins' death by drowning in California was reported in the colonial press.[28] Bertelsen remained on the run and in mid-1852, he was listed among thirty-six licensed occupants of crown lands paying assessment on stock in the Burnett District.[29] At the beginning of January the following year, however, Boonara was advertised for sale, complete with "12,000 sound sheep, more or less, enquiries to B. J. Bertelsen, proprietor, residing on station."[30]

What had happened in the three years or so after Hawkins left for America seems to have driven an articulate, positive, experienced bushmen like Bertelsen to near madness. Murphy and Easton, in their local history, record that Ned Hawkins had followed a policy of "scrupulous humanity in dealing with blacks" and that this policy had secured him "immunity from native attack."[31] That this immunity did not extend to Bertelsen may have less to do with Bertelsen's own approach towards them than with the declaration of war on white invaders of indigenous lands, a war that had been growing in intensity since the middle of 1849.

In December 1850, part of Boonara's flock was taken by Aborigines.[32] In August the following year, Bertelsen, referring to himself as "Squatter of Burnett Gentlemen," addressed the commandant of the Native Police via the Sydney press:

In the course of a week I have nearly had all my rams roasted by the blacks setting fire all round them, and leaving no way for the shepherd to extricate them from their dangerous position. Several of the sheep died from the effect, and the wool of the remainder is more or less damaged. Twice the blacks have cut off 300 to 400 at a time, which I fortunately partially rescued from their hands by getting early notice of it. If this state of affairs is to continue, and we are left to our own resources, to protect our property the best we can, what, may I ask, is the use of the [Native] Police? They certainly become no more nor less than a mere nominal and perfectly useless force.[33]

It was not indigenous hostility, however, that forced Bertelsen to sell up and leave the Burnett. The real cause of his downfall was his shameful treatment of the Chinese indentured labourers on Boonara. In September 1852, in the Gayndah courthouse, Bertelsen charged four Chinese workers in his employment with assault. He claimed that he had been knocked down with an iron dray pole pin and his nose was broken. On cross-examination, according to the press, Bertelsen admitted that at the time of this occurrence he had "a private lock-up, or a Chinese tied upright in a little meat safe ... by the throat, arms and legs, and without food or water for two or three days and nights."[34] He argued that he had been given to understand that "this was found an efficacious mode of discipline upon stations where Chinese are employed." From the Bench, Henry Herbert, J. P., remarked that a Chinese in Bertelsen's employment had lately come over to his station marked from head to foot with a stock whip, to which Bertelsen replied that it was very likely, as they were in the habit of fighting together. Herbert said he was not aware that the Chinese fought with stock whips and that this man was marked with the cuts of a stock whip all over his body. After the hearing, the Bench committed the four Chinese workers for trial, stating that this was as much for their protection as for Bertelsen's.

This was not the end of the affair. The newspaper report continued:

> Since [the hearing], the Chief Constable from Gayndah has been summoned over from Boonara to apprehend a lot more Chinese, charged with a revolt upon the station and threatening to burn the head station down. On his arrival

he found a tribe of blacks encamped right round the house, in order to prevent the Chinese from burning it down; and Mrs Bertelsen in a fearful state of alarm, with four double barrelled guns loaded, in the parlour, ready for action. Ten of Mr Bertelsen's Chinese are now in the lock-up, or outside the Court House at Gayndah, waiting to obtain or receive justice. Such doings require no comment.[35]

Within weeks, Bertelsen had acknowledged defeat. He withdrew the charges against his Chinese servants and transferred their agreements to other squatters in the district. Nevertheless, more shepherds on Boonara left their flocks, "leaving nineteen thousand sheep to be divided into three flocks; four thousand ewes lambing down together."[36] The situation was irremediable and Bertelsen's reputation in the district was worthless.

Aboriginal Resistance

The indigenous inhabitants, the original owner-custodians of the territory proclaimed by the colonial governor as the Burnett district, knew their country as Wakka Wakka.[37] Their lands coincided with the country drained by the Burnett and its tributaries behind the coastal range. In 1859, according to Jill Slack, thousands of Aboriginal clanspeople occupied this region, including those of the Thibura clan of Gayndah, the Yarmbura clan of Boonara, Warbaa of Monduran, Yawai of Walla, and Nukunukubura of Mount Perry. By 1880, it was estimated that fewer than 150 men, women and children were left.[38] Their numbers were decimated by infectious diseases that the Europeans brought with them, such as smallpox, measles, tuberculosis, influenza, and venereal diseases. Their culture and traditions were violated by the sexual demands of white men (and Chinese men) who neither knew nor cared about the intricate laws surrounding marriage and progeny. An untold number were deliberately poisoned with strychnine and arsenic, both in plentiful supply on all runs and used for the eradication of native dogs in the first instance and for the treatment of scab in sheep in the other. Many of the leaders among them were shot or trampled to death by horses during the frontier war.

For four years, between 1849 and 1853, the various clans of the Wakka people engaged in a war of resistance to European occupation of their lands. The number of aboriginal deaths during that war is not recorded; the deaths of

Burnett Valley seen from McConnell's Lookout near Gayndah

Part of Boonara Station, 2012.

squatters, overseers, shepherds and other station hands, however, were carefully collated and avenged and were made the subject of inquiries by parliamentary committees and endless discussion in the colonial press.

There were some earlier instances of Europeans attacked and killed in the Burnett but these were isolated incidents that had an immediate and discernible cause. In August 1847, for example, a shepherd named John Rogers was struck by a tomahawk and killed on Barambah station, while later that year, the lessee, George Furber, survived an attack which sparked wild rumours of a general massacre on his station.[39] B. J. Bertelsen dismissed those rumours as malicious, explaining,

> Mr Furber's own men state the reason why the blacks attacked him was because he had failed to provide them with sufficient rations, according to his promise for stripping bark and doing other work for him; and that in serving out the flour to them it was spread over a large surface, to make it appear a greater quantity than there was in reality; at which the blacks were greatly dissatisfied, and which, no doubt, was the reason for their seeking revenge for what they conceived to be an injury.[40]

Furber had also supplied them with alcohol and the effects it produced caused them to believe that he had tried to poison them. Bertelsen believed, with good reason, that some Europeans invited trouble on themselves.

Towards the end of 1848, however, the squatters were reporting "savage outrages" committed during incidents which obviously involved both organization and careful planning. In one incident, for example, a Burnett station was attacked, men driven off it, huts burned to the ground, and bales of wool set alight.[41] Renewed calls were being made for the assistance of the Native Police:

> The complete impunity with which the natives are indulging their savage and bloody propensities in this unprotected district, calls for the prompt interference of the Government, and we hope that the appeal for help, now made for the hundredth time, will not be made in vain.[42]

When their demands fell on deaf ears, the Burnett squatters took matters of justice into their own hands. Perhaps the worst act of European violence against the indigenous peoples of the Burnett and Wide Bay districts was one of revenge for the killing of Gregory Blaxland, son of the New South Wales pastoralist best remembered for opening a route from Sydney across the Blue Mountains. He and his nephew, William Forster, had moved their stock north from the Clarence District following an incident during which an aboriginal man was shot.[43] Both men, former magistrates of the territory, were subsequently removed from the Commission of the Peace, although Forster later claimed that he had never been informed of the grounds for his dismissal. They settled on the Kolan River, on the seaward side of the Burnett coastal range and submitted tenders for a large run, Tirroan (later Gin Gin). In fact, their tender was invalid because the Kolan area remained beyond the boundaries of either Wide Bay or Burnett districts until 1854, and Blaxland and Forster's occupation of the run was therefore illegal.[44]

In mid-1849, two young shepherds were speared to death on Tirroan. Blaxland organized a punitive expedition with neighbouring squatters and pursued the Taribelang clan he considered to be responsible, trapping them on the bank of the Burnett at the place now known as the Cedars, about twenty kilometres from the station.[45] The clan suffered heavy casualties. Almost exactly one year later, servants found Blaxland's mutilated body only two hundred metres from the Tirroan homestead. Within a week, according to Tony Matthews, "a huge force was gathered from Walla, Yenda, Barambah, Booubyjan, Kolonga, Eureka, Boonara and Ideraway - bristling with arms and violent determination ready to avenge the death of this aristocrat of pioneer squatters."[46] This force of squatters and their servants, led by Forster and W. H. Walsh of Degilbo, was sworn in as special constables by Captain O'Connell, the commissioner for crown lands, before they hunted down the suspects near the mouth of the Burnett River, on Paddy's Island. It is said that the assembled aborigines there numbered "about one thousand."[47] This rough figure may have been an exaggeration, but deliberate efforts were subsequently made to downplay what was undoubtedly a massacre. Many years later, Les Hopton who was born on Paddy's Island in 1907 and grew up with the aboriginal people there recalled,

> One of the main things one old black fellow would say was, "Don't go over that river. Debil. Debil." The hummock used to smoke, he'd say. It came down through the ages to him;

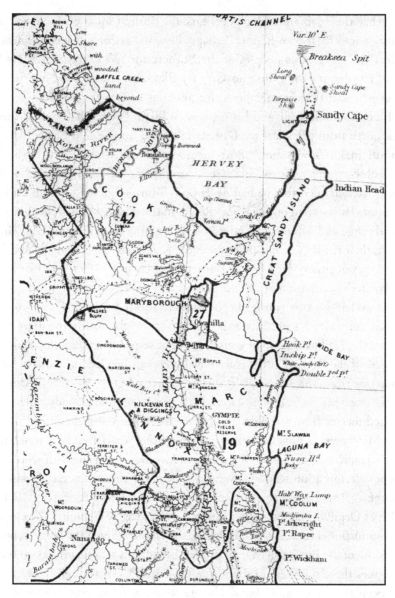

Figure 4 - Map of Queensland census districts, 1871:
Wide Bay District

Source: L. E. Skinner, *Police of the Pastoral Frontier* (St Lucia: University of Queensland Press, 1975.)

This map adjoins Figure 3 on the east. It shows the early settlement of Bundaberg town and "Sloping Hummock", or simply the Hummock, which is referred to in the text.

his people must have told him. I think that was why they didn't cross over, the time they were all rounded up and shot on the Island. My granny used to mention it. Two of the blunderbusses were still on the farm when I was there; we used to use them for shooting crows.[48]

Throughout 1851, the newspapers reported several attacks that were similar in detail to those that Bertelsen had complained of: sheep cut off from the flock and destroyed or stolen. The pattern was very much the same in the Burnett, the Wide Bay and especially in the Dawson Valley that bordered the Burnett district in the northwest. There were more fatalities among the white population. A Legislative Council Paper entitled "Murder by Aborigines in the Northern Districts" was tabled in May 1853, providing details of the number of deaths during the five years from 1847 to 1851, inclusive.[49] In the Burnett alone, there had been fourteen victims in that period: nine labourers and the wife of one of them, two graziers, and two Indian Coolies (a hutkeeper and a shepherd). These numbers did not include those of Blaxland and his three servants, a further one having been killed in a subsequent attack on the station.

During the first six months of 1852, there was a dramatic escalation of conflict with a further nine deaths, and fears that there would be a "general rising" among the Aborigines during winter. Stations on the river had been attacked at three different points almost simultaneously.[50] In March, there came news of an attack on Rawbelle station in the far northwest of the Burnett. Adolphus H. Trevethan and two Chinese shepherds were killed in the raid and 1,700 sheep were driven away. The bearer of this information continued,

> [T]hey marched on the head station, some five hundred strong and with loud voices and gesticulations, demanded that Mrs Thompson, the wife of the overseer, should be given up to them. On this, Mr Trevethan ran out of his hut, unarmed, to hold a parley. He was in the act of picking up some tobacco he had given which they threw with vengeance to the ground, when he was speared in several places. The unfortunate man succeeded in getting back to his hut, where he expired in about two hours.

The blacks then drove away the whole of the rams, with
the rest of the sheep. This station is the same as that on which
Mr Street was killed some months ago. Only last shearing
the blacks bailed up all the shearers and took the whole of
their blankets, tea, sugar, quart and pint pots, and clothing
away; the men not being able to resist for want of arms and
ammunition.[51]

From this account, the reader should infer that relations between the
newcomers and the original inhabitants had been bad for some time. The
demand for the handing over of the overseer's wife was a sure indication of
sexual transgression committed against the indigenous women by the white
men on the run, but there were other factors involved. Six years after the death
of Trevethan and the two Chinese shepherds, during evidence given by James
Blair Reid before the Select Committee of the New South Wales Legislative
Assembly on "Murders by the Aborigines on the Dawson River", he was asked
to give his opinion about why the terrible murders at Hornet Bank and Cullin-
la-ringo stations that had left thirty Europeans dead, including women and
children, had occurred. Reid replied,

I suppose they must either be a more determined race of
blacks there [in the Dawson Valley]; or, in many cases, from
what I hear, it has been traced to aggression on the part of
the whites, such as firing salt at them at night. That was the
case in poor Trevethan's murder.[52]

The effect of the salt pellets, he said, "would cut the skin and irritate
them - make the blacks mad almost."

Writing about the peculiar race relations on the frontier, Eric Rolls made
a salient point:

When a shepherd in a lonely hut was speared, if he saw the
man who threw it, he knew him by a name. And, when
stockmen rode out to shoot Aborigines in retaliation, they
counted the dead by name. But the names they called them
were cursory and degrading: Bobby, Saturday, Sunday, King
Billy … in choosing names for Aboriginal acquaintances they
took less trouble than teamsters in naming their working

bullocks. The whites were often more savage than the Aborigines who were sometimes simply outraged, sometimes bewildered into violence by persistent transgressions against their moral codes.[53]

The ringleader in the attack on Rawbelle was at first thought to be "Jacky". The dead man's older brother, W. Trevethan, deposed that the man they called Jacky, shot dead by the police during the course of an arrest, was known to him for three years and that he was the leading man in the attack on Adolphus Trevethan; this was also sworn to by a servant on the station.[54] Another Aboriginal man, "Davy" was committed for participation in the murder and stood trial in the Brisbane Circuit Court in May 1854. He was found guilty on the evidence of only one witness, a workman on Rawbelle, and sentenced to death. His execution in front of Brisbane Gaol was reported in the *Moreton Bay Courier* on August 26 that year as the "one such public example" of justice for the killing of "about fifty white men" in the Northern Districts. "We consider that the Executive acted with proper firmness and judgement in carrying out the sentence of the law upon this occasion," the newspaper said. "The aboriginal natives had so frequently escaped the punishment of their crimes that they had begun to look upon the sentence of death as a mere bugbear and a farce." The journalist ignored the obvious fact that when white men went out to avenge the death of one of their kind they killed with impunity, as they had on Paddy's Island. By the end of 1853, only one white Burnett resident, James Smart, a shepherd on Booubyjan station, had been tried and sentenced for the wilful murder of an Aboriginal person, a woman named "Kitty". He was found guilty of manslaughter and sentenced to six years' hard labour, two of them in irons.[55] During the same session of the Brisbane Circuit Court that convicted James Smart, two Maryborough men were found not guilty of the manslaughter of an Aboriginal man, "Diamond", who had allegedly robbed their hut. The dead man was found with a head wound and a rope tied tightly around his neck. The two white men were discharged with a caution to show more discretion in future.[56]

The open hostilities, however, were over. The press reported in April 1853, "It is the general opinion of the settlers in the Wide Bay and Burnett Districts that war is at an end."[57] More than that, an indigenous labour force was proving to be both reliable and productive on some of the runs:

Men and boys are now shepherding without arms, and travelling along the roads with their blankets on their backs, as unconcerned as though they were in Sydney streets. The sheep on some stations are being shepherded by blacks, - stations with sixteen thousand sheep and the salvation of the masters ensured by their help when their Chinese servants bolted. On others, the whole of the washing was done by them; on one station, thirty thousand sheep were washed by natives with one white man; on others, the masters acknowledge that they, by their assistance in shepherding, in lambing down, in sheep-washing, and in shearing, effect a saving of from £150 to £250 per annum on their establishments.[58]

Although the regular tirades in the colonial newspapers may have suggested a state of total confrontation between the European newcomers and the indigenous inhabitants, in fact, the majority of Burnett squatters had generally followed a policy of "letting in" the original inhabitants on the runs. The local clan members taught the squatters the contours of the bush and helped with the early tasks of stripping bark and erecting rudimentary shelters. They were paid with rations of tea, flour and perhaps tobacco. It was only after the war started that the policy became contentious, and, oddly, especially after the policy was urged on all the squatters by Frederick Walker, the commandant of the Native Police. Some of the squatters, especially Forster and Walsh remained so opposed to any form of authority that they refused to acknowledge advice that was simply common sense. Others, such as the Strathdees of Cooranga, had worked their whole run with indigenous labour from the start, and the Archers persisted with their open-door policy, although the farther north and west one went in the Burnett, the less this was likely to be the case.

Despite the rare exceptions, however, from the beginning of white settlement in the Burnett, it had always been obvious that Aboriginal labour, even when willingly offered, would be insufficient for the needs of the expanding pastoral industry in the Burnett. There was no existing pool of surplus white labour in New South Wales to draw on either. Throughout the colony, according to James Boyce,

By 1846 fewer than six thousand permanent workers were tending three million sheep and a third of a million cattle. These men were shepherds, shearers, bullock drivers, builders, carpenters, splitters, sawyers, fencers, hunters and mercenaries, often all in one. The squatters did not let moral judgments distort their verdict on the capacities of emancipist bushmen.[59]

Given the blood-curdling stories in the colonial press of Aboriginal atrocities on the northern frontier, neither these experienced bushmen nor the free immigrants who started to arrive in Moreton Bay in 1848 could be attracted to work on pastoral runs in the Burnett. The urgent need for labour would require some novel solutions and original sources that would frequently test British law and the patience of the British Colonial Office in almost equal measure.

CHAPTER 4

Labour Issues

The last ship from England transporting convicts to New South Wales arrived in Moreton Bay in May 1850. The *Bangalore* carried 290 Pentonville exiles, all young men, who were to serve out the remainder of their sentence in the Northern Districts on a conditional pardon, the condition being that they should not return to Britain within the term of the original sentence, seven years in most cases. At almost the same time, 108 Chinese indentured workers on five-year contracts disembarked from the *Favorite* that had brought them north from Sydney. The arrival of the convicts especially revived the spirits of the squatters, it was reported, and it was assumed that all would be engaged by various agents within one day, "so that in fact not one-half will get supplied to the number required."[1] The northern squatters, hungry for labour and ever querulous, blamed the government for the lack of available workingmen in their districts. They accused Sydney of appropriating land sale revenue for the benefit solely of the Middle District. The land fund was used to attract migrants from the British Isles, but hardly any of them came to Moreton Bay, let alone to the unsettled districts farther north. So disgruntled were the northerners that they let it be known they were forming a league to petition Queen Victoria and the House of Commons to separate the Northern Districts from the Sydney government.[2]

The Burnett district squatters may have been in urgent need of labour but as in the rest of the colony, for them it was not simply a case of labour at any cost. In fact, there were some colonists who argued that there was no lack of labour at all; rather, there was not enough of the type of labour that the squatters wanted—docile, submissive, reliable, intelligent, preferably single and male, and above all, cheap. It is hardly surprising, therefore, that every attempt to solve their labour problem failed to engage their ideal workingman: the perfect convict servant.

Labour Demand

British convict labour in Australia had never been a chattel that could be bought and sold, transferred, or otherwise mistreated at will by those to whom it was assigned. The British Government, as Coghlan explains, handed over the convicts' indentures to the persons who were contracted to transport them to Australia and, on arrival, these indentures were transferred to the governor of New South Wales.[3] When the governor assigned prisoners as servants to his military and civil officers, they remained his responsibility. He regulated the conditions of their employment and he could grant them conditional or absolute pardon; in theory, only the governor could punish assigned convicts with severity but appealing to the local magistrates against the brutality of their masters was futile for the assignees since the magistrates, in all instances, were themselves employers of convicts.

Organized sectors of public opinion in Britain, buoyed by the success of the anti-slavery campaign, strongly opposed the assignment system. To abandon it, however, would have been expensive; it cost almost as much to support a convict in New South Wales as it did in a British prison. Assignment of convicts, if the masters housed, fed and clothed them, eased the cost to the British government's satisfaction but it denied the colony the public labour force required to build roads and other essential infrastructure that those same masters demanded. Successive governors trialled various balances of assignment and government employment. Under Governor Darling, in 1827, for example, there were ten convicts working for the government compared to every twenty-six of them in assignment, but the trend was moving inexorably towards the latter arrangement.

The convict system in New South Wales reached its peak in the 1830s when a total of 31,200 prisoners arrived, compared to only half that number (15,030) who had arrived in the previous decade.[4] The ongoing controversy surrounding the whole issue of convict transportation also accelerated and in 1837, a parliamentary select committee of enquiry into transportation, chaired by Sir William Molesworth, recommended that the transportation of

British convicts to New South Wales and the settled districts of Van Diemen's Land be discontinued as soon as possible. Coghlan notes that when it was announced in 1839 that the system would end, there were about twenty-five thousand convicts on assignment, and as many more could have been placed had they been available.[5] "Six years later," he continues, "the number had fallen to less than one thousand; there was a very large deficiency in the class of labour that the pastoralists demanded." Furthermore, as the convicts finished their sentences or won their tickets-of-leave, just as many left the districts where they had been employed as remained there, leaving the landowners even more short-handed.

Pastoralists were forced to switch to paid, free labour just as their profits were declining as a consequence of the severe drought of the late 1830s and the economic depression that affected wool prices from the beginning of the 1840s. Wages, however, were also affected by the depression. In the older settled districts, a shepherd at that time earned £16 annually with rations and a hut, while in the farther reaches of the unsettled districts, a shepherd's annual wage was between £25 and £30.[6] Raw figures like these must be treated with caution, however, because cash rarely changed hands. Away from the towns, wages were paid by orders drawn on merchants or agents in Sydney and they were liable to heavy discounts when surrendered. Furthermore, in remote districts, workers had little option but to purchase their clothing and extra rations at the station store where prices were often marked up far in excess of those at normal retail stores. Consequently, it is difficult to estimate with any accuracy what rural labour was actually worth in money terms. There were two steady indicators of wage levels: wool prices and the level of migration. The following table shows how fluctuations in the price of wool throughout the 1840s affected the average wage of a shepherd or agricultural labourer in the Middle District of New South Wales:

Table 1: Wages in relation to wool prices and exports, 1839–1850[7]

Year	Annual Wages of shepherds and agricultural labourers (average)	Wool price per pound (average paid in London, in pence sterling)	Wool Exports in pounds weight
1839	£15-25	14.75d.	7,213,584 lbs
1841	£24-27	15.75d.	12,959,671 lbs

1842	£16	15d.	17,433,780 lbs
1843	£14-15	13d.	17,589,712 lbs
1844	£14-15	11.5d.	24,150,687 lbs
1845	£17-18	14d.	21,865,270 lbs
1846	£20	15d.	26,056,815 lbs
1847	£23	13.5d.	30,034,567 lbs
1848	£21	13d.	35,774,671 lbs
1849	£17-18	10.5d.	39,018,221 lbs
1850	£17-18	12d.	41,426,655 lbs
1851	£17-18 (until gold discoveries)		

As the table shows, apart from some instability between 1843 and 1845, wool production throughout eastern Australia increased steadily despite fluctuations in price, and while wages also fluctuated according to wool prices, the trend was towards sustained higher wages. The demand for labour rose commensurately with production and it was a loud and immoderate voice, a newspaper editorial of 1846 declaring,

> In all parts of the interior, agricultural and pastoral, there is an urgent and increasing demand for more labourers. Wages are rising so rapidly that unless checked by a competition of which we see no prospect, they will soon have reached a point at which they will leave no profit to employers. It is to be feared, indeed, that in some districts this point has already been attained; and still, even at those unbearable rates, the number of hands absolutely required for immediate operations cannot be procured.[8]

Some wondered, all things considered, if transportation was really as bad as it had been portrayed. Even those so recently critical of the convict system began to make excuses for it, noting that of the forty-three thousand transportees who then numbered among the total New South Wales population of 187,413, only about two thousand had been "troublesome".[9] The anti-transportationists were more specific in their argument. Detailed calculations were undertaken to estimate the exact labour requirements of the pastoral industry. Between 1841 and 1846, the number of sheep had doubled but the number of shepherds had hardly increased at all. At the same time, however, the colony's population had also increased at the rate of between four thousand and five thousand males added yearly to the labour force, or, more precisely, to the future labour force. The colonial press, taking up the anti-transportation cause, concluded that the needs of the labour market had been exaggerated. It argued against the "wretched impolicy" of transportation "which would pour into our sheepwalks the criminal outcasts of Great Britain and brand the life of a shepherd as the especial vocation of convicts …".[10]

Another side of the argument, that of the landed gentry, proposed that the problem was really about over-production of wool and the greed of squatters whose assumption was that flocks could increase indefinitely. "The squatting districts now in occupation, 1,600 miles in length and 300 [miles] wide," wrote an established Sydney pastoralist, "are capable of supporting thirty millions of sheep. But were we to continue multiplying our flocks as we have done, we should, ultimately render them valueless."[11] Renewed transportation would provide merely temporary relief to a problem that had no real solution, he argued, until land prices were reduced and the country was thrown open to permanent occupation, inviting immigrants with capital who would provide both a market and a labour force for a diversified economy. This was the sort of "virtuous immigration" that other permanent settlers in the colony espoused. In the Northern Districts, however, the voice for renewed transportation was unequivocally pragmatic:

> Revive that system,—let us have cheap labour, and prosperity unexampled in the previous history of this colony will most assuredly follow… We are not of those who would wish to see transportation renewed, if it were practicable to get free labour and plenty of it.[12]

The Molesworth Report had done its best to highlight the so-called depravity of the convict system in New South Wales, accusing the convicts of being given to "unnatural crimes." The Brisbane press derided this objection, simply arguing that the state of morality in the colony was the same as it had been under the old system. In fact, the free society might be less moral since, the editorial continued, "the higher the wages the more troublesome the men become and the less regard they have for character."

In 1849, transportation to New South Wales resumed. This was done in direct contravention of the resolution carried by a majority of eleven to seven in the New South Wales Legislative Council in September 1847 repudiating the recommendations of the report of the select committee on the renewal of transportation and declaring that "a return to the system of transportation and assignment would be opposed to the wishes of this community and would also be most injurious to the moral, social, and political advancement of the colony."[13] Those who opposed resumption of the system, including the governor, Sir Richard Bourke, were understandably outraged by the decision despite the Home Government's assurance that "it was not intended to send any convicts but such as were considered would become useful labourers in the colony."[14] The first ship, the *Hashemy*, arrived to organized protests in Sydney in May that year and forty-five of the prisoners were sent on to Moreton Bay, along with others from the *Rudolph*, where they were landed at the end of June. In November, a further 225 prisoners disembarked in Brisbane from the *Mount Stuart Elphinstone* amid a slowly growing protest movement led by those free immigrants who had started to arrive in the north under the scheme initiated by the radical Protestant minister, John Dunmore Lang. After the *Bangalore* discharged its 290 Pentonville exiles in May the following year, there were no more convict ships from Britain. In fact, the *Bangalore* arrived a month after the governor had received the despatch from London informing him that "Her Majesty has been advised to rescind the Order in Council making this colony a penal settlement."[15]

In the interim between the debate leading to the Molesworth Commission and the brief resumption of transportation to New South Wales in 1849, Britain's penal system had undergone major reform. The number of capital offences had been reduced to only four, compared to more than two hundred at the end of the Napoleonic Wars in 1815, the police force was properly organized, new gaols had been constructed, notions of behavioural reform were entering the rationale for state-sanctioned punishment, and juries were becoming more impartial. In short, there should have been no argument at all in Britain for renewed transportation to New South Wales; the very notion itself was outmoded by these utilitarian reforms.

Migration Issues

Prison reform was only one feature of the major social restructuring that was conducted by the British government in the 1830s in response to dramatic developments taking place in the economy in conjunction with the rising political power of a new middle class and its urgent need for a mobile labour force to work factories in the northern industrial cities. Members of the 1832 royal commission of enquiry into the operation of the Poor Laws found what they were predisposed to believe: that parish relief and allowances were harmful to the recipients' moral character, a financial burden on those who had to contribute through Poor Rates, and a brake on industrial development. Poor Law relief represented a financial burden that could be eased, it was argued, through economic rationalisation and professional, centralised administration. The Poor Law Amendment Act of 1834 sought to reduce dependency on relief in several ways: by making able-bodied paupers less eligible than independent workers, by worsening conditions in the workhouses in order to deter the poor from entering them, and by putting an end to welfare benefits for those living outside the workhouse, including the elderly, orphans, the sick, and the disabled. Fierce resistance from the likes of the Chartists to the harshness of the Act's regulations and the abruptness of their implementation served only to swell the numbers of Pentonville exiles, products of the new rational and efficient prison system. Britain's response to the commission's report in 1834 to make workhouses unattractive as refuges, according to Noel Butlin, was in line with its enthusiasm for assisted migration and closely timed with it. "From the British government's point of view," he reasons, "the more dependent paupers were, the better did they appear as candidates for emigration."[16]

Emigration, in the context of the Poor Law reforms, originally referred to internal migration, that is, of paupers away from their home parish to the manufacturing districts. This scheme was largely ineffective but overseas emigration grew markedly in the same period. According to Arthur Redford, the annual average of Poor Law emigration between 1835 and 1846 amounted to only 1,400 persons, while the total recorded emigration from the United Kingdom during the same period averaged 84,700 persons annually. Simply put, Poor Law emigration was almost insignificant as a factor in the more general problem of movement overseas.[17]

The deep economic depression that affected New South Wales in the early 1840s had already been detected in Britain by mid-1836 and several important business houses in England had collapsed under the strain. In the following year, Redford notes, "The full force of the economic collapse was felt both in America and in England, and the next six years were a time of almost unrelieved commercial depression on both sides of the Atlantic."[18] Massive unemployment, misery and riots consumed the manufacturing districts of northern England. By the summer of 1845, there was a revival of trade and prosperity but, he notes,

> A damp summer was developing into a soaking autumn and while the corn was rotting in the ear news came from Ireland that a blight had fallen on the potatoes. The failure of the Irish potato crop led to a famine the horrors of which were unprecedented even in that most distressful country.[19]

A great wave of overseas migration set in, especially to the United States of America. New South Wales, however, was not a popular destination for those who considered emigrating. It was too far, the voyage too long and too expensive, and its reputation as a penal colony for the worst offenders hardly added to its appeal. Nevertheless, after 1836, all land revenue of New South Wales was earmarked for immigration purposes. Immigrants were selected by authorities in England or they arrived under a bounty scheme; there were also unassisted immigrants, usually small capitalists who were attracted by special concessions. In the years before the gold rush, the largest number to arrive, in 1841, was 22,483, but this was exceptional.[20] Due to the depression, there was no government money to assist immigration during 1845, and there were no assisted immigrants at all in 1846 and 1847.

Evidence given to the New South Wales Legislative Council's select committee on immigration in 1847 revealed the extent of the colonists' anguish over the labour shortage.[21] In Melbourne, one witness said, the scarcity of domestic servants was so severe that ladies were forced to do their own domestic work. Everywhere, it seemed, the power of demanding extravagant wages was leading servants to insubordination and carelessness. "In fact," the wealthy pastoralist James Macarthur of Camden submitted, "the natural order of society is reversed—the servant becomes the master, and the master may be said to be a slave."[22] If the situation was bad around Sydney and Melbourne, it was far worse in the rural districts, according to R. V. Dulhunty, a colonist of twenty years' standing who noted, "In the interior they are obliged to pay the men anything they ask. The wages of shepherds have risen ... from £20 to £25 a year; of farm labourers from £18 to £22; and in fact all labour is on the increase in the same proportion."[23]

In the latter part of 1847, the colonial secretary of state, Earl Grey, informed Governor FitzRoy that he would direct the emigration commissioners to send out five thousand "statute adults" to New South Wales, the number to be divided equally between Sydney and Port Phillip, at a total cost of £100,000 to be raised by the sale of debentures secured separately on the crown revenues of those two destinations.[24] Apart from this, other privately supported schemes involving Irish orphans (mainly women from the workhouses), English lacemakers in France, and selected candidates from the Ragged Schools took the total number of assisted immigrants in 1848 to 7,885 at an average cost to the colony of just over £11 per person. More than half of them were from England and Wales, while the rest were almost evenly divided between Scotland and Ireland.[25]

Rather than being encouraged by the news that the assisted immigration scheme had been revived, potential employers in the Northern Districts were bitter and aggrieved. It was carefully calculated that of all the immigrants who arrived in New South Wales in 1848, not more than 130 found their way to Moreton Bay.[26] Even worse, the few who did make their way north either remained in the environs of Brisbane or soon absconded from the stations where their labour was most needed:

> What few men did come to the [Moreton Bay] Settlement did not care to move out of it. A local labour fund was established here by stock-holders, who subscribed at the rate of 10s. for every 1,000 sheep or every 250 head of cattle they owned. During the four months this was worked Mr Robert Graham, the agent, introduced 150 labourers. These, however, like the rest, cared little for the agreements they had signed, and deserted as soon as they became tired or a hint was dropped that somewhere else they could get an advance on their wages, and the only satisfaction derived by the troubled squatter was the payment of a reward of from £2 to £5, and if captured to give the object of his search a month in Sydney.[27]

The first emigrant ship chartered by the British government commissioners that was specifically destined for Moreton Bay, the *Artemisia*, set sail at the end of July 1848 with 209 passengers, more to be taken on board at Plymouth. On arrival, it brought news that the *Fortitude*, the first of the three ships under the migration scheme of the Rev. Dr Lang, would arrive within a month or so. All the migrants were quickly engaged in Brisbane, the Moreton Bay district generally and on the Darling Downs. The districts of Wide Bay and

Burnett, according to J. J. Knight, an early editor of the *Brisbane Courier*, were "systematically tabooed" by the immigrants.[28] Knight attributed this to references in Dr Lang's brochure, "Cooksland", about "certain affrays with the blacks which occurred there about six or seven years ago."

Under the circumstances, the northern squatters' resentment was justified and their response was typically extreme. A meeting calling for the resumption of transportation was held at Ipswich in January 1850 where "the squatters mustered pretty strongly," it was reported.[29] Francis Bigge, MLC, declared that "he for one would rather have the pick of gaols than the refuse of workhouses," while another speaker made the observation that the working classes were "a selfish race, extorting from their employers high wages for the purpose of spending their earnings in brandy, rum and champagne." They believed that they had been denied immigrants under the government-assisted scheme—"except the orphan girls and a few drafts of exiles"—although they had regularly paid their squatting licences and assessments for stock. If they were defeated in getting convicts, they warned, they would send for Chinese. The squatters of the Wide Bay and Burnett were particularly resentful about being taxed but not represented and they repeated the call for separation:

> There is no member in the Legislative Assembly to represent them. No money has been laid out for making and repairing bridges and roads. Not a single immigrant has been sent unless at the expense of the settlers themselves; and the only protection the two districts have is six constables and two chiefs. We do not wish to raise the cry of separation, because we want to have nothing to do with Brisbane. But we want our just rights.[30]

Early Experiments with Non-European Labour

In 1847, so urgent was the demand for labour and so great was the distress experienced from the want of labour, landowner Charles Cowper told the Legislative Council, that "the colonists have, in some instances, been induced to have recourse to the importation of Coolies from India, and savage natives from the Polynesian Islands."[31] Adding China to the list of sources for this type of labour, the member moved:

That this Council cannot regard the prospect of an immigration of this character without feelings of the deepest regret and alarm, arising from the apprehension that it would expose the colony to all the evils of a mixed and coloured population, and lead to the pre-occupation of the territory by a semi-barbarous or savage race, to the prejudice of immigrants from the United Kingdom, and to the injury of the purely British character which it is so desirable the colony should continue to maintain.

Inherent in this motion, however racially biased it appears, was the growing divide between the native-born, landowning gentry that included the likes of Charles Cowper and James Macarthur among others who had a long-term vision for Australian society, and the big squatters like Benjamin Boyd and Philip Friell who were more often than not short-term speculators who came to New South Wales for fortune and adventure and needed reliable economic resources to secure their capital investments. In short, to protect their investment in livestock they needed shepherds, and if Britain could not supply them, they would seek them elsewhere and at the lowest cost to their own pocket. The social implications did not concern them.

Hill Coolies

Some early colonists arrived in New South Wales with servants they had acquired elsewhere in the empire during their tours of duty for the Crown. William Browne, for instance, was accompanied by nine Indian labourers who supplemented the convicts assigned to work his three thousand-acre land grant in the colony and they were later joined by thirty more.[32] In 1819, they complained to Governor Macquarie about cruelty and the governor ordered that they be returned to India. Browne refused to pay the return passage and the government failed to recover the cost, the Supreme Court justice arguing that Browne's responsibility had ended when the Indians left their place of employment and the government had not intervened. The publicity surrounding the case no doubt discouraged further interest in Indian labour until rumours that transportation was about to end created renewed demand. The governor appointed a committee to investigate and advise on the Hill Coolie proposal in 1837 and its report reluctantly concluded that this type of immigration be permitted to help relieve the labour shortage. Around forty Indian labourers arrived in Sydney under indenture to John Mackay, a colonist with almost thirty years' experience in India, who leased them to various employers, but he was held responsible when fifteen of them absconded. Their grievances were obviously related to ignorance of terms of contract, a problem with the Indian labour trade that was far more widespread than simply in New South Wales. The British Colonial Office placed a general ban on the traffic at the end of 1838, disappointing those potential employers in New South Wales who had placed an order for 1,200 Coolies in October.[33]

There was, however, a loophole. Sailors and menial servants were exceptions to the ban. Alan Dwight notes the arrival of the *Minerva* in October 1844 from Calcutta with a group of forty-one "servants," accompanied by Gordon Sandeman as their "master" who was probably acting for Philip Friell, a squatter in the Northern Districts with Indian experience, whose name was also on the passenger list.[34] This may have been a test run because the following year, Robert Towns, William Charles Wentworth and Robert Campbell commissioned a Calcutta firm to obtain "about a hundred menial servants," quoting Sandeman as precedent. The numbers are not exact, but approximately sixty Indians, including some women and children, reached Sydney in March 1846. The result of this experiment was a debacle. Towns complained to the magistrates' court that they refused to work, while the Indians claimed that they were promised more than was being offered. The Bench dismissed Towns' complaint on the grounds that there was no clear evidence that the agreement had been explained to them. Six of those assigned to Wentworth absconded and complained to the magistrate that they were being made to eat meat because the agreed rations of rice and dholl were not provided.

Meanwhile, Philip Friell, for a time, seemed satisfied with his labour experiment on his run, Tent Hill, in the South Burnett and he published a pamphlet, "The Advantages of Indian Labour in the Australasian Colonies", explaining the pros and cons along with the cost of importing Indian labourers from Calcutta.[35] Those at Tent Hill were engaged for five years, and the contract guaranteed them return passage to India at the end of their indenture, unless the agreements had been cancelled by magistrates for misconduct. The cost of bringing one labourer to New South Wales was £14, including what he called the "engagement fee." An adult male labourer was paid four rupees, or four shillings, a month. Friell claimed that their wages were paid in silver and monthly, and that an average labourer could save four-fifths of his wage. Rations included staples of rice, dholl, onions, et cetera, but if these were not available, meat, flour, and maize meal could be substituted. He described the Coolies as "headstrong and self-willed ... determined to follow their own course regardless of such punishment as the Magistrates had power to inflict" but in terms of their moral habits, he believed they were not "inferior" to the Europeans. In particular, he noted, "drunkenness is a vice not practised amongst them."

A peculiar piece of advice offered by Friell and supported by the Brisbane press was that the Indian indentured labourers should be employed only at stations where there were no Europeans apart from bullock drivers. This "exclusive" system was best, the editor of the *Moreton Bay Courier* concurred, because it prevented the Indians from being "tampered with." This, no doubt, was a reference to the huge difference in the wage the indentured labourer was contracted to receive and the actual bargaining power of the pastoral worker in the remote frontier districts of New South Wales at the time. The introduction of non-European labour was clearly intended for the purpose of suppressing rural wages and awareness of this fact was undoubtedly a cause for grievance among all bush workers on both sides of this artificial racial divide.

It was not organized protest over wages, however, that soured Friell's attitude to imported Indian labour. In November 1846, the overseer at Tent Hill brought two of the Coolies before the magistrates' bench on a charge of absconding.[36] Violent disputes among the Coolies had caused these two to flee to Brisbane. When the police magistrate told the overseer that he should have applied to the commissioner of crown lands for a remedy to the dispute, the overseer replied that he always declined to interfere, "for had he done so, he would have had little else to do than settle their disputes."[37] The pair were ordered to return to the station, but they refused to go and began to make complaints about rations. They were sentenced to a fortnight's imprisonment for contempt of court. Friell claimed that they had conspired to protest before leaving India on free passage, that they were naturally indolent, and "notorious in their disregard of law." Above all, he blamed the women for being the chief instigators of discontent.[38]

Like the others before him, Friell's experiment with Indian indentured labour did not live up to his expectations. Alan Dwight claims that he "disposed of them to Sandeman." Gordon Sandeman, by far the largest employer of non-European labour in the Burnett, giving evidence before the 1854 select committee on Asiatic Labor said that he had employed at least forty Indians, including the twenty-five formerly engaged by Friell and a further fifteen who had been employed on another run before it failed.[39] By the time of that committee hearing, the Indians who had participated in Friell's venture had finished their indentures and were employed elsewhere in the colony except for one who had remained in Sandeman's service at Burrandowan and nine who had returned to India in accordance with the terms of the original contract. Two or three, he believed, had purchased land in Brisbane, and others followed small business occupations such as driving horses and hiring out carts.

The Indian labourers may have been less than satisfactory but the northern squatters would have recruited many more if the law had permitted them to do so. At the 1854 committee hearing, Robert Towns, who identified himself as "the principal mover in the matter" in that it was his ships that carried the Coolies to New South Wales, admitted that the ruse he and his partners employed to evade the 1839 law against contracting Indians labourers overseas had given them so much trouble that they never attempted it again. A number of squatters, however, had petitioned the home secretary to induce the Bengal government to relax the law on the Indian indentured labour trade so that the exemptions that applied to Mauritius and British Guiana should also be applicable to New South Wales.

In 1861, two years after the establishment of Queensland as a separate colony, the Indian government consented to the petitioners' request on the condition that laws be passed by the colonial legislature that contained provisions for the protection of the Indian labourers similar to those already in force in Mauritius and the West Indies. In the despatch, the secretary of state for the colonies advised the Queensland governor that "the Emigration must be considered as liable to be discontinued, if experience should show that either on account of such legislation, or for any other reason, it is found to be prejudicial to the immigrant."[40] The "Act to give the force of Law to Regulations for the Introduction and Protection of Laborers from British India," otherwise known as the Indian Laborers Protection Act (27 Vic., No. 5), was given assent on July 2, 1862. It would have permitted the squatters to commence recruitment from March 1863 but there is general agreement amongst scholars that no Indians arrived in Queensland under this regulated indenture system. The reasons for this are not clear. The regulations and restrictions may have been prohibitive, the costs incurred may have been greater than the perceived advantages of hiring such labour or the new Queensland government, despite passing the enabling legislation, may have shared the reluctance shown by the former New South Wales government to assist the introduction of Asiatic labour that was obviously used as a wedge against wage demands by the (preferred) European immigrants. Furthermore, during the 1860s when this law was passed, the demand for labour in Queensland had shifted more towards that required for plantation culture, especially sugar cane, and the islands of the South Pacific once again became a recruiting ground.

South Sea Islanders

In northern Australia, indentured Melanesian labour is associated almost entirely with the sugar industry that boomed in the decade after Queensland separated from New South Wales in 1859. The little-known earlier experiment that employed men from islands in the New Hebrides and the Loyalty Group as shepherds in the pastoral industry was short-lived but it had echoes in the far more substantial labour trade that began in the 1860s.

Within a year or so of his arrival in Sydney in 1842, Benjamin Boyd, chairman of the Royal Bank of Australia which he founded in London, was the biggest of all the squatters in New South Wales paying licences on vast runs in all but one squatting district in the colony, stretching from Colac southwest of Melbourne to Laidley Plains in Moreton Bay. The headquarters of this pastoral "empire" was at Boyd Town on Twofold Bay, near the present town of Eden on the south coast of New South Wales. Given the scale of his squattages, he was also one of the colony's largest employers.[41] Like all squatters, Boyd had the problem of both attracting and keeping workers on remote stations while paying the cheapest possible rate of wages. His objective, according to Marion Diamond, was to lower wages to £10 per annum, a rate usually exceeded even during the depths of depression in 1843.[42] Failing to achieve this with the labour force still available to him in the colony, at the beginning of 1847, he sent his ship, the *Velocity*, to recruit and import Pacific Islanders to employ them as shepherds on runs located in the hinterland of Boyd Town, in what is now the Monaro district in the foothills of the Snowy Mountains, and also well inland on stations along the Murray and Edward rivers.

About three months later, the ship returned with sixty-five Melanesians from Lifu in the Loyalty Group and Tana and Aneityum in the New Hebrides (Vanuatu). "The pressures which led [them] to board *Velocity* and to put their mark to a document which bound them to five years' indentured labour," Marion Diamond remarks, "remain unclear."[43] They were to be paid twenty-six shillings a year, and provided with some clothing and a weekly ration of ten pounds of meat. Within a week of their arrival at Twofold Bay, a party of them started inland, but almost immediately some of them absconded and drifted back to the coast. Boyd was not prepared to admit defeat, however, and in May that year sent the *Velocity* and a second ship to the New Hebrides to recruit more labourers. Altogether, between April and October 1847, Boyd imported 190 islanders, including seven women.[44]

As the ships sailed, far away in Moreton Bay, the press was extolling Ben Boyd's efforts to source labour in the South Sea Islands:

> No undertaking too extensive or costly that wealth and labour cannot accomplish, ... Mr Boyd's experiment is a bold and startling one and should it turn out successful will render the stockholders entirely independent of the mother country as far as the importation of labour for pastoral pursuits is concerned.[45]

The editor was at pains to depict the South Sea Islanders as "much more tractable than most other barbarous tribes," having "considerable intellectual capacity and inclination to work" although, he admitted, "it remains to be proved whether a shepherd's life is congenial to their habits." He attempted to downplay the stereotypes of cannibalism and infanticide that had been built up in widely-read explorers' accounts by arguing that the islanders were driven to such extremes by starvation. The captain of the *Velocity*, he wrote, had explained that "the men of lower caste than the chiefs are frequently reduced to the greatest extremities to procure food and that many of these miserable beings are necessitated to share a simple coconut amongst three or four for the day's meal." The *Velocity*'s objective, therefore, was not kidnapping but liberation for these unfortunate islanders "anxious to leave countries where starvation stared them in the face." Using an argument that would be used again later among Queensland cane farmers, the editor prated, "They will be lifted from a state of degradation and gradually reconciled to labour—to such labour as they can readily perform without toil—for the sake of a certain reward." The Tahitians, he believed would also be glad to leave their country and "flee from French persecution to a land where the people whom they have been taught to look up to as their natural protectors are living in peace and plenty." More practically, he concluded, "These people can be brought here at the trifling expense of £5 per head and there would not be the slightest difficulty in procuring any number of them."

By the time those comments were published, however, there was growing concern over the presence of the Melanesians in the colonial society and also about their obvious distress. Some of them reached Sydney where in one incident, a group entered a shop "and, having closed the door, went round the counter and began to make free with the bread and other eatables."[46] The time for state intervention was obviously overdue.

In June, the New South Wales Legislative Council went into committee on the Masters and Servants Act Amendment Bill. The third clause of the bill, that dealing with contracts made outside the colony to engage indentured labour, was subjected to long discussion. This clause gave external contracts the same force and effect as those undertaken within New South Wales, and made them subject to the same penalties and system of justice, provided that they were not binding for a period longer than five years.[47] The colonial secretary and the attorney-general argued that the Hill Coolies and the South Sea Islanders should be excluded from the operation of the clause. At the second reading of the bill, W. C. Wentworth moved that the clause should stand as printed and that a proviso should be added which allowed natives of China and India to come within the provisions of the Act as long as it was proved before two justices of the peace that they understood the nature of their agreements. The colonial secretary moved an amendment on the proviso excluding the introduction of "savages" into the Act, which was passed. Thus, the Act (11 Vic., No. 9) when it took effect from August 1, 1847 included the stipulation in Clause 15:

> Provided always and be it enacted, that nothing in this said recited Act contained, shall be deemed or construed to apply to any native of any savage or uncivilized tribe, inhabiting any Island or Country in the Pacific Ocean, or elsewhere, anything therein or herein to the contrary notwithstanding.

Consequently, when Boyd's ships arrived back in Sydney in October with another fifty-four men and three women on board, their indentures were no longer valid. According to Marion Diamond, "This left the new arrivals under no authority and no one's responsibility, for Boyd, once denied their labour, took no further interest in their plight."[48] Those already working as shepherds on Boyd's stations found themselves in the same situation and suddenly freed from their indentures, they left en masse for Sydney, the local magistrates having no power to intervene. They remained around Sydney Harbour, begging for transport back to their islands. Boyd employed some of them in shipping, some took work with other Sydney employers, and most of the rest finally gained passages to the islands, but it is doubtful, Marion Diamond concludes, whether many of them reached their own islands again.

At the end of that year of the first experiment with Melanesian indentured labour, Governor FitzRoy forwarded a report on the matter to the British government. His main conclusion was that Boyd's agents had not kidnapped the islanders but he added, with obvious satisfaction,

> It is right that I should add that this speculation on the part of Mr Boyd has turned out a complete failure, and is not likely to be followed by others of the same nature; and that Mr Boyd is gradually removing these people from the Colony, not more than fifty or sixty of whom now remain.[49]

The governor was wrong in his prognostication because from 1863 to the eve of the First World War perhaps as many as one hundred thousand islanders drawn from a number of island colonies in the South Pacific, but especially from the New Hebrides and the Solomon Islands, went as indentured labourers to Queensland, Fiji, Samoa and New Caledonia to work on sugar and copra plantations, in the mines, and on the colonies' sheep and cattle stations.[50] Until 1904, when racially exclusive legislation forced their repatriation, more than sixty thousand Melanesians were introduced to Queensland.[51] The "Kanakas" as they were locally known, worked mainly in all the sugar districts along the coast from Cairns in the far north to Maryborough in the Wide Bay district but before legislation limited their hire to tropical and sub-tropical agriculture, some were engaged as shepherds on Queensland sheep stations, in the Burnett district, for example. During those years, the same concerns arose over methods of recruitment, of a revival of the slave trade, and so on, as had surrounded Ben Boyd's ventures. While indentured Melanesian labour played an incalculable role in the development of the sugar industry in the new colony, its second experiment in the pastoral industry was as disastrous in the Burnett in the 1860s as it had been on the Murray in 1847.

In important ways, however, the second experiment was very different from the first because it had the active support of the state with the provision of administrative machinery and financial assistance, and the all-important penal sanctions that could enforce labour contracts. By the turn of the twentieth century, when the trade was coming to an end, it was heavily regulated by several Acts of Parliament, schedules, regulations and instructions. Even if the laws were not always supervised or enforced, their mere existence served to moderate abuse. State involvement, A. T. Yarwood argues, is vital to the success of the indenture system and because similar state measures were absent in the early experimental stage, "the importation of coloured labour in the era before gold was numerically insignificant, and for the employers financially disastrous."[52] Whether that was true for the importation of Chinese indentured labour to the Northern Districts between 1848 and 1853, however, is debatable.

PART II

Among the Pioneers

The protection by the State of indentured labour was not a democratic domestic compulsion as is our own industrial legislation; it was a paternal and humanitarian compulsion, imposed from without by the circumspection of the Indian and British Governments. Without going so far as to suggest that in the absence of these external authorities the condition of indentured labourers in British Colonies would have been as bad as on the San Thomé plantations, it is quite certain that had this protection been absent there would have been a great deal of oppression and cruelty to indentured Coolies. Injustices and ugly incidents occurred in our Colonies notwithstanding those safeguards. There is in communities of dominant white men employing coloured labour neither the disinterested humane public opinion, nor the democratic self-interest and organised power to check abuses.

Lord Olivier.[1]

CHAPTER 5

Celestial Shepherds

Chinese indentured labourers arrived in New South Wales at a critical juncture in the history of their own country amid the mayhem there created by internal rebellions, and also in the history of what was soon to become two and then three separate, self-governing colonies of eastern mainland Australia. Between 1848 and 1853, approximately three thousand Chinese labourers were imported, about half of them to the Northern Districts. Their arrival helped bridge the labour gap in the pastoral industry immediately prior to the 1851 gold discoveries and the years immediately following the gold rush when labour could not be found anywhere at any price until the gold fever dissipated and the colonies discovered that they had a workforce that had paid its own way to the country and would work on its own terms.

The importation of Chinese labour had repeatedly been issued as a threat by the squatters, even while arrangements were being made by some of them to recruit and import Indian Hill Coolies and South Sea Islanders between 1845 and 1847. Unlike the former who were British imperial subjects and the latter who were already the focus of concern at Exeter Hall, especially the London Missionary Society, the Chinese had no champions in the colony. During the First Opium War that had concluded in 1842, China had militantly if ineffectually resisted British imperial designs on its territory and institutions. Therefore, while not quite an enemy nor even a perceived threat, China was hardly an imperial ally and its citizens were regarded as undeserving of British sympathy. In short, the Chinese indentured labourers arrived in Australia simply as "aliens," without the same rights to protection enjoyed by the Indians who preceded them but, thanks to the 1847 amendment to the Masters and Servants Act, and unlike the South Sea Islanders, subject to the same laws and penalties that applied to all employees in New South Wales and bound firmly to their contract of indenture.

Overtures

In March 1847, the *Sydney Morning Herald* published a letter from Adam Bogue, friend and entrepreneurial fellow-traveller of Ben Boyd. He had recently been to China and had visited Amoy, one of the first treaty ports. He proposed a labour scheme that was, he believed, "worthy the attention of the Australian public," noting,

> The dense population of the city and surrounding district, the great poverty of the majority of the inhabitants, their civility and kindness to Europeans, their general quiet and inoffensive manners, the tractability of their character, and their indomitable industry in agricultural and other pursuits, induced me to suppose that it would be of the first advantage to New South Wales in her present condition, if she could be supplied with labourers from that province.[2]

He had already discussed the matter with Francis Darby Syme, a merchant of Amoy, he said, "who is in the habit of annually shipping many thousands of Coolies to Mauritius, Bourbon, and also to the various settlements in the Straits of Malacca."

The term "coolie" was rarely used in relation to the Chinese indentured labourers who came to Australia, the term being chiefly reserved for the Bengali Indians who arrived via Calcutta. In Australia, they were referred to as "Celestials," a perfunctory term of address that was certainly derogatory but neither more nor less deliberately racist in its intention than "Kanakas" would be later in the century towards the South Sea Islanders on Queensland's sugar plantations.[3] In terms of the trade, however, they were "Coolies," and whatever its etymology, the word acquired its own definition. "What are Coolies as distinguished from other Chinese?" an American visitor to Hong Kong wondered.[4] "They are just muscle," he decided, "... born to toil, to carry burdens, to pull rickshaws, to do the menial work, to bear without alleviation the Primal Curse. Never can they rise or change their condition... They and their women and children for all time must do the same."

Syme's company was one of the main brokers in the Chinese coolie trade. The other was Tait & Co., the leading British house in Amoy which was the first and most important port from which Coolies were sent overseas. James Tait had the additional privilege of acting as consul for Spain, Holland and Portugal and could therefore personally guarantee the legality of the indenture contracts he issued to those despatched to their colonies. The intercontinental trade in Chinese indentured labour was, Robert Nield notes, big business.[5] In front of his company headquarters in Amoy, Syme established a barracoon, a term borrowed from the African slave trade, to hold the recruits before they were shipped overseas, while Tait used a floating ship for the same purpose. The local people called the large wood and bamboo shed a "pig pen" and the comparison was apt. In November 1852, the barracoon was stoned by a crowd angered by abuses committed by Syme's broker who was accused of abducting men for sale to the shippers. Syme was himself attacked in the rioting that continued for several days until it was put down by British marines. Some local people were killed and many more were wounded in the incident.

A court of inquiry into the riot was instituted in December by Sir John Bowring, acting superintendent of British trade and soon to be governor of Hong Kong. He later reported on the horrifying scene he witnessed inside the barracoon where hundreds of men were gathered together in pens, stripped naked, and stamped or painted with the first letter of their destination. Syme was charged with a breach of treaty regulations with China and fined the meagre sum of $200 (£40). Given the international nature of the trade and the disinterest of the Chinese government in regulating it, there seemed little else that the British authorities based in Hong Kong could do to check the blatant abuses that marked it. A British vessel in Amoy harbour only had to run up the flag of another country, Peru, say, or the United States of America, to avoid investigation. Nevertheless, the riot of 1852 and the subsequent inquiry, the first and only one of its kind in Amoy, had important consequences for the labour trade there. Only three vessels left Amoy with Chinese labourers during the rest of that year because, according to Wang Singwu, "labourers could hardly be obtained at Amoy."[6] Tait, meanwhile, moved his floating depot south to Swatow/Shantou, and Amoy was soon overtaken by Canton, Macao and Hong Kong as an emigration port for the intercontinental labour trade. It remained, however, a major departure point for Chinese leaving to work in various parts of Southeast Asia.

Margaret Slocomb

It is necessary to separate clearly the Celestials, that is, the Fujianese men who arrived in New South Wales between October 1848 and mid-1853 from Amoy under the intercontinental scheme for indentured labourers who were contracted to work for pastoralists in the interior, from the thousands of Chinese miners who arrived on the Australian goldfields after 1851 under their own locally sponsored credit-ticket or other schemes, as well as from other Chinese men who were recruited in small numbers by individual Australian employers for a variety of purposes throughout most of the nineteenth century, or who arrived independently. A Cantonese man had arrived in Sydney as a free settler as early as 1817, and was allotted thirty acres of land by Governor Macquarie; there were Chinese cabinetmakers and artisans in early Sydney, Melbourne and Van Diemen's Land; and there were even three Chinese convicts transported from Mauritius where Cantonese men had been indentured by British planters after slavery was banned.[7] In the year before the arrival of the Celestials, South and West Australian pastoralists had imported from Singapore small numbers of men to work as shepherds and farm labourers, and as late as March 1848, seven freemen from Hong Kong, according to Eric Rolls, arrived in Sydney on the barque, *London*.[8] In the years after the end of the organized trade in indentured labour for the pastoral industry, the scale of Chinese migration to the goldfields almost erased the memory of the earlier arrivals. In the first quarter of 1854 alone, almost as many Chinese arrived in Melbourne as had arrived during the four or five years of the Amoy trade, and during the period 1855-67, more than sixty-two thousand miners were shipped from Hong Kong to Australia.[9]

The Celestials were part of the intercontinental trade in indentured labour at a specific point in world history. This was a large-scale commercial venture that involved the trafficking of millions of people, mainly from India and China, to other countries where a surplus, disciplined labour force did not already exist for the needs of European colonisation. This trade was organized on rational, capitalistic lines and the numbers involved in the traffic were significant at this time of unprecedented human migration, even in New South Wales where the number of men imported, although comparatively few in relation to the global trade, must be compared with the total population of the colony in the era before the discovery of gold and particularly with the size of the European population in the squatting districts where most of them were employed.

The total number of Celestials remains somewhat imprecise. Eric Rolls warns that "no one kept count of the numbers who came in [to New South

Wales] and every historian gives a different estimate."[10] His figure is 2,666 from Amoy alone, bringing the total estimate by the end of 1852 to around three thousand. According to the British consuls in Amoy, Charles Winchester and then J. Backhouse, between 1848 and 1851 inclusive, the number of Chinese men exported to New South Wales was either 2,666 (Rolls' source) or 2,260, respectively.[11] The number of Fujian labourers shipped to other countries during the same period was 2,101, making Australia the leading customer at that time.[12]

By studying *The Shipping Gazette* and *Sydney General Trade List*, Wang Singwu was able to provide a breakdown of imports of men to New South Wales by ships out of Amoy according to arrival years, as follows:

Table 2: Chinese Emigrant Ships from Amoy for New South Wales, 1848–53[13]

Ship	Tonnage	Passengers	Arrival Port	Arrival Date
Nimrod	234	120	Sydney	2 Oct. 1848
London	338	149	Sydney (ex- Hong Kong)	22 Feb. 1849
Cadet	376	138	Sydney	23 Apr. 1850
Gazelle	242	131	Sydney	14 May 1850
Duke of Roxburgh	498	242	Sydney	6 Feb. 1851
Duke of Roxburgh	498	225	Moreton Bay	9 Nov. 1851
Arabia	387	179	Sydney	21 Dec. 1851
Ganges	430	213	Sydney	26 Jan. 1852
General Palmer	571	264	Sydney	16 Feb. 1852
Statesman	345	180	Sydney	20 Feb. 1852
Amazon	370	290	Sydney	17 Mar. 1852
Eleanor Lancaster	480	67	Sydney (ex Swatow)	16 Apr. 1852
Spartan	364	240	Sydney	29 Apr. 1852
Royal Saxon	620	224	Sydney	16 Feb. 1853
Spartan	364	161	Sydney	3 May 1853

To the total number of 2,823 according to this list, Maxine Darnell adds further arrivals by the *Eleanor Lancaster* in March 1853 at Newcastle and another of Robert Towns' ships, the *Rhone*, in the same month.[14] She estimates that just over three thousand indentured Chinese labourers arrived in New South Wales ports between 1847 and 1853, the majority of them during the first six months of 1852, as is borne out by figures in the table above. In fact, she adds, their arrival rate approximated that of European immigrants in the same period:

> ... in February and March of 1852, 1097 immigrants from
> Great Britain on nineteen vessels and 787 immigrants from
> China aboard five ships arrived in the colony.[15]

As further noted by the table, Robert Towns, a co-conspirator in the brief attempt to introduce Indian indentured labour from Calcutta, played a major role as agent in the China trade. In fact, his role continued beyond the supply of Celestials to the pastoral industry because, according to Wang Singwu, Towns was still importing Chinese labourers, presumably destined for the goldfields, right up to May 1860.[16]

In his early correspondence with Adam Bogue, Francis Syme had suggested that it would be more economical to charter vessels from New South Wales than from China, conceding, "but then again you must send her up empty. On this you must use your own judgment and give me a little timely notice of your intention; perhaps better write me to get a ship in Hong Kong, and I will always be able to fill her with freight for Amoy."[17] Robert Towns once famously boasted that he could turn a profit from any venture. During the brief Indian labour trade experiment, he had filled his ships with horses out of Sydney, returning with Hill Coolies; on the run up to Amoy, his ships' captains were instructed to take on a cargo of sugar at Manila, a profitable ballast for the return voyage.

During his evidence before the New South Wales Legislative Council Select Committee on Asiatic Labor, on August 29, 1854, Towns declared that he had been the chief importer of Chinese, bringing about eight shiploads, averaging three hundred persons, to the colony until after 1852 when it had become too difficult to attract mechanics and labourers because the Chinese preferred to make their way to Melbourne and California under their own schemes.[18] Before the same committee, the immigration agent, Hutchinson H. Browne, said he thought that no more than seven or eight shiploads had arrived in Sydney from where the immigrants were trans-shipped to other ports; two shiploads had gone to Port Phillip and most of the men on the other ships were destined for Moreton Bay. Only the *Duke of Roxburgh*, on its second voyage, sailed directly to Moreton Bay, arriving on November 9, 1851, with 225 Chinese labourers on board, but many more went there via Sydney so that by 1852, according to Wang Singwu, about one thousand had disembarked in Brisbane and a depot was built there to accommodate them until they found their masters.[19]

The special attraction of the trade in Chinese indentured labourers according to Robert Towns was that there were no restrictions at all with respect to them. The terms of the trade were set down by the British firms of Syme and Tait, but these were only business terms between agents and before the 1852 riot in Amoy there was no official supervision of the conduct of the trade at any point in the process from recruitment to arrival. There was even confusion over whether or not the Passenger Vessels Act that set out the minimum standards of space, ventilation, sanitation, and so on for those on board British ships should apply to vessels out of China's ports. China expert, Andrew Shortrede, before the select committee of 1854, was adamant that the Act extended to "every man who ships in a British vessel, or proceeds to a British port."[20] Paul Pax was equally adamant that "the British Government has no power over [this immigration]. It does not come within the range of the Passenger Act."[21] Kathryn Cronin notes that coolie dealers evaded the Passenger Vessels Act by confining the trade to non-British ships and sailing from non-British ports such as Macao but this was later, when the intercontinental trade had generally moved away from Amoy and when British authorities had begun to show some interest in supervising the traffic.[22] As mentioned previously, ships only had to fly the flag of a foreign country to avoid the notice of authorities if they sailed within the radius of British jurisdiction over Hong Kong, and consular officials in Amoy were hardly disinterested parties, being profitably involved in the trade themselves.

In the initial correspondence with Adam Bogue, Francis Syme outlined what he referred to as "my terms":

> A man engages to serve me, or the contractor, as the case may be, in Sydney, for the space of five years, at the monthly wages of two to three dollars. I engage to find him a free passage to, and a free passage back, on the expiration of his term, should he wish to return. He is allowed his rations and

two suits of clothes a year. The expenses here are two dollars per man, paid to the collector; advance before leaving, eight to ten dollars, to be repaid on arrival in Sydney, in monthly instalments; and of course rations, water; and between decks fitted in the vessel and bunks in the between decks large enough to stow eight or ten men.[23]

The shorter version, translated into local currency, was soon circulating in Moreton Bay as

They can be brought here at an expense per head of £8 to be indented for a term of five years, at the annual wage of from £4 16s. to £7 4s., with two suits of clothes and rations.[24]

Given the then current wage rates of between £20 and £25 paid annually to shepherds, the scheme represented a great bargain to the squatters in the north. The only problems the squatters could foresee were "the fact of the Chinese being unable to speak any intelligible language ... [and] the anticipated antipathy of the Europeans on account of the reduced wages."[25]

The cost estimates presented by Francis Syme in 1847 were, in fact, considerably higher by 1851 and 1852 when most of the Chinese labourers were imported so, instead of £8, the colonists paid around £13 to bring each man to New South Wales, with annual wages starting at the higher end of Bogue's estimate. Given that they were contracted for five years at a static rate of wages, however, they still represented a huge saving in labour costs.

Information passed by word of mouth or by letter from one interested party to another. Orders were then placed on a list and when the numbers constituted a shipload, the agent in Sydney chartered a vessel to Amoy that returned with its human cargo.

Between Recruitment and Indenture

When the ship arrived in Amoy, the captain contacted the nominated firm and arrangements were made to procure the number of labourers required. European merchants were still forbidden to travel freely inside China and for many practical reasons, recruitment for the labour trade would have been impossible without the assistance of local brokers, "crimps", who were employees or servants of the foreign firms. The merchant guaranteed to pay his crimp a commission of around £1 for every recruit. The crimp, in turn, promised a portion of the head price to his own touts who went into the countryside or around the poorest parts of the town and brought the recruits to the depots located in and around the harbour.

Then, as now, controversy surrounds the definition of means employed in the trafficking of persons. For Andrew Shortrede, newspaperman and China expert, the business was "a great deal like kidnapping... These brokers have gone out and procured young men on the most false and specious pretences."[26] Wang Singwu expands on this, arguing,

> A great number of Chinese labourers were obtained from the southeastern provinces of China using illegal means such as gambling, temptation, deception, purchase, et cetera. When all these methods of recruiting were exhausted, they resorted to open kidnapping along the coast and some parts of inland China.[27]

At the other extreme, Paul Pax described the trade as an opportunity for destitute men to change their lives:

> Some escape to the towns, such as Amoy, for the purpose of emigration and think themselves happy if they reach it; and it is from these poor creatures, bowed down by a grinding despotism or starved from their homes, that the emigration depots are fed.[28]

A more balanced view was given by the New South Wales immigration agent, Hutchinson Browne who, even though he had no legal jurisdiction over these vessels, had boarded each one that arrived in Sydney, and through the interpreter who generally accompanied the voyage had enquired about their treatment on board. He had deep personal reservations about the trade but he did not believe that the men had been deceived or forced into boarding the ships. He told the 1854 select committee,

> [T]he information that has come under my knowledge has led me to believe that there is a great inclination on the part of these people to come down, knowing that they will better their condition... I do not think there has been any

difficulty in catching them, but I cannot say that I think the agreements which are supposed to be entered into so formally, are very correctly explained to them.[29]

The failure of brokers to explain fully the terms of the agreement that was entered into by the recruits was the crux of the matter. It was this concern that had caused the British officials in India to put a halt to the trade in labourers from that country to Mauritius and Réunion. Trafficking in persons is indeed a despicable crime and it is reasonable to sympathize with Wang Singwu's ire towards the crimps and touts as "men of the lowest character, their hearts hard and their deeds inhuman; no really respectable Chinese would engage in a trade regarded as the selling of men to foreign merchants."[30] At the same time, it is wrong to deny the independence of human will and agency, or the blind leap of faith that is every emigrant's experience. No doubt some men were tricked into the depots and others entered somewhat more freely but none could genuinely have known what the future held for him.

Once they were recruited by the broker and had entered the depots, the labourers were reduced to mere commodities. They were stripped, inspected for health and fitness, and, as Sir John Bowring observed, painted with the first letter of the destination intended for them. They had no say in this matter, as Paul Pax confirmed,

> They do not select Sydney in preference to any other country, but all depends upon the first ship wanting emigrants. Singapore, California, Batavia, the Philippine Islands, the Polynesian Islands, Sydney, are all the same to them, it being the interest of the broker to get them off his hands with all possible despatch.[31]

The men remained in the depots until the ship was ready to receive them for a period of between three weeks and a month. During this time, they were charged for their board and lodging at the rate of fifty cash per day so that by the time they were ready to board and were paid the promised advance on their wages, there was little or nothing left except the obligation to repay it. In this matter, they must have felt sorely cheated. The promise of an advance was undoubtedly the lure used by the crimps to entice them to engage with the foreign brokers; the money should have been used to repay old debts and to help provide for family members that the men were leaving behind. The men could not have known how long they would be detained or that they would be forced to pay for their keep during that time. It is highly likely that the "unpaid" advance was the real cause of the 1852 riot in Amoy, and also what Hutchinson Brown meant when he said that the terms of the contract had not been properly explained to the men when they entered into the formal agreement with the foreign firm in Amoy.

When the ship was ready, early in the morning, the head broker assembled perhaps twice the required number of men in a large yard in preparation for an examination by the ship's doctor, the surgeon-superintendent.[32] If they passed muster, they moved to the right; if not, to the left. "Men of advanced years pick out their grey hairs and make themselves look as young as possible," Paul Pax observed, "[and] boys try to appear men, the ages at which emigrants will be accepted being well known to them all. Consequently no one is under nineteen nor more than thirty-three, according to their own account."[33] Nevertheless, he admitted, "A few under as well as over the age specified, one or two men halt or lame, several opium smokers, and a 'gong,' that is, an idiot, have managed by aid of the brokers to elude the vigilance of the medical examiner and his coadjutor."[34] When the numbers were made up, the men were placed on board the waiting ship where they were again examined for fitness and then, if finally accepted, they passed on to the advance table to be indentured and receive their money which soon left their hands:

> Every man now signs his agreement if he can write, and there are few exceptions, he gets his $6 and nearly all of them hand the $6 to the broker who has fed and clothed him… The men now having obtained perhaps two suits of clothes, tobacco, sweetmeats, and other little delicacies for the voyage, they are now richer in worldly goods than they have ever been.[35]

The indenture agreement was signed by each man and counter-signed by the ship's captain as witness. The contracts were printed in Chinese on one side and in English on the reverse and each indentured labourer kept a copy. How many of the men could actually sign their name to a contract they could read and understand is a matter of conjecture. It is a specious to argue, as Paul Pax did, that the scheme offered hope to the most destitute when these destitute men, with few exceptions, were unable to comprehend the contract conditions. When the 1854 select committee asked Andrew Shortrede if he thought they could understand the agreement, he replied, "I think they very seldom do. I suspect few of those who come here, boors taken from the fields, have more than a smattering of education, and many of them, probably, can neither read nor write." The contract, for those who could comprehend it, read:

> Memorandum of agreement made and entered into this ... day of..., in the year of our Lord one thousand eight hundred and..., between..., a native of China, of the one part, and.... of... in the territory of New South Wales, of the other part: witnesseth that the said... agrees to serve the said..., and such person or persons whom he may place in charge over the said... in the capacity of shepherd, farm and general servant, and labourer in the said territory, for the term of five years, to commence from the date of the arrival of the said... in the said territory, and to obey all his lawful orders and the orders of such persons as may be placed in charge over him. And the said... agrees to pay the said... $3 per month, the said amount to be paid in dollars, or in sterling British money at the exchange of 4s. per dollar. And also to provide the following weekly rations, namely:- 8 lbs flour or 10 lbs rice at option; 8 lbs meat; 2 ozs tea.
>
> And the said... having received at Amoy from the agent of... the sum of... dollars advance, agrees to repay the same in NSW, to..., by a monthly deduction of $1 from his wages.
>
> Signed by Messrs Tait & Co., as agents and the contracting Chinaman.

Wang Singwu notes that the men who arrived in New South Wales on the *Nimrod* and the *London*, that is, before 1850, were paid $2.50 a month, not the $3 that appeared on the contract above, but otherwise the terms were consistent until the trade ended in mid-1853.[36] It is important to note that there was no requirement in the agreement for the contracting party to pay the cost of the return passage at the end of the indenture. Nor is there any mention of the two suits of clothes per year that Francis Syme had also stipulated in his original correspondence with Adam Bogue, although there is some evidence that a suit of clothes and boots were usually provided, along with rations, by their masters in the colony. Nowhere in the literature, however, is there any discussion of the number of men who returned to China on completion of their contracts, and although Paul Pax confidently boasted that "Chinese women will soon follow their countrymen, as they have in different parts of the world, and even now some of those immigrants who were married ere they migrated are returning for their wives, having saved means for that purpose," this was not borne out by the colonial census statistics.[37]

Were the names of the eventual employer included in the contract at that point in the process? This is not clear. The Sydney immigration agent said that he had seen men on board some ships partitioned off in groups of eight or ten by small spars or studding-sail booms and these partitions were marked with chalk to make the groups of men more recognizable to their importers. "The importers," he said, "professed that they knew them, and knew all the different signatures and handwritings, but I had grave doubts on the subject, and the arrangements appeared to me to be anything but satisfactory."[38] If the Chinese labourer had no control over his destination or even the exact nature of his employment, the term "labourer" covering a multitude of possibilities, the future employer also lacked choice, receiving the labourer that was simply delivered to him at the wharf or depot in Moreton Bay or elsewhere in the colony. The venture was profitable to some but risky to many more.

The Passage

Despite the pious maxims of proponents of the trade such as Paul Pax, conditions on board the ships were governed purely by commercial interest: every man lost during the voyage cost the importer £12 or £13, so it paid to keep them all alive.[39] Mortality rates were very high on one ship, resulting from an outbreak of dysentery caused by contaminated drinking water, and there was something like a mutiny on another, but for the most part, and despite the absence of regulations and official supervision, the Celestials survived the voyage to Australia thanks as much to their own habits of social organization as to the weather, the goodwill of the captain, and the skill of the doctor on board.

The average length of the voyage from Amoy to Sydney was eighty-five days, or roughly three months; the fastest run was fifty-nine days, by the largest of the ships, the *Royal Saxon*, which docked in Melbourne.[40] Depending on the prevailing winds, the ships either took the easterly route through the Coral Sea or sailed due south through the Indonesian Archipelago, around Cape

Leeuwin and across the Great Australian Bight, with a stopover in Manila, Singapore or Bali en route for fresh water.

The ship's captain and the doctor each received explicit instructions regarding rations, water, and the management of the men during the voyage. There were, however, no stipulations regarding the outfitting of the ship to accommodate the men. It was only in hindsight that a rough guide to the number of men per ton was suggested as three men to every five tons, which was already about twice the allowable rate under the Passenger Vessels Act, and as shown in Table 2, in some instances, most alarmingly in the *Spartan* where the men rioted, there were three men to every two tons. The conditions were so over-crowded that instructions to the captains and doctors stressed the need for ventilation and for one-third of the men to be constantly on deck to allow more room and air for those below. The between decks where the men were held had no sleeping facilities, no berths or fittings of any kind, "simply the open deck on which they spread their mats and lay down," Hutchinson Browne told the inquiry. There was a small batten nailed to each side so the men could brace their feet against it during bad weather to keep from slipping. Given these descriptions, it is little wonder that the ships were condemned by liberals in the colony as slavers.

The rations, for the men who were not affected by seasickness, seemed adequate. In fact, as detailed by Paul Pax, the daily allowances were not significantly different from the dietary scale that was incorporated into the Chinese Passengers Act of 1855 that eventually gave some protection to emigrants from China's southern ports.[41] Nevertheless, as the 1854 inquiry confirmed, many of the men landed in New South Wales in a sad state of scurvy. A far more serious problem was dysentery. Paul Pax blamed the salted fish that he said was insufficiently prepared. Indeed, it was, he wrote, "highly objectionable. It is salted down uncleaned; a large proportion of it is early decomposed, and is thus one of the chief causes of dysentery."[42] Once dysentery broke out in the overcrowded conditions, there were insufficient medicines on board to cope and not even water closets where men could relieve themselves safely.

Among all the ships, the *General Palmer* suffered the highest rate of mortality. Of the 333 Chinese men who boarded that vessel on October 15, 1851, only 264 survived the voyage. Many of those survivors were in such a debilitated state that they could barely make their own way from the ship and even more died while the ship was in Sydney harbour. In fact, four or five deaths had occurred before the ship reached Bali where it stopped to take on fresh water, which had been lacking for some time. It was the wet season, and the water in Bali was contaminated. Not long after leaving port, dysentery broke out with terrible effect, eighty or ninety men ill at one time and up to seven or eight men dying in a single day.[43] The Sydney immigration agent reported the circumstances and the government instituted a board of inquiry that absolved the captain and the ship's doctor of any blame while it called for improvements in rationing, clothing, and accommodation on board the ships involved in the Chinese labour trade. Hutchinson Browne was so upset by the plight of the men on the *General Palmer*, he told the 1854 select committee, that had the immigration continued, he intended to pressure the government to introduce a bill that would give him the same legal jurisdiction over the coolie ships that he had over all the other passenger ships, adding,

> I contemplated also that the ships should be fitted properly, in the same way as all other passenger ships, and that they should have, if not bed places, at least a sufficient framework to keep the people off the deck in case of wet. I also intended to suggest that they should have suitable water closets erected on the deck, to prevent the necessity of the immigrants being obliged to go into the chains. The Coolies would not use them except in case of illness, but it was given in evidence by Captain Simpson [of the *General Palmer*] that several of these poor unfortunate wretches, for the want of closets, dropped from the chains, being unable to hold on from weakness.

The other notorious ship and its passage that brought public attention to the abuses of the trade was the *Spartan*, another of Robert Towns' vessels that left Amoy towards the end of January 1852. A barque of 364 tons, it was inspected later that year by the British Navy in Amoy harbour while preparing to take on a further cargo of labourers. As a result of that inspection, and according to the passenger space of 2,300 square feet, the number of Chinese it was permitted to convey was 153.[44] In approximate compliance with that order, it landed 161 men in Sydney on May 3, 1853. During the controversial voyage of January to May 1852, however, there were 254 Chinese on board in intolerably overcrowded conditions that allowed less than ten square feet of space per man.[45]

Not long after leaving Amoy, the human cargo revolted. The captain and several ship's officers were seriously wounded in the mêlée, one fatally. The *Spartan* put into Singapore where a charge of murder was brought against nineteen rioters, eleven of whom were found guilty and sentenced to death. A local newspaper took up the cause of the condemned men and it was able to demonstrate that the riot had resulted from cruel treatment by the captain and his crew. Consequently, all but two of the men had their sentences commuted to a few weeks' imprisonment.[46]

The problems were not over for this ill-fated voyage, however. An epidemic broke out on board while the ship was lying at the wharf in Sydney Harbour and there were many deaths. The immigration agent was not invited to hold an investigation, but, he told the 1854 select committee, "I believe it was a fact that bodies were thrown overboard into the harbour from that vessel." Robert Towns acknowledged that there had been a considerable number of deaths among the Chinese on board the *Spartan* at the wharf in Sydney. He told the committee, "I believe this disease on board the *Spartan* may be accounted for by their having had the dysentery when they went into Singapore; and after they were cured of the dysentery, it settled into a species of debility and a relaxed state of the system generally, which terminated in dropsy." For Towns, the episode represented merely a loss of profit, "I sent several of them to the Infirmary, until at last they refused to receive them, and levied a tax upon me of five shillings a day," he complained.

Of all the white men who commented on the shipping trade in indentured labour from Fujian to New South Wales, the most reliable and the one least self-interested was the immigration agent, Hutchinson Browne. The Celestials, of course, were not invited to comment publicly and formally about methods of recruitment, their indenture agreements, or the conditions on board the vessels that transported them from one hemisphere to the other. The mutiny on the *Spartan* was undoubtedly a comment of a violent sort, but we are left without the details as to its cause. Paul Pax in his voluminous submissions to the Sydney press was obviously sensitive to suggestions that manacles were used on the ships and to any other suggestion of harsh and cruel treatment. Hutchinson Browne told the 1854 inquiry that he had never ascertained that there had been ill-treatment as such and because he visited the ships when they docked and made a point of speaking to the men through their interpreters, his assessment should be respected as trustworthy.

He judged that the merchants and shippers were guilty of neglect rather than outright cruelty. The poor fittings of the vessels to accommodate the men—the absence of bunks, the open space that was often wet, the lack of water closets so that sick men had to hang from chains over the open sea when attacked by bouts of dysentery—and the overcrowding were a sufficient indictment. The men frequently complained to him of cold, especially during the leg of the journey across the Southern Ocean from Cape Leeuwin which was the route most of the ships took. Their clothing was thin and inadequate, just "dungaree frocks and trowsers" and no underclothing. The men paid for the two suits of clothing out of the $6 advance and Hutchinson Browne believed that they were cheated by the brokers. He considered the ships' doctors to be good men and skilled in their profession but he also felt that there were inadequate medical supplies on board to cope with outbreaks of illness that were inevitable.

Paul Pax argued that no matter how stringent the measures were to ensure good hygiene on board, sickness would inevitably break out a few days after leaving Amoy. A major cause was debilitation among some of the men during their withdrawal from opium addiction. He calculated that ten percent of all the emigrants were addicts, not surprising, he said, when "about one-third of the adult population of China use this drug more or less."[47] There were also other men who made repeated attempts to commit suicide by jumping overboard. "The first death on board," he wrote, "will exercise a material influence on the spirits of the men, as it has invariably been found that others soon follow."[48] He did, however, admit that the clothing might have been inadequate or insufficient. In this matter, he blamed "the rapid manner in which the men are shipped" at Amoy.

Ultimately, he blamed the Chinese themselves. "The imprudent habits of the Chinese make them totally incapable of taking care of themselves, and they must consequently be treated as so many children," Paul Pax wrote in the conclusion to his series of long articles in the press. But this surely was not true. The three-month voyage to New South Wales would have been an unrelieved nightmare without the systematic arrangements they made among themselves and the care and support they gave to the sick among them. Andrew Shortrede spoke from experience when he told the 1854 select committee, "[I]f there were twenty or thirty Chinese on board a ship or anywhere else, they would select a headman, a cook and other persons for different duties … they are used to combinations among themselves … in every ten houses in China there is a combination for honest ends…". Wang Singwu confirms this and elaborates,

Headmen (corporals), cooks, and barbers were chosen from among the Chinese for enforcing discipline among their people, washing their clothes and bedding, cleaning the decks, and cooking food, tea, and other purposes.[49]

There would, of course, have been fights and disputes among them, necessitating good organization and discipline. We can assume that the men spent much time gambling during which arguments and fights would have arisen. They would have brought on board all the same rivalries, conflicts, and suspicions that different groups and villagers would have shared on land. Boredom and cramped space, if nothing else, would have sparked tension. "But if we see much to condemn in some of them, in their deficiency in point of humanity one to another, we also see much to praise," Paul Pax conceded,

We shall find many of them attending on their sick comrades with brotherly fidelity, boys of sixteen performing the most menial offices for their fellow-youth, with no prospect of reward, and this will go on for weeks, night and day, until a sight of the Australian coast breaks upon them, when a loud shout announces the first appearance of the promised land.[50]

No doubt they were greatly relieved by the sight of land, but how did they appear to those on shore? Kathryn Cronin recounts the scene at the Geelong pier, Port Phillip district, in December 1848 when a boatload of Indian, Malay, and Chinese Coolies arrived there from Singapore. By the following account, the appearance of the Chinese attracted the most curious attention:

Their heads were shaved with the exception of a patch on the crown about four inches in diameter, from which depended a tail two feet long... A very few of them had the large hats which we are acquainted with, capital substitutes for umbrellas, being nearly three feet in diameter. Their dress appeared invariably black ... cotton, wide drawers, and an upper dress like a sailor's duckfrock, but wide in the sleeves and rather larger. Their square-toed shoes were ornamented with silk on the uppers, and with soles an inch and a quarter thick.[51]

The "tail", the wearing of the hair in a plaited queue, was the most singular eccentricity of Chinese dress. Wearing it was said to be a mark of subjection to Qing rule and removing it was, by corollary, an act of rebellion. The initiation ceremony for those seeking membership in the secret societies involved cutting off the queue, so the "tail" was not simply a hair fashion; it was highly symbolic and it was unthinkable for a Chinese man to appear in public in the nineteenth century without it. Ordinary Sydneysiders were not unaware of the significance of the queue, so when many of the men arrived in Sydney without it, they assumed that the men were outcasts of the Chinese jails. This was put to Andrew Shortrede at the 1854 inquiry, and he had dismissed the notion, advising the committee that it would be as unlikely for a magistrate in China to remove a prisoner from jail and transfer him to a labour ship to New South Wales as it would be in the reverse situation. To put the matter to rest, Paul Pax assured the readers of the *Sydney Morning Herald* that "every man when he was shipped in Amoy possessed one [i.e. a queue]." The haircuts took place during the voyage as a matter of hygiene and efficiency, he wrote,

> Scalp diseases, arising chiefly from want of cleanliness, are very rife among the Chinese, the health and comfort therefore of the men will, as stated, be very materially promoted by denuding them of the "pig-tails".[52]

Letting go of the queue must have been as terrifying to most of the men as losing sight of land as they sailed from Amoy. It surely was an admission to themselves that they would never return to China. None of this sentiment bothered Paul Pax. "Tact is all that is required," he added confidently, "one by one, they will all or nearly so yield this outward emblem of their barbarism; the most potent argument is to assure them that they are no longer Chinamen but Englishmen, that they must dress and act like Englishmen...".

Public Reaction

If the colonial press is to be believed, there was outrage in New South Wales society over the importation of these three thousand or so Chinese indentured labourers. Most of the reports, letters and editorials were hate-filled, racist, homophobic, and hysterical. "[W]e shall have introduced amongst us vices of the most horrible description; vices which cry to heaven for vengeance, and which will render the interior of the colony a place fit only for the abode of savages," thundered the editor of the *People's Advocate*.[53] The most stinging remarks, however, contained the charge of slavery. "One thing is very certain—the whole class of these men is destitute of the capacity of British freedom. There is not a single circumstance in their condition which defends them from the inequality which is the prime characteristic of slavery," contended the *Empire*.[54]

There was even a half-hearted attempt to introduce legislation for the regulation of immigration from China to the colony. In November 1851, Dr Henry Douglass, member of the Legislative Council for the counties of Northumberland and Hunter, asked the colonial secretary in the House if he had any information concerning the attempt to open up a "Chinese slave trade" to the Northern Districts.[55] When the colonial secretary replied in the negative, Dr Douglass, amid laughter, gave notice of his intention to ask leave to introduce a bill against what he regarded as "a speculation ... among the class of flesh-dealers in this colony."[56] In reply, one of the leaders of that very class, William Charles Wentworth, said he believed the bill would be a violation of the law of nations and a breach of the amity existing between the two nations. He suggested that Dr Douglass was responding to populism, as he surely was. The editor of the *Sydney Morning Herald* called the proposed bill "a peg whereon the mover might hang a speech, and thereby elicit the opinion of the House on the question thus ingeniously raised."[57] The colonial government could not countenance a bill that was opposed to the law both of the colony and the empire, a house member pointed out, and Dr Douglass withdrew the motion. The ruse had its desired effect, however, and with the exception of those members who had participated in the trade, Chinese immigration was roundly condemned and the Chinese labourers already in the country thoroughly denigrated:

> Their notions of morality and of justice are so utterly
> repugnant to ours, so subversive of law and order, so deeply
> tinged with a ferocity which pants for blood, and scruples
> at no means for glutting its savage appetite, that to speak of
> them as a mild and inoffensive people, of whom shiploads
> may be brought to the colony without detriment to our
> social well-being is to insult our common sense not less than
> our national pride.[58]

Thus, it was the opinion-shapers and the legislators who placed the Chinese indentured labourer beyond the pale of normal society. They would never be allowed to become "Englishmen," no matter how they dressed or otherwise behaved. The legislators, all of them men of wealth, power, and property were themselves, more often than not, both avid importers and employers of the trade. The solidarity that the Celestials had developed on board the ships, little better than slavers, that had brought them to New South Wales, would be all that they could rely on for the long five years of their indenture.

CHAPTER 6

Labour

The business of importing Chinese labourers to New South Wales between 1848 and 1853 was regarded at the time by those who engaged in it merely as an extension of the general trade in commodities, one that was no different from that in coal or sandalwood, for instance, or on an international scale, in tea and opium. The rapid expansion of the pastoral industry had created a demand for labour, one that could not be met by local supply, or so the squatters argued. The market in cheap human labour sourced in Amoy would help to satisfy that demand. The colonial shipping industry also stood to gain handsomely from the trade, as did the local agents, typically owners of wharves and wool warehouses who acted as middlemen and brokers.

For the most part, the labour trade to the colony during these years consisted of sixteen shiploads of men, all except three of which departed from Amoy.[1] Around two hundred of the men who embarked in China died during the voyage, mainly from dysentery, and others debilitated by their sickness died shortly after arrival in Sydney or en route to the coastal port nearest to their place of assignment. Half of those deaths occurred during two voyages: seventy on board the *General Palmer* that arrived in Sydney in February 1852, and thirty-three who died aboard the last of the ships, the *Spartan* that arrived via Melbourne in April 1853. Some ships' voyages suffered no casualties at all and, generally speaking, the rate of mortality on board was low. Thirteen of the sixteen ships ended their voyages in Sydney, two of them via Melbourne. On two voyages each, the *Duke of Roxburgh* and the *Eleanor Lancaster* were commissioned to sail directly to Moreton Bay and to Newcastle respectively but bad weather forced the *Duke of Roxburgh* to change course for Sydney on its first trip. According to Maxine Darnell's figures, excluding those who almost immediately proceeded from Sydney to the new gold-rich colony of Victoria, around 3,043 Chinese labourers arrived in New South Wales aboard these vessels, of whom 1,452, or almost half, were contracted to work in the Northern Districts that included New England, Clarence River, Darling Downs, Moreton Bay, Maranoa, Wide Bay, and the Burnett.

Shipping lists indicate that around 755 labourers disembarked in Brisbane (Moreton Bay), the vast majority of them arriving by the end of 1851. From Brisbane, they would have been conducted to stations and other places of employment in the Northern Districts, including some who would have travelled overland to runs in the lower Burnett. A further 158 at least were transferred from Sydney, or from Newcastle in one instance, to Maryborough (Wide Bay) by coastal shipping, generally by schooner, especially after port facilities improved there around 1851.[2] Most of those arrivals in Maryborough occurred between October 1851 and mid-1852. Some of those men remained in the Wide Bay district while others made their way to Gayndah and the Burnett district along the dray roads that ran between the port of Maryborough and the pastoral runs inland.

The figures from shipping lists, however inexact, are likely to be more reliable than those from official statistics. Time taken to count heads for commercial purposes was surely considered better spent for the squatter than form-filling for a distant, resented government in Sydney. Using the results of both the 1851 and 1856 census, as well as statistical returns for the Legislative Council, Maxine Darnell notes that according to official records, in all the Northern Districts (including Maranoa where there were only two and then three Chinese by the latter census in a total non-indigenous population of 110, and Stanley where the city of Brisbane was located) there were 620 Chinese in 1851, increasing to 702 by the second census.[3] These figures are probably under-estimates. Nevertheless, away from Brisbane, the census results showed that the numbers of Chinese in the districts were significant in relation to the overall settler population and especially to participation in the pastoral economy. In the Burnett, ranked third in regional sheep production after the Darling Downs and New England, almost one person in eight counted by the census in the years 1851 to 1856 inclusive was Chinese, and one out of every four shepherds in the district was Chinese.[4] These were critical years for the pastoral industry when gold fever sparked by discoveries in Bathurst and Victoria all but stripped the Northern Districts of their labour force while simultaneously increasing demand for meat and other products of the industry. This is not to say, however, that the introduction of Chinese labourers was a response to the gold discoveries. It was not. Arrangements for their importation had already been made before the first large claims were struck at Bathurst in New South Wales in 1851.

How the Celestials found their way to their place of work in the Wide Bay and Burnett districts, the nature of the jobs they performed during the five years of their indenture, the general conditions and remuneration for their labour, and an attempt to measure the cost or benefit of their employment to their employer and, in purely material terms, to themselves will be the subjects discussed in this and the following chapter. The period under study will be late 1848 to 1860 by which time even the most recalcitrant or unfortunate of the Chinese labourers would have completed his five-year contract.

From Ship to Shore

In late October 1848, the following advertisement appeared in the *Sydney Morning Herald* under the caption "Chinese Immigrants":[5]

> Some of the Chinese immigrants per *Nimrod* from Amoy being still open for engagement, parties desirous of obtaining their services can see them on board the vessel alongside Deloittes' wharf and will be assisted in entering into agreements with them on application to the undersigned.
>
> These men can be engaged for a period of five years at £6 p.a. with rations and clothing on payment of their passage money.
>
> Henry Moore, Agent for the *Nimrod*
> Miller's Point, October 17.

The arrival of the *Nimrod* with 120 Amoy men on board marked the beginning of what Maxine Darnell refers to as "sponsored importations".[6] Squatters had placed an order with the ship's agent in Sydney for the number of men required for their own needs and the total number was made up in Amoy under the auspices of James Tait.[7] A little over half of this first human cargo, or sixty-two labourers, were transferred by coastal shipping to Moreton Bay, so it appears that the northern squatters had initiated this first buying trip. Among them, Richard Jones of Barambah and Mondure stations in the lower Burnett employed sixteen of these men, all purchased for £8 15s. each.[8] Those who remained in Sydney had not been contracted to a specific employer before embarking in Amoy, and Darnell notes that Henry Moore had to advertise for almost seven weeks to clear his stores of the last of the men in this first consignment.

In January 1849, the *Moreton Bay Courier* reported an incident which it thought might amuse the readers. This account describes the earliest recorded impressions that the Chinese made on the small Brisbane community:

> On Sunday morning last, as some of the lately-arrived Chinese labourers were passing down Queen street, they encountered about six or eight aboriginal blacks who saluted the Celestials with some observations, in the mixed gibberish formed by the patois of the natives and the elegant language of their earliest instructors. The subjects of the Moon's Brother did not understand the words, but, as the actions of the blacks were tolerably significant, without being equally flattering, several of the offended parties tucked up their sleeves, and prepared for a bout at fisticuffs *à l'Anglaise*. This was opposed to the tactics of the blackfellows, and they hastened to possess themselves of waddies, to the infinite disgust of their antagonists, who in vain strove, by voice and gesture, to convince the grimy savages of the unfairness of such a contest. At every fresh expostulation, the man-eaters opened their jaws to a frightful width, and flourished their weapons with increased glee. A crowd soon collected, and the influence of the mischievous might have been sufficient to have caused an affray between the parties, but that some well-disposed persons contrived to separate them. Certainly the Chinamen displayed considerable game, and their adversaries an equal amount of the chicken.[9]

The *London* out of Hong Kong brought a further 149 men, a third of them destined for Moreton Bay, in February 1849. After that, there were no large-scale consignments for more than a year; then, from April 1850 to February 1851, three more shipments arrived with the men on board already under contract to specific employers. Almost all of the labourers on these three voyages were engaged in the Northern Districts. There was then another hiatus in the trade with no arrivals for nine months until November 9, 1851 when the *Duke of Roxburgh* brought its second cargo of men from Amoy directly into Moreton Bay. The terse reporting on its arrival reflected the change in mood and the growing antipathy of the press and, according to it, of the general public, towards the importation of Chinese labour:

> By the arrival of the barque *Duke of Roxburgh*, at this port on Sunday last, 225 labourers have been imported into Moreton Bay and who are, I understand, to be obtained from the agent for a term of years upon payment of the passage money—£13 per head; a sum by the bye, more by £2 than would bring out an emigrant from the United Kingdom or Germany. Several deaths had occurred on the passage, including the Doctor. The Schooner *Toroa* has been engaged to bring the Chinese up to Brisbane; she went down the river yesterday for that purpose.[10]

This voyage marked the entry of entrepreneur Robert Towns into the trade and a change in its general nature, Darnell suggests, to one of pure speculation, and thus inevitably to over-supply.[11] In the six months between November 1851 and the end of April 1852, eight shiploads of Amoy men arrived, or half the total number of ships and more than half the total number of labourers for the whole period from 1848 to 1853. Towns was the agent responsible for five of these shipments and he used his own ships, including the *Arabia*, *Statesman*, and *Royal Saxon* which had been fitted out specifically for the trade.[12] He wrote directly to his customers, assuring them of the value of the product he had to sell, as this extract from a letter to Adolphus Trevethan on Rawbelle station in the upper Burnett, then the northwest outpost of European settlement in New South Wales illustrates:

> [The Chinese] will be your salvation in shape of labour not so much for the six men but it will teach your other men a wholesome lesson viz. that others are to be had if they persist in demanding such wages as you cannot pay … you have the services of these men for five years at a rate not exceeding one-quarter you are obliged to pay your own countrymen and I find I can get more work out of a Chinaman than a European even in Sydney.[13]

Far from representing "salvation", however, two of those six men, along with Trevethan himself, were killed during an Aboriginal raid shortly after they took up work at the station.

Soon after the *Duke of Roxburgh*'s arrival in Brisbane in November 1851, the editor of the *Moreton Bay Courier* commented sarcastically on this form of commerce that had become analogous to slaving:

> [I]t seems, nevertheless, likely that Moreton Bay is destined to cultivate extensive mercantile connections in the ports of his [Chinese] Majesty... Accordingly, it is not surprising that the demand for labour in this colony should have called forth some sagacious commercial speculators who have shown their willingness to supply certain quantities of blood, bones and sinews wherever they could be picked up for a profitable consideration.[14]

The northern squatters' newspaper had clearly changed its tune from the not too distant past when it had defended the call for cheap labour wherever it could be sourced. It now demanded regulation of the trade, although not solely out of concern for its victims. It accused the government of behaving "in the deceptive manner of a Revenue officer who shuts his eyes so that he may not see the smuggler ... [and] peopling this fine country with male Tartars":

> The nature of the arrangements by which the services of these Chinese labourers are secured—the previous occupations and characters of the men—and their treatment while on the voyage are circumstances which, we presume, the Government... have never taken pains to ascertain. There seems to be nothing known... on those subjects. All that appears is that a vessel enters this port and the captain reports that he has on board so many Chinamen, that such a number died on the voyage and that he has no sickness on board. This appears to be all the inquiry deemed necessary and the vessel forthwith discharges its freight.[15]

The men who were discharged onto the wharves in South Brisbane were lodged temporarily in the warehouses belonging to the local shipping agents, principally William (John) Connolly, proprietor of the Union Wharf and

Store. The *Toroa* that had transferred the men from the *Duke of Roxburgh* to Brisbane was one of the schooners belonging to the shipping line that Connolly represented. Henry Buckley, agent for the Hunter River (later the Queensland, then Australasian) Steam Navigation Company among other enterprises, was another agent. The squatters shipped their wool through these wharves in South Brisbane, so there was a well-established personal and commercial link that facilitated the quick despatch of the Amoy men to their contracted employers. At the same time, these and other businessmen on the south side of the Brisbane River, among them J. and W. Orr who had a slaughterhouse near Connolly's wharf, and Henry Hockings, general merchant, engaged some of the Chinese labourers as porters, dockers and general hands.

Between 1851 and 1853, the Amoy men employed in and around Brisbane were occasionally mentioned in the press, usually by the court reporters. At least five men who worked for Buckley absconded during that time; three of them said they objected to the cruelty of his overseer and another, after offending for a second time, preferred spending three months in Brisbane Gaol to returning to Buckley's service.[16] Some of the charges brought against these men were petty, including one of indecent conduct, another for stealing a pair of trousers left drying on a fence overnight (for which one of the thieves, Tean/Teon, received six months of hard labour), and even stealing mulberries hanging over a town fence (a week's imprisonment). In one rare instance, Gan Som, a frequenter of the Brisbane courts as a rather inefficient interpreter, succeeded in bringing an assault charge against his employer, Henry Hockings, who admitted to having pushed Gan Som into the Brisbane River in a fit of "momentary irritation" and for this received a fine from the Brisbane Bench.[17] In January 1853, Seikh/See-eth was charged in the Brisbane Police Court for the second time with vagrancy and punished with three months' hard labour.[18] Seikh was reported to have no master. Presumably he was one of those were men brought from China to Moreton Bay without guaranteed employment, as part of a speculative venture by Towns or some other entrepreneur. Unwanted and unable to return to China, the only home for these cast-offs was Brisbane Gaol.

For the men who came to Moreton Bay and who were not engaged by squatters on pastoral runs in the interior but who remained in Brisbane and its environs, the most serious threat to their well-being came from white co-workers. In nearby Ipswich, around thirty Chinese were involved in a terrible fracas at the boiling down works owned by R. J. Smith in March 1851 when six white butchers assaulted eight or nine Chinese workers with sharpened staves and iron bars, leaving some so grievously wounded that "their lives were despaired of".[19] Other Chinese in the area then became involved in a revenge attack. Four of the white men received gaol terms ranging from nine months to one year.

This was a rare instance of justice. When there was conflict with Europeans, the Chinese almost invariably came off second-best, not because of lack of courage or endurance on their part but because they were an unwelcome minority and there were few men in authority who cared enough about their welfare to take their side. Solidarity was their only hope. When Oohee was charged with assaulting fellow seaman Frederick Richards of the brig *Brothers* moored at South Brisbane after Richards had allegedly called him a "black devil," the fine and court costs were made up by his countrymen.[20] Those who worked without the company of their countrymen had to rely on good luck and happenstance. Almost a year after Oohee was charged, Hawk, named only for the mail steamer on which he was employed that plied between Sydney and Brisbane, was discharged following an appearance in the Brisbane Circuit Court on charges of stabbing, wounding and cutting a white hand on the steamer. The evidence suggested extreme provocation by two white hands and the jury found him not guilty but the judge expressed only regret that he could not charge the Chinese labourer with common assault and warned that "if [Hawk] ever came again before him and was found guilty, he would be most severely dealt with."[21]

The most serious incident, one that almost had fatal consequences, occurred at Ferry Wharf, South Brisbane, in February 1852. Tshow, recently arrived and "waiting for engagement," was arrested and charged with indecent conduct. The incident itself was trivial and the following day the Police Court ruled that the prisoner "appeared not to be in perfect possession of his mental faculties," that he was unaware he was committing an offence, and he was discharged. Tshow, however, was immediately followed into the dock by three compatriots, Pooun, Taw and Seong who were charged with assaulting James Gorman. From the evidence, it became clear that it had been a man named Fisher, a sawyer, who had alerted the constables to Tshow's misdemeanour. When Tshow was apprehended, a number of Chinese gathered and threw stones and a glass bottle at Fisher who ran to a nearby blacksmith's shop pursued by the Chinese. Gorman, Fisher's mate, took up an axe, which he was persuaded to relinquish for a stick, to fend off a crowd of Chinese estimated by witnesses as between twenty and seventy, and which the newspaper judged as "probably between twenty and thirty." The three accused got the better of Gorman and witnesses, including Hockings, told the court that they believed Gorman would be murdered. The ineffectual Gan Som acted as interpreter for the prisoners who, it was reported, appeared to have no satisfactory defence to make. The magistrates ordered each of the three prisoners to pay a fine of forty shillings and costs, amounting to about four months' wages, or spend a month in prison.

This, however, was not the end of the affair. At the Brisbane Assizes in May, Fisher had his revenge. On the basis of his testimony alone, Teeam/Tekam of South Brisbane was found guilty of having committed the "unnatural act" of bestiality on a dog, and at the Brisbane Circuit Court of May 21, a sentence of death was recorded against him with a recommendation from the judge that this be commuted to twelve months' hard labour at Newcastle Breakwater.[22] At those court sittings, another Chinese labourer was found guilty of theft and sent to Newcastle for six months on the evidence of the same man, Fisher, "the witness with eyes everywhere," who bore a deep grudge and waged a very successful personal vendetta against the uncomprehending Chinese.[23]

The editor of the *Moreton Bay Free Press* considered the appearance of so many Chinese labourers at the Brisbane Circuit Court during May 1852 and decided

> It is highly probable that … the Chinamen resident in this district do not possess in the gross the turbulent and vicious character which has been generally ascribed to them… [T]he solitary and uneventful life led by shepherds and hut keepers in this colony must be exceedingly monotonous and dreary to them… [I]t is in the interior and especially in the very remote stations where they seem to have been found most unruly and intractable.[24]

Therefore, in the short space of little over three years, the indentured Chinese workers had gone from being "game" in the eyes of the general public to being "turbulent and vicious," and worse, in the interior, to being "most unruly and intractable." No doubt a few of them were all of those things but given the conditions they had to endure on the frontier, these were also the human qualities that helped them to survive the odds they faced there.

From Shore to Sheep Station

Most of the Amoy men remained in South Brisbane for only a short time after their arrival because, according to their contracts, wages commenced from the date of arrival. It was in the interest of the importer, therefore, to have the men taken off his hands as quickly as possible. The transfer, as noted previously, was a simple commercial transaction. The employer paid the passage money, including the advance which the worker had to repay his employer in monthly instalments, at a cost of £13 for each of the men who disembarked in Brisbane from the *Duke of Roxburgh* on November 9, 1851, and, most probably, now had his name affixed to the contract that had been entered into in Amoy. The price varied according to vessel. Maxine Darnell notes that the price started at £15 per head for individuals hired off the *Nimrod*, the first ship, with the price reduced to £10 each if they were sold in batches of five or more.[25] During the purely speculative era of the trade, Robert Towns was pleased with the disposal of his cargo of 213 labourers that arrived in Sydney on the *Ganges* on January 26, 1852, declaring, "We had no difficulty in hiring all we could spare at £12 per head and the advance …".[26] This, Darnell explains, represented a total cost of £13 4s. to the employer.

Before leaving Brisbane, the men were fitted out with work clothes and boots, usually at Henry Buckley's store, at a cost of roughly one pound a head. According to the contracts of the early arrivals, this cost was borne by the employer but as the trade progressed, the clothing provision was removed from the contract and the cost of work outfits would have been put against future earnings.[27]

The Chinese labourers who disembarked in Moreton Bay and who were contracted to work on the Wide Bay and Burnett runs made the journey from South Brisbane by bullock dray. These were two-wheeled flatbed wagons, pulled by fourteen or sixteen bullocks per team with perhaps six drays making the journey together to the head station. The heavily laden drays eventually wore tracks through the bush and across the hills that became the regular communication routes between the city and inland towns. In the early days, the drays left from the south bank of the Brisbane River and passed through Limestone (Ipswich) before joining up with those that left from North Brisbane at Ferriter's station, Durrundur. This north road was about a week's journey by full dray, or some thirty miles/fifty kilometres shorter than the other. From Durrundur, the tracks went to Kilcoy station and then over the Manumbar Range to Goode's Inn, ten days by dray from North Brisbane.

This hostelry, famous in the South Burnett, stood at the junction of the main inland routes, now the town of Nanango. One dray track continued southwest over Cooyar Creek to Rosalie Plains and the Darling Downs while the other led north to Gayndah. Jacob Goode secured a publican's licence in April 1851 and until his death in 1859, he and his establishment drew custom not only from the dray trains that rested their teams there but also from the squatters competing for the pastoral labour that might arrive on some of those drays.[28]

There is no way of knowing what the Amoy men comprehended of the strange new world they encountered. They had spent about three months on board a sailing vessel, been emptied into a warehouse, and then put on a dray that dragged through dense scrub and dusty plain for several weeks before their journey ended. On board ship, they would already have discovered that the seasons were reversed and that the night sky revealed constellations different from those so familiar at home. There was also little in the landscape, the flora and fauna that was recognisable. As they traversed the savannah of the Burnett, they would have taken note of the common trees: the bunya and hoop pines gradually giving way to the spindly black ironbarks and pink bloodwoods, the clumping brigalow, the strangely womanish brachychitons, and the strongly scented eucalypts, grey-leafed with ragged trunks and threadbare limbs, some with bulbous protuberances resembling large weeping warts. By a strange twist of fate, however, they found themselves at around twenty-five degrees south, the latitude identical to the one they had left in the northern hemisphere and therefore in a climate not essentially different from that of Fujian province, although farther from the sea. The rocky hills and shallow soil would also have been vaguely familiar to them. The strangest sensation would no doubt have come from the vastness and seeming emptiness of the land itself, especially the absence of close human settlement, of manmade order over nature.

The Jobs They Did

In 1852, when most of the Chinese labourers were already at work in the districts to the north and west of Moreton Bay, white labour was very scarce on the runs. The gold discoveries in the south of New South Wales and in Victoria, the escalating violence against Europeans from organized indigenous resistance, and the terrible solitude of pastoral work left many stations in the remote Wide Bay and Burnett districts almost totally dependent on indigenous and Chinese labour. Therefore, the Chinese labourers were more than shepherds. Shepherding may have been their primary task, but they were general station hands and performed many roles from domestic servant in the squatter's kitchen to shearer in his woolshed.

Shepherding in the Australian bush, according to Russel Ward, was an occupation held in tremendous contempt by stockmen, bullock-drivers, shearers and other skilled bush-workers and one that experienced bushmen would usually accept only as a last resort.[29] Until the end of transportation, assigned convicts and then those on conditional pardon had provided this sort of labour. It was not, in other words, a job willingly undertaken, paid or unpaid, but one reserved only for "crawlers," the derogatory term for diseased and decrepit sheep. Ward explains,

> The shepherd's duties consisted of little more than to wander about with his flock by day, remaining wakeful enough to see that none of them strayed too far away from the main body, and to count them at night into a temporary fold made of brushwood hurdles. Usually he shared his bark hut with a mate, the hut-keeper, who slept in a kind of portable sentry-box beside the flock to protect it from dingoes. But much of what active work was required of both shepherd and hut-keeper was performed by their dogs. The life was so lazy, lonely and monotonous that many shepherds became a little mad. These ... came to be known as "hatters".[30]

Nevertheless, shepherds were indispensable on the Northern District runs that were vast and unfenced, and they accounted for a large proportion of the workforce of every squattage there. Jan Walker notes that on Rosalie Plains in 1860, there were twenty-six employees, of whom fifteen were shepherds.[31] One of the largest stations on the Darling Downs, Jondaryan, had fifteen outstations in 1859, most of them worked by between two and four shepherds each.[32] The size of the flocks were in inverse proportion to the availability of labour. Until the end of transportation, one shepherd was put in charge of around four hundred sheep; at double that number, it was calculated, disease was common and the wool deteriorated.[33] This was therefore the optimum ratio. Coghlan argues that in 1853, however, three shepherds were frequently entrusted with as many as four thousand sheep without harm arising.[34] This assumption is, to say the least, dubious.

The harm to the worker when flocks reached that size, not to mention the environmental damage, was obviously not a consideration at that time. On Burrandowan, where the head station and numerous out-stations covered hundreds of square miles of unfenced territory stocked to maximum capacity, with the strong-willed Gordon Sandeman in charge and around forty Chinese shepherds employed along with the remaining Indian Hill Coolies and sundry Europeans who also served as overseers and superintendents, work relations were always fractious. The behaviour of the Chinese frequently verged on the mutinous in situations that were provoked by the high-handedness of young white overseers.

In March 1855, Sub-Lieutenant Keene of the Native Police handed over five Chinese men to the constable in Gayndah and charged them with disobedience of orders. The first of them to appear before the Gayndah Bench of magistrates was Kong Kaw, a shepherd and watchman who had responsibility for two flocks of 1,300 sheep. For this onerous task, he was paid "an increased rate of wages" that was not specified in the court.[35] On March 6, the record states, "he absolutely refused to shepherd his sheep or to return to his station with them when ordered." Kong Kaw, not unexpectedly, offered no defence and was given three months in Sydney Gaol. His compatriots, Toan and Lim Hein, were found guilty of "intentionally mixing the sheep and refusing to draft them and refusing to take them out the next day" and received the same sentence. Ny Li and Tan Shai were similarly charged and sentenced. With flocks so large and wages so low compared to European rates, strikes and go-slows, absenteeism, and feigned sickness were all inevitable consequences of gross exploitation. Simple human error was also understandable under the circumstances, especially when language difficulties are taken into account.

Large flocks were susceptible to the disease known as scab. Mixing flocks, deliberately or not, therefore, was tantamount to spreading the disease. When there was an outbreak of scab, some of the northern squatters believed the Chinese shepherds were taking revenge for their poor working conditions. The work of treating and dressing animals with the disease, however, was punishment enough for a shepherd's mistake. Each individual sheep, kicking and struggling, had to be dipped in a solution of corrosive sublimate, or arsenic, that turned the labourer's fingers and nails black, and left his hands sore and swollen.

The only variation in the diurnal round of following sheep to pasture, tending and culling them, was the arrival of the weekly ration-cart

Drovers and farm hands, Jimbour Station, 1869. (John Oxley Library, State Library of Queensland, Neg:74272)

along with the storekeeper or the overseer who counted the flock and inspected the animals for disease. The shepherd was required to collect the ear-marks of dead sheep to account for them; otherwise, it was assumed the sheep were lost and the shepherd's wages would be docked accordingly for his negligence. Once a year, usually in late September after lambing, the shepherd drove his flock into the head-station to be washed and shorn. Shorn wool was much lighter to transport than that shorn in the grease, although washing was costly in time and labour. Until the 1860s when more complicated plants came into general use on the runs, the washing was done in a washpool in a creek a few miles from the shearing shed. Roy Connolly describes the process as follows:

> Driven in a crush kept to the narrow limits by the sturdy barking dogs, the sheep were moved to a sloping race. One by one in rapid succession, the sheep were dragged into the water, given a ducking, and then thoroughly rubbed with soft-soap. They were passed from man to man [standing up to the waist in cold water] and the wool thoroughly cleansed. When sufficient of them had been washed to form a flock, a waiting shepherd moved them to the shearing shed three miles away; they grazed a leisurely mile a day for it required three days to dry a wet fleece.[36]

At the time, there was scepticism among the Europeans that the Chinese labourers could shear. The following piece written by a correspondent from the Burnett appeared in the *Moreton Bay Courier* on March 3, 1855:

> The *Sydney Herald*'s correspondent says that some Chinamen have been shearing, and going about from shed to shed in a quiet manner, etc., etc. Disgusted with the drunken white man, he puts forward Mr Chinaman as a specimen of what white men should be. Don't you believe it. Such a thing as a shed of Chinese shearers never existed in this district, except in the fertile brain of the *Sydney Herald*'s correspondent. I have heard it was attempted in one shed but signally failed. Instead of the Chinamen being the respectable characters he would have us believe, they are the greatest nuisance we have in the Burnett District. What do you think these respectable Chinese did to Mr Lawson? Why, when they had a quarrel

> with their master, they mustered together and brought in the
> whole of their flocks to the head station, and mixed them
> with a flock which was known to be scabbed.

There was more than one factual error in this account. The Lawson brothers of Boondooma station had indeed suffered a devastating outbreak of scab among their sheep, but they blamed a fellow squatter, and not one of the Chinese shepherds in their employ with whom they had no quarrel. Some months after this article appeared, the negligence of some of them was blamed, in part, for a further outbreak of the disease, but this report at the time it was written was both unfair and inaccurate.

The Lawsons had purchased twenty-two indentured Amoy men in three batches: nine from the first voyage of the *Duke of Roxburgh* who started their contract in February 1851, seven from the same vessel that arrived in Moreton Bay in November that year, and a further six who arrived on one of Robert Towns' ships, the *Ganges*, in January 1852. There were also at least two Pentonville exiles from the *Bangalore* on the station, and a number of German indentured labourers.[37] The Lawsons were fair, if occasionally irascible employers who had generally good relations with their Chinese servants, which was a far cry from the simmering hostility that persisted on neighbouring Burrandowan. On September 18, 1853, the Lawsons sent a letter of reply to the superintendent there who had complained about "visitors" on his run:

> Sir – we are duly in receipt of your letter of today's date
> and in answer beg to inform you that we were not aware
> that any of our Chinamen had visited Burrandowan; and
> we may mention we never allow any of them to leave their
> occupations without a written permission which they take
> with them.
>
> We are ... (illeg.) of the necessity of keeping our
> respective men apart and would willingly adopt any move
> to do so. We need not allude to the difficulty of keeping these
> people at their stations as they are fond of visiting and will
> do so without our knowledge.
>
> However we shall be not only satisfied but obliged to
> you if you will inflict such punishment upon them when

you get them on the Burrandowan run as will prevent a nuisance in future.[38]

The Lawsons had no serious problems with their servants, regardless of where they came from; their main problem was hiring and keeping a sufficient supply of labour. In 1853, their prospects were for a heavy wool clip: "Now is the winter of our discontent made glorious summer...," they assured a correspondent.[39] Towards the end of that bountiful summer, they urged their Sydney agents to engage more shepherds for them "and forward them as soon as possible say at wages from £20 to £25 per annum. Chinese, Germans or any other labour would be most acceptable, the former we would prefer having a number on the station."[40] Towards the end of the 1854 lambing season, they assured their agents that scab had been eradicated in the Burnett district and that all the diseased sheep had been boiled down.[41]

Two months later, however, Robert Lawson was advising his neighbours, agents, and clients with sheep on agistment at Boondooma that scab had infected almost all the stock, numbering about thirty thousand sheep, adding "–all our hopes to be blasted as it were at once."[42] He blamed T. L. M. Prior who had traversed Boondooma while moving his flocks from the Logan River south of Brisbane to his new run, Hawkwood, on the Auburn River in the Burnett district for the latest outbreak. A Boondooma shepherd had picked up several of Prior's sheep and from those sheep the disease had been propagated. By the end of 1854, more than half of Boondooma's stock, or seventeen thousand sheep, had been destroyed. Lawson advised his Sydney agents to commence legal proceedings against Murray Prior.

At the end of May 1855, the clerk of petty sessions in Gayndah was advised of a further outbreak of scab on Boondooma. This time, Lawson did blame his Chinese shepherds–"those d–d scoundrels", he called them. Short of men and busy with lambing, he had put three flocks of wethers at one station and the shepherds had mixed their sheep, spreading the disease.[43] There was no suggestion, however, of malicious intent on the part of those shepherds.

The destruction of so many sheep reduced the need for labour, but whether this was the reason why five Chinese shepherds at Boondooma were paid up and discharged in 1855 with more than a year and a half of their contracts remaining is not recorded. It is quite likely, however, that these five men were held responsible for the outbreak of scab that year. Nevertheless, fifteen of the remaining seventeen Amoy men on the station completed their indentures there, including two who returned after finishing their six-month prison sentences in Sydney Gaol.[44] Many Chinese labourers were employed at Boondooma in the post-indenture period, including some of those who had been discharged, confirming the impression that it was one of the better-managed stations in the district and amenable to this sort of labour.

The newspaper article of March 1855 had scoffed at the idea of a Chinaman shearer in Burnett woolsheds. On Booubyjan station, however, in February that year, Twan/Twang had been paid £15 8s. 3d. for shearing 1,544 sheep.[45] Compared to the wages that the Amoy men still under indenture were earning, this represented a fortune and no doubt acted as a powerful incentive for those soon to finish their contracts. Shearers were itinerant labourers and they were paid by the score of sheep shorn. It was not, therefore, considered as work to be undertaken by indentured men, although Twan would no doubt have gained the skills and necessary experience while under indenture. In the following years, he was a regular shearer at Booubyjan station and also at Boondooma.

It may be difficult for Australians to imagine a Chinese gun shearer. The stock image of the heroic bronzed and bearded bushman is so ingrained in Australian folk memory that it does not allow for one with a Chinese face. Roy Connolly, however, confirms that some Chinese labourers in the Burnett were adept with the thin, narrow-bladed, hard-tempered shears. He notes, "A number [of shearers] were Chinese who, having acquired some skill as shearers during the contractual period of their bush labours, had now finished their indentures and were free to earn the rates which the squatters would pay them."[46]

Bush life imposed uniformity, if not equality, on all who engaged in it. In the bush, shepherds and itinerants of different ethnicities all wore the same outfit that was stocked by the station store. According to an article that appeared in the *Mount Perry Mail* in 1872,

> The dress of the shepherd comprises a "cabbage-tree" or felt hat, a blue serge shirt, and moleskins, confined by a strap round the waist: on this he carries a pouch to hold his pipe, tobacco, matches, flint and steel, etc.[47]

When Coon absconded from Coorangah station in July 1853, a notice appeared in the newspaper with his description as "about 45 years of age, tall and ill-looking with large front teeth, and when last seen was wearing a blue serge shirt, moleskin trousers, and a cabbage-tree hat, riding a very old and nearly blind dun-coloured horse."[48] Apart from his ethnicity, this Don

Woolshed at Booubyjan Station, c.1865. (John Oxley Library, State Library of Queensland, Neg:86330)

Quixote-like character in standard shepherd uniform fits well with the image of the eccentric, solitary Australian bushman drawn by Russel Ward in *The Australian Legend*. The most important human qualities for survival in the bush, or successful assimilation with the outback, in Ward's words, were "adaptability, toughness, endurance, activity and loyalty to one's fellows ...".[49] These essential characteristics were as true for the Chinese bushman as they were for any other pastoral labourer of the era.

The Company of Chinamen

What comfort there was on the job came from being in a group of fellow countrymen, men of the same dialect, perhaps from the same clan or lineage group, and especially close relatives, even siblings. As noted previously, the price of an indentured Chinese labourer was cheaper if purchased by the dozen, or at least in batches of five or so. Richard Jones on Barambah and Mondure hired sixteen men from the very first consignment, and Trevethan on Rawbelle, we know, purchased six men from Robert Towns. The Lawsons on Boondooma employed around twenty, and there was a similar number at Booubyjan. The Archers had employed Chinese labourers as far back as their occupation of Cooyar in the South Burnett. Maxine Darnell notes that eight men off the *Nimrod* started work with the Archers in February 1849. In the first half of 1850, they purchased nine men who had arrived in Sydney on the *London*, and the following March, eleven more from the *Duke of Roxburgh*.[50] These twenty-eight men were all despatched to Maryborough and, apart from those off the *Nimrod* who may have been originally contracted for Cooyar, their destination would have been Eidsvold in the upper Burnett or one of the many runs, including Tellemark, Mundowran, Geumga, and Malmoe that were associated with this huge prestigious holding settled by four of the Norwegian-raised Archer brothers: William, David, Tom, and Charles. Tom Archer recalled how that settlement was made,

> From [Cooyar], Charlie and I set off with all our belongings and about half a dozen men and ... in about a fortnight we arrived at Ban Ban, Humphries and Herbert's station on the Baramba, where the road came to a stop. For the rest of the way I had to act as guide to the party, riding ahead of the dray, which had the honour of making the first wheel-tracks

through the site of the future town of Gayndah, and so onward over the broken country … up the Burnett… [W] e unanimously agreed to call our new run "Eidsvold", after the village in Norway where the first Storthing passed the Norwegian Constitution about 1815. The lower part of the country, which fell to D. Archer & Co, we afterwards called "Coonambula", … where we formed the head station.[51]

In late 1853 after his ill-fated adventures in California, Tom Archer made the journey to Eidsvold again, this time with his newly-wed wife. It was then an eight-day trip from Maryborough in a spring cart covered with a canvas tilt to keep off sun and rain which was hardly the sort of comfort that would have been afforded to the Chinese labourers one or two years before.[52]

Tom Archer's close friend, Ned Hawkins, included two of the Chinese he employed on Boonara along with three indigenous men in their party that went to the California goldfields. Hawkins' death by drowning there late in 1849 or early 1850 left more than ten Chinese at Boonara to the abuse, already noted, of his overseer, Bertel J. Bertelsen. Indeed, all the big squatters, those with more than one lease and who could most afford to hire this sort of pre-paid labour, employed Chinese by 1853. The largest employer of Chinese labour in the Burnett was Gordon Sandeman, on the largest run, Burrandowan. He told the select committee in 1854 that he then employed "upwards of forty" Chinese, which would have represented between one-quarter and one-third of all the statistically recorded Chinese labourers in the Burnett at that time, and he had employed them as shepherds for "upwards of four years".[53] According to his evidence, answering the question about the total number of men imported into the Moreton Bay district, he stated, "From first to last, I should say about six hundred—there may have been more."[54]

The company of fellow countrymen did not always make for harmony, however. There were inevitable quarrels that occurred on the job, perhaps resulting from the forced proximity of two or three shepherds responsible for vast flocks in remote and isolated out-stations. One of the earliest appearances of a Chinese labourer before a rural bench was on a charge of having killed another Chinese shepherd named Kou. On October 8, 1850, Ang/Ong, employed in the Burnett on the Ideraway run of James Blair Reid, was taken before the Ipswich Bench and in the absence of witnesses or a competent interpreter was committed for trial at the Brisbane Circuit Court in November. While in prison awaiting trial, Ang impressed his gaolers with detailed drawings, accompanied by Chinese script that described the events leading to the shooting death of the victim.[55] He was convicted of manslaughter on November 16 and sentenced to three years' hard labour at Cockatoo Island. According to Shirley Fitzgerald, when he became eligible for parole in October 1852, he chose to remain on the island in the company of Eu, a shepherd from Mondure station who was serving seven years' hard labour for shooting and wounding a European on the run.[56] In fact, Ang had petitioned the authorities to allow him to work out a portion of Eu's remaining sentence—"a bizarre suggestion at law," Shirley Fitzgerald admits, "but one which was apparently accepted."[57] Both men were off the *Nimrod*, and both had been committed at the same Circuit Court sittings in Brisbane in 1850; their shared prison experience had made them inseparable. In May 1853, they made a joint submission for remission of (Eu's) sentence and were given free pardons on the anniversary of the Queen's birthday in June.

Other clashes were deemed "old quarrels" that may have had their origins in Fujian, or on board ship. One of these flared up on Boondooma in 1854. There were several Chinese men at the head station one day in March and around nine o'clock that night, one of them went to Lawson, the lessee, and his superintendent, James Rogers, to say that there was going to be a "row." They checked and everything seemed to be quiet but after five minutes a shot was fired at the Chinamen's hut. According to the Gayndah Bench record, five Chinese accompanied Rogers to the hut and five shots were fired at them. Two men, Ong Ceo and Con Chiam ran way from the hut, both of them armed. The case was dismissed, but these two men were extremely fortunate to have avoided long gaol terms.[58]

The case of Eu and Ang, prisoners on Cockatoo Island, may have been an exceptional case of fraternity among these Amoy men. There are, however, suggestions in the literature, particularly in the post-indenture period, that the long working partnerships of some men were, in fact, sibling relationships. This is partly because of names—Dem Chi and Dem Whan, Tan Chan and Tan Yang, Har Sin and Har Coo—but especially because they operated small businesses together, worked together on runs for many years, and even, in the case of Tan Chan and Tan Yang, were naturalized on the same day before the Gayndah police magistrate. If it could be proved that there were siblings among the shiploads of men from Amoy, this would surely be proof that not all of them were tricked or forced into the trade. For obvious reasons, it is impossible to verify that long-standing partnerships of men with the same clan name were family-related. There was, however, one rare recorded instance of brothers, veterans of the original indentured labour experiment with twenty years' experience in the country, that was published in the *Brisbane Courier* in 1870. This was the report on the double suicide of Ah King and Ah Chong in May that year on Dyngie station, due west of Gayndah in the Burnett district. According to the station owner, the older brother, his mind wandering, believed that "some of his countrymen would come and kill him, and that some of them had written threatening to do so."[59] While arrangements were being made to take Ah King to Gayndah because he was not considered safe to be at large, the overseer found both brothers in his hut hanging from the one piece of greenhide from a rafter, "Ah Chong's foot doubled under him, and the other almost sitting down… They must have watched me away, as I suppose it was not more than an hour until they were seen," the station owner wrote.

CHAPTER 7

Reward for Labour

It is unlikely that any of these men from Amoy ever had previous experience tending sheep. There were sheep in China in the mid-nineteenth century, of course, but they were herded on the Mongolian steppes and in the remote northwest provinces, and certainly not by Han Chinese. Those places were probably as distant from the imagination of Fujian people as were the sheep runs of the Burnett and Wide Bay. Nevertheless, they were good shepherds, despite the scorn and vitriol regularly poured on them by the colonial press and the opportunities their occasional misdemeanours gave to populist politicians to present an immigration restriction bill before the Legislative Council, using the parliamentary motion as a ploy or "a peg whereon the mover might hang a speech." In the years before self-government was granted to New South Wales in 1856, British law placed no bounds on the free movement of peoples within the Empire and of other peoples who shared friendly relations with it, and the British Colonial Office had little patience with the posturings of these shallow opportunists.

The size of the physical presence of Chinese labourers in the Northern Districts, however, was enough to warrant public attention and the frequency of stories about them in the local newspapers suggests that reporters and the reading public alike found them interesting. According to Maxine Darnell's research, in 1852, Chinese labourers were herding about two million sheep, or between one-third and one-half of all the flocks grazing in those districts north of the thirtieth parallel.[1] The majority of other shepherds at that time were Pentonville exiles from the *Bangalore* and the *Hashemy*. By the end of

1851, most other bushmen in those districts not tied to employers by tickets-of-leave or other forms of indenture had already headed south to the Bathurst diggings and when the rich gold discoveries were made in Victoria, as Tom Archer remembered, labour could not be procured "for love or money."[2] The timing of the arrival in the Northern Districts of the Chinese shepherds who were already bound to contracts which guaranteed the squatters a permanent low-wage labour force for terms of five years was therefore a stroke of great good fortune for the squatters, and one that some exploited to the hilt.

The Legality of Contracts

When the men were placed on board ship in Amoy harbour and had passed their final fitness examination, they were handed the promised advance ($8 or £1 12s. in the case of the *Nimrod* and *Cadet* passengers, and $6 or £1 4s. for those in later shipments) and then signed the indenture agreement which was witnessed and counter-signed by the ship's captain. The contract specified the duration of hire (five years), the monthly wage (generally $3 or 12s.), the weekly food rations, and the conditions for repayment of the advance.

From their perspective in Amoy, the men must have considered the conditions offered in the contract as generous. Even allowing for the exaggeration of a publicist for the trade like Paul Pax, the nominal wage prescribed by the contract was far more than anything these men could earn at home:

> What will the reader think when he is told that for one dollar per day (five shillings sterling), he can obtain the labour of ten Chinese carpenters on ship-board, and for this sixpence a day they would work twelve hours and find themselves!!— that for half that amount he can obtain Chinese labourers to work for the same period, and happy are they if they can get it.[3]

That the wages offered these indentured labourers were inequitable when compared to the wages then being paid to European labourers for the same work in New South Wales or when compared to the cost of living in the colony, had no bearing on the legality of the contract. Moreover, thanks to the 1847 amendment to the Masters and Servants Act, the agreements signed by the men in Amoy harbour were binding in New South Wales, and it was expediently assumed that the men who were hired were fully cognisant of the terms and conditions in the contract. Once again, in the words of Paul Pax:

[T]he matter stands simply thus, that according to the Masters and Servants' Act, passed by the Colonial Legislature in 1847, agreements made in a foreign country are held to be binding on the parties when they arrive in this colony, and the law appears to be especially directed to the object of introducing foreign labour into this country upon a system of apprenticeship, for a term of years, as is done in other parts of the British Colonial Empire. The contract is perfectly fair and legitimate, and is perfectly understood by the Chinese themselves...[4]

The legality of the contract does not appear to have been contested, at least in the Northern Districts, until May 1852 when the trafficking of Chinese labourers to Moreton Bay had almost ended. This case that was heard before the police magistrate and two justices of the peace on the Ipswich Bench concerned a charge for absconding brought against Lim Poh who had arrived in Moreton Bay on the second voyage of the *Duke of Roxburgh* on November 9, 1851. For six months, he had been employed by Richard Watson, lessee of Tarome station near Cunningham's Gap. It was argued in the court that Lim Poh was not Watson's servant because according to the agreement, he was engaged to serve Captain Kirsopp, master of the vessel that had brought him to New South Wales.[5] The following is the agreement that was signed by Lim Poh (perhaps with a circle if he could not write) and G. J. F. Kirsopp:

Memorandum of Agreement made and entered into this fifteenth day of August, in the year of our Lord one thousand eight hundred and fifty-one, Between Lim Poh, a native of China of the one part, and G. J. F. Kirsopp, of Sydney, in the territory of New South Wales, of the other part: Witnesseth, that the said Lim Poh agrees to serve the said G. J. F. Kirsopp, and such person or persons whom he may place in charge over the said Lim Poh, in the capacity of shepherd, farm and general servant, and labourer, in the said territory, for the term of five years, to commence from the date of the arrival of the said Lim Poh in the said territory; and to obey

all his lawful orders, and the orders of such persons as may
be placed in charge over him. And the said G. J. F. Kirsopp
agrees to pay the said Lim Poh at the end of every three
months, wages at the rate of three dollars per month, the said
amount to be paid in sterling British money, at the exchange
of four shillings per dollar. And also to provide the following
weekly rations, namely,—1 lb. of sugar, 8 lbs. of flour, 9 lbs.
of meat, 2 oz. of tea. And the said Lim Poh agrees to pay to
the said G. J. F. Kirsopp, out of the first monies or wages to
be received by him, by four equal quarterly payments, the
sum of six dollars, now advanced to him.[6]

On the back of the agreement was the endorsement, signed by Kirsopp
and witnessed by John Connolly at Union Wharf, South Brisbane, where Lim
Poh stepped ashore.

In the Ipswich court, the captain's endorsement on the back of the
agreement transferring Lim Poh's services was said to be illegal as property
only, and not services, was transferable and, it was argued, Lim Poh had
entered Watson's service in ignorance. The prosecutor, on the other hand,
declared that Lim Poh was indeed Watson's servant by an implied agreement.
Moreover, he had gone to the station, worked there for some time, received
rations, clothing and money; his passage had been paid and he had accepted
an advance. The case was controversial. Lim Poh eventually received a sentence
of one month in Brisbane Gaol for absconding, despite the total absence of
agreement among the magistrates concerning the legitimacy of the contract.[7]

Later that month, a squatter from the Darling Downs, identified only by
the initials F. Z., continued the discussion in the Brisbane press.[8] He had had
a similar experience regarding one of the sixteen Chinese labourers employed
on his station, he wrote, and he had sought out "a high legal opinion" which
held that if the endorsement on the back of the agreement had been properly
explained by an interpreter to the Chinese servant, it was legal, as it amounted
to another agreement. This seems to have ended the debate, although no proof
was ever forthcoming that proper, detailed explanation had been given by a
competent interpreter at any stage in the contractual process.

The contract may or may not have been legitimate, but it certainly was not
fair. Every article of the contract was in the buyer's favour, and if it were not,
it could easily be made so as the big squatters were also the colonial legislators
and the district magistrates. Station ledgers and eyewitness accounts from the

1850s in the Northern Districts, however, suggest that the original contracts were observed in the main by both parties. Some squatters increased salaries a little after the first six months or so of service in order to keep and encourage their bonded servants, but there is nothing in the records to indicate that this generosity was a general practice. Writing of Jondaryan station on the Darling Downs, Jan Walker notes,

> [O]ne of the first to have reportedly tried the indentured labour experiment was Robert Tertius Campbell. Campbell bought his Chinese labourers at £8 a head, hired them for a term of five years, paid them between £4 16s. and £7 4s. a year and supplied them with two suits of clothing and rations. Thomas Hall (a pioneer settler) estimated that there were three hundred Chinese on the Darling Downs in the early 1850s. They were engaged principally as shepherds for a term of five years, were to be paid twelve shillings a month at the end of every three months, were to receive a weekly ration and were to "obey" all their employers' orders.[9]

These men at Jondaryan had most likely arrived on the *Nimrod* in 1848. A surviving contract from that voyage awarded the worker ten shillings per month or six pounds per annum, a sum which Campbell appears to have averaged out among the men performing different jobs. Each servant was supposed to receive two suits of clothing, three pairs of boots and a cap, along with relatively generous rations of ten pounds of meat and flour, a pound of sugar and four ounces of tea. Over time and in line with the more speculative stage of the trade, the wage increased a little to twelve shillings per month, but after the arrival of the *Duke of Roxburgh* in November 1851, there was no clothing provision and the rations also decreased.[10] By then, the gold rush had set in and prices of all commodities had started to rise. So too had the wages paid to European workers, a fact that would not have been lost for long on the Chinese. Inflation must surely have had an impact on them, driving some into debt at the station store, another factor which was very much in the squatter's favour.

The Price of Labour

It was usual practice in colonial New South Wales for an agricultural worker to receive rations and a hut in addition to his wage. The quantities of rations were almost identical to those offered by contract to the men from the *Nimrod*, with the addition perhaps of a little salt and soap. Wages had always fluctuated according to season and markets but the trend was steadily higher. Before the international financial crisis that reached New South Wales in the early 1840s, the pastoral industry had made strong and steady progress. Wages reflected this growth and had peaked in 1838 when immigrant farm labourers were engaged at an average wage of £30.[11] Shepherds' wages were not much different from those of ordinary agricultural workers, Coghlan notes, but they were paid a minimum wage plus a premium for other services in addition to mere shepherding. This practice no doubt explains the discrepancy in wages paid to the Chinese employed by Tertius Campbell at Jondaryan. For example, in 1836, the wages offered were £16 per annum with rations and a hut to ordinary shepherds, £20 to those who could shear, and £30 when a shepherd could dispense with a watchman.[12] In the peak year of 1838, sixty immigrant shepherds were engaged at the average annual wage of £32 5s., but these men, Coghlan concedes, were of superior general qualifications.

For the most part, little was expected of the shepherd, apart from docility. Convicts and ex-convicts had fulfilled this role, and when transportation ended, the demand remained for this class of shepherd for whom the pastoralists were prepared to pay a wage of about £10 or £12 a year. Apart from Ben Boyd's abortive experiment with men from the South Sea Islands, however, wages never fell as low as that before the arrival of the Chinese labourers. In 1843 and 1844, according to Coghlan, shepherds were hired at relatively low rates of £14 and £15 in most districts of the colony.[13] These were years when immigration had resumed and about three thousand agricultural labourers, shepherds, and domestic servants arrived in Sydney, their labour supply forcing down wages. After immigration ceased again in 1845, wages for agricultural labourers and shepherds began to rise from an average of £17 to £18 a year, to £20 in 1846, and £23 in 1847. Even higher wages were paid in the more remote districts as optimism returned to the pastoral industry with rising prices for wool in London.[14]

Typically, as wages rose, so did the pastoralists' demand for renewed immigration. Along with the bounty immigration scheme, shepherds' annual wages fell to £21 in 1848 and even further to £17 or £18 the following year and they remained at this level, according to Coghlan, until the gold discoveries in 1851 forced all wages to rise. By 1852, the year when most Chinese labourers arrived, a shepherd's average wage was between £25 and £30, and in the Burnett it was £26 a year.[15] Desperation could force the price of labour even higher than this as the following paid notices from a Darling Downs squatter that appeared in the *Moreton Bay Free Press* of November 1, 1853 illustrate:

> Notice by J. C. Pearce, 18 October: To good and careful shepherds, the under-signed will give £35 per annum and to hut-keepers, £30 per annum (J. C. Pearce, Perseverance).
>
> Notice 2: Whereas, within the last five weeks, I have, by my agent in Ipswich, hired seven men as shepherds and hutkeepers all of whom have received advances in money and payment of other expenses and none of whom have arrived upon the station; and from circumstances which have come to my knowledge, I am induced to believe these men have absconded through the representations of designing and malicious persons, the above reward of £10 will be paid upon receipt of such information as may lead to the prosecution to conviction of such parties so offending.

For an indentured Chinese labourer like Lim Poh on a static wage of £1 10s. per quarter for the first year, rising to £1 14s. once the advance was repaid for a further four years, making a total of £33 4s. for the full term of his contract, the disparity between the value placed on his labour and that of a European for the same work was glaring. The period covered by their contracts coincided with sharp rises in the cost of free labour forced on the squatter by the southern gold rushes. European shepherds who were earning between £25 and £30 annually in 1852 could demand £45 to £50 by 1860, with hut and rations included, and more than that in the interior.[16] Comparable figures for the Burnett were £26 per annum in 1852 and twice that, £52, in 1860.[17] At a modest estimate, we can say that during this period, on average, a European shepherd earned in one year what the indentured Chinese shepherd earned in five years. The European shepherd or hut-keeper, however, was hardly well remunerated. According to Russel Ward,

> Before the Gold Rush... shepherds and hut-keepers were
> rarely paid more than £25 a year plus rations. More highly
> skilled bush-workers such as shearers and stockmen were
> of course paid somewhat more, but like the shepherds they
> too had to pay, often at inflated prices, for "all clothing and
> extras" issued from the squatter's store. Even the most highly
> paid and virtuously abstemious worker could hardly have
> had more than £25 cash left to show for his year's work.
> From 1831, when land was normally sold in minimum 640
> acre lots at a minimum price of 5s. an acre, the shepherd
> who saved every penny of his wages would have been able
> to buy his own "block" after seven years... Perhaps another
> seven years' self-denial would have provided sufficient initial
> working capital for stock and implements. And from 1842
> onwards, when the minimum price of land was raised to £1
> an acre, the quantum of initiative would have been increased
> accordingly.[18]

Suffice to say that none of the 3,043 Chinese labourers would have been able to save even enough money to pay his fare to return to China by the end of his indenture. Unlike the contracts for the Hill Coolies of India who had been introduced to the Burnett in the 1840s and for the South Sea Islanders who laboured on Wide Bay sugar plantations from the late 1860s, theirs contained no clause providing for return passage. The Chinese labourer must have soon realized that he had placed himself in exile when he boarded the ship in Amoy harbour; for some, the despair must have been acute, while for others, there was opportunity. The most fortunate among them were those who sensibly remained debt free and avoided the court.

Luck played a critical role in the life of an indentured Chinese labourer. Those twenty-two men who found themselves working on Boondooma station, for example, were fortunate to have fair employers who used incentives rather than physical coercion, and clear guidelines rather than the court to extract labour from their Chinese servants. There were incidents on Boondooma, but there were no organized strikes and no charges of violence laid against overseers as occurred on other runs in the Burnett, especially on Burrandowan, the adjoining run. This suggests, above all, that the men were satisfied with the way that they were paid. The Lawson brothers adopted a practice of paying the men what they called "cumseongs" that were gifts or rewards for good behaviour. Contract rates were paid for the first six months, then half a dollar per month extra was added until two years had been served; then throughout the third year, an extra one dollar per month, and in the fourth and final years, one and a half dollars and two dollars per month supplemented their wage. They were also paid a one pound bonus at lambing.[19]

Thanks to the cumseongs and other extras that substantially increased their contract wages, the Chinese shepherds on Boondooma could make ends meet and still enjoy some of life's luxuries. Goe Lit, for example, was among the earliest Chinese arrivals on Boondooma, with his contract due to expire in February 1856. Almost halfway through his indenture, by May 1853, he had paid off his advance and was spending his quarterly wages at the station store where he bought six yards of calico and five and a half yards of salampore (9s. 6d.), tobacco and soap (one shilling), boots (eight shillings), thread (nine pence) and flour (six pence). The following month, he bought socks, a belt, more calico, pipes and tobacco, tape, two rings and a small chain, sugar, thread, and rice, and withdrew four shillings in cash. When he was next paid on August 10 (at $4.50 per month, this amounted to £2 14s.), he was in debt for 1s. 9.5d. Fortunately, however, he had earned extra for two months' "watching" at $2.25 per month and he also received his one pound for lambing duties, leaving him comfortably in the black.

As Goe Lit would have clearly understood, it was important to avoid debt because as long as the servant was in debt, the master could use the law with greater severity. Debt, as the Chinese would already have learnt at home, was their real master. What caused great confusion and controversy, however, was the payment method known as promissory notes or orders.

Payment Issues

Both press reports and squatter memoirs ascribe much of the discontent among the Chinese labourers to the fact that they were not paid in silver as specified in the original contract. In all of the contracts that remain, spanning the most intensive period of shipments of labour to the Northern Districts, 1850 to 1852, the condition was that payment of wages should be made quarterly in (Spanish/Mexican) dollars or the equivalent in British sterling; in other words, the men had to be paid in silver. Given the problem with the availability of currency in New South Wales since the beginning of European settlement, a problem that had become acute by the time of the

Boondooma Station Homestead, 2012

Original Boondooma Station Store, 2012

importation of Chinese labourers, this was a rash undertaking. In fact, it was a deliberate deception as neither the facilities for securing and distributing cash generally let alone a regular supply of silver existed in Moreton Bay. On the other hand, given the regularity of commerce with China, it was a problem that was generally known abroad and the brokers of human labour in Amoy understood that it was in their own best interest to demand payment for the men in silver and not in any of the diverse and frequently unreliable forms of exchange then practised in New South Wales.

In 1940, in the language of those times, Roy Connolly, a direct descendant of the man at Union Wharf who as agent endorsed the transfer of the Amoy men to their squatter owners and who was also a pioneer and leading merchant of Gayndah, wrote,

> Of all the troubles encountered by the stockholders in the handling of [indentured Chinese servants], none was more frequent than that which followed the failure to pay them, as promised, twice a year in silver... [But] there was the problem of transporting, say, eight hundred half-crowns over hundreds of miles of lonely road—had that number of coins been available at the bank—in order to pay twenty Chinese. Such a departure was sometimes made, but to have attempted it regularly would have been asking for an outbreak of bushranging. The squatters in a body repudiated the promise made on their behalf by their agent in Amoy.
>
> Occasionally, the Chinese were induced to accept the station orders and cheques without open rebellion, but these were exceptional cases... On almost every station they revolted, their sense of injustice forcing them frequently to demonstrations of violence, threatening their white overlords with the blades of the shears.[20]

When the first Chinese labourers arrived in New South Wales, only sixty years had passed since the founding of the colony as a penal settlement and therefore without any need, the authorities believed, for a currency or financial institutions. Nevertheless, trading had commenced almost immediately and vessels that were not always British in origin or on British business had landed in Sydney and exchanged coins of all types for goods purchased there. The supply of coins, however, was always insufficient and in the interior, it was unlikely that cash was ever used at all. Wages for assigned convicts, and in turn for ticket-of-leave, expired and emancipist convicts were paid in cash and kind, with standard equivalents where no cash was available. Measured quantities of rum and tobacco were commonly part of wages, but the main currency was promissory notes that circulated for as little as one shilling in New South Wales and threepence in Van Diemen's Land.[21] An Act of 1826, generally referred to as Sir Ralph Darling's Currency Act, aimed to prohibit the issue of notes under one pound in value, but orders for smaller sums remained in use and forgeries were common.[22] As Roy Connolly explained,

> The orders circulated with the good will of all, based on the good faith of the men who drew them... That said, occasional resource was had to trickery. One common form was to bake an order before issuance. This made the paper extremely brittle, so that it tended to crumble to dust in time, and therefore could never reach the bank or mercantile house on which it was drawn. Thefts were numerous....[23]

For a time, it had seemed that New South Wales would have a dollar-based currency. In 1812, Governor Lachlan Macquarie received a supply of forty thousand silver dollars. In an attempt to retain the silver in the colony, he ordered that the centres be cut out and the two pieces circulated at separate values; the so-called "holey dollar" was valued at five shillings and the "dump" at one shilling and threepence. The first bank was established in 1817 and the coins gradually gained circulation but never enough to eliminate promissory notes, despite the governor's proclamation towards the end of 1817 that all reckoning should be made in sterling.

The promissory note was "currency", locally acceptable money but the repeated efforts of governors to control it failed and this failure only proved the vitality and growth of private enterprise in the colony intended as a prison.[24] The notes were written on any handy scrap of paper and accepted in the most casual manner, according to S. J. Butlin. They were usually issued in terms of pounds, shillings and pence but they were clumsy to use because they were sometimes issued in broken amounts, for specific debts, and their acceptability depended on an estimate of the drawer's worth. Consequently, they were accepted only at a substantial discount. Before being "cashed in" at a store or a pub, these notes or orders had probably passed through many hands. As Butlin notes, the transactions could be expensive and complicated:

The issuer had to meet a collection charge of two and one-half per cent from his agent and the local shops took them at up to twenty per cent discount. Negotiation was often difficult and sometimes had to be achieved by advertisements such as this: "The undersigned has for sale on advantageous terms two I.O.U.s signed R. H., one for the sum of £6 0s. 3d. and the other for 18s. 2d., or the above will be given in exchange for turtle, salt beef, tallow, hides, sheepskins or any other colonial produce."[25]

In Moreton Bay district, at least five hundred miles from Sydney, the first full branch of the first bank in the colony, the Bank of New South Wales, was not established until 1850, and the Burnett district had to wait until 1864 for a bank, so the promissory note was long-lived in the Northern Districts and later Queensland. In 1850, the usual problems associated with money supply in the north were compounded by a monetary crisis. The large gold discoveries in California and Russia had sparked fears in England of a reduction in the standard value of gold and of subsequent currency depreciation. In a situation like this, the Brisbane press reported, "[I]t need not cause surprise that some uneasiness has been created by the lately published opinions of his Honour Mr Justice Therry and the Attorney-General, not only that the small paper currency of Brisbane is worthless, but also that any person negotiating it is subject to a heavy pecuniary penalty."[26] The merchants and squatters of the Northern Districts were forced to face the consequences of having largely ignored the 1826 law prohibiting the issuing of notes under one pound in value. Given the peculiar structure of the judicial system where justice was largely decided by the same merchants and squatters who sat on the benches of magistrates, they were no doubt less concerned about being penalized for having issued the small orders than with the loss of trade that would follow the withdrawal of these orders from circulation. This, the editorial judged, would be merely a "temporary inconvenience" given the substantial basis of commerce at Moreton Bay. On the other hand, the editor cautioned, there was the problem of paying the Chinese labourers:

The recent introduction of considerable numbers of Chinese labourers will add not a little to the embarrassment as those men must be paid in silver, and thus the demand for coin will be greatly increased in one direction, at the very time when it becomes more than usually necessary in another.[27]

That "recent introduction" was a reference to the 169 men who had arrived in Moreton Bay on the *Favorite* in the first week of May that year from the *Cadet* that had carried them from Amoy to Sydney. They were all engaged at three dollars per month, at the exchange of four shillings per dollar, "to be paid in dollars or in sterling British money."[28]

The crisis proved to be a blessing in disguise for the Northern Districts because a judicial decision in Sydney in July confirming the opinion of Judge Therry and the attorney-general meant that the Bank of New South Wales would have no competition from private issues of currency notes and it subsequently opened a full branch in Brisbane that commenced business in November 1850. This helped to reduce the local discount rates and the bank gradually replaced many of the orders with its own notes.[29]

In these circumstances, the Chinese labourers were completely justified in demanding to be paid in silver as their contracts stipulated. It was soon apparent to them that they were being grossly underpaid for their labour, and to be forced to accept payment in station orders that they were unable to read or to negotiate was a further breach of contract and trust. Roy Connolly claims that they sought their own means to redress the balance:

> The yellow servants found a variety of ways to revenge themselves for the repudiated promise of payment in silver. Sometimes they taught the big, savage German collies to attack the very sheep they had been trained to guard, or, before decamping from a station, would leave the untended flocks where the dingoes worked unimaginable slaughter. There were stations where the Chinese sullenly accepted their station orders and decamped in a body within a week.[30]

On this matter, we have only Connolly's word. When a Chinese labourer was charged with absconding, negligence, or deliberately mixing sheep in order to spread disease among the flocks in his care, he gave no defence for his behaviour or, more precisely, no defence was ever recorded. The Gayndah Bench in those early years when summary justice was dispensed by squatter magistrates never employed the services of an interpreter, so there is no way of knowing what motivated such behaviour. The Chinese shepherd rarely had either the power or the means to prosecute a case for the proper payment of wages, so direct action of the vengeful kind that Connolly describes is plausible. At the same time, there is no proof that the men refused to accept payment in orders during the period of their indentures. This, again, is not to say that Connolly is wrong. It does, however, beg the question of payment of wages in general and there were, in the record, many instances when the men claimed they were denied their wages. The Chinese shepherds were not alone in experiencing abuse like this from their employers, and under the law they had the same rights of appeal to justice as all other hired servants, if they could make that appeal and if they could defend it. T. A. Coghlan notes,

> The Master and Servants Act gave a servant the right to seek redress from the courts of summary jurisdiction if his wages were not paid, and numerous appeals to the magistrates are on record, especially during the troublous period of 1843. Indeed the difficulty of recovering wages when due was, for a time, so general as to induce a strong disinclination on the part of immigrants and other genuine workers in Sydney to seek country employment, even when they could obtain none in the town.[31]

Because it was unlikely that the Chinese shepherds would make a direct appeal to the local court if their wages were unpaid or rations wanting, these complaints usually only arose during the course of court hearings where the Chinese worker was typically the defendant on some charge of breach of the Act brought against him by the employer and the complaint was thus recorded in the court and also by the press. For example, Achem, Tokay and Asson told the court that they refused to return to the service of Captain Collins of Logan River, south of Brisbane, after their discharge from prison for a breach of the Masters and Servants Act.[32] They said that they had been made to pay for their rations. This was denied by the employer, but the men returned to gaol rather than go back to service. Three shepherds at Wetheron station, Tan Guie, We Hok and Tan Teng, appeared before the Gayndah Bench in January 1853 charged with absconding.[33] They complained of poor rations, but their employer, William Humphreys, claimed that they could get rice or flour whenever they wanted it. No mention was made of other ration entitlements included in their contracts and the bench could hardly question the word of a fellow magistrate, especially a well-connected one like Humphreys.

On rare occasions, the Chinese labourers won a case against their employer for the non-payment of wages. When Loy took his claim for wages against Alfred C. Thomas before the Gayndah Bench in November 1853, the matter was settled out of court.[34] It is possible, however, that Loy had completed his indenture by then, which would have strengthened his claim. Only two months later, the Brisbane Bench gave a verdict for Kim, the plaintiff in a case for unpaid wages.[35] He had engaged with his employer, W. D. White, in June 1853 at £26 per annum, so he would have been among the first of those to complete their indenture. Not all post-indenture claims had favourable outcomes for the Chinese labourers, however. A lot, it seems, had to do with the might and status of the employer against whom the charge was laid. In July 1856, before the Gayndah Bench, Ang Tee charged James Wilkin of Yenda station for non-payment of wages.[36] He had hired with Wilkin in June for the lambing season at twenty shillings a week, but after the lambing finished, when he asked for his wages, Wilkin refused to pay him and instead told him to go and shepherd. Ang Tee said he had not hired to shepherd, so he left the station and, the record states, "gave the sheep over to a blackfellow who had been employed as Ang Tee had and had a flock to mind." Wilkin complained that he had found ten sheep missing and Ang Tee also owed money to the station store. The complaint was dismissed, but Ang Tee had his wages forfeited as compensation for the loss of sheep.

During the indenture years, it was only when breach of contract was accompanied by acts of cruelty or violence that the matter came to public attention. In the Brisbane Circuit Court of May 1852, Sang, a shepherd, was charged with assault and battery on Robert Fleming, manager of Hawkwood station in the Burnett where Sang had worked for twenty months.[37] The interpreter was the rather less than proficient Gan Som, but he told the court that during a period of three months, Sang had received only two pounds of sugar instead of the ten pounds of flour or rice that had been promised in the agreement. When he went to Fleming and complained, the manager had shut the door in his face and Sang had threatened him with the blade of shearing shears. In his defence, Sang said that he was owed £10 in wages and was kept overnight in handcuffs without a blanket. The jury found Sang not guilty and the judge told the court that the wages owing "ought to be paid although he did not have the authority to enforce this."

On the final day of those sittings in May 1852, Dim Cheong approached the court and complained that he had been shot in the arm and could get no redress.[38] He showed the judge his right arm which had received a charge of heavy shot; the wounds were healed but the elbow and fingers were bent, leaving him crippled and unable to work. A charge had been laid against John Murray, overseer to Simon Scott of Taromeo station, but Murray had absconded and could not be found. When this was explained to Dim Cheong, he said that he had one year and four months' wages due, at £7 4s. a year. The Chief Justice told him to apply to a magistrate. The press reported, "He [the judge] trusted that if the person who had shot him should be apprehended and found guilty, he would be severely punished; indeed he had no doubt of that... The circumstances commented on by his Honour were some of the fruits of the system."[39]

One of the worst cases of cruelty, reminiscent of the barbarity practised by B. J. Bertelsen at Boonara, was committed against Liqua, a shepherd, who appeared in the May 1854 session of the Brisbane Circuit Court charged with assaulting Edward Weinholt, brother of the owner of the station on the Darling Downs where Liqua was serving his indenture.[40] Liqua had brought in his flock an hour ahead of time, and when reproved by Weinholt, according to the press report, he became insolent and said he would do so as he had not had a settlement of his wages for some time, used threatening language and said he would kill his master. According to Weinholt, the shepherd had seized him by the throat and struck him on the mouth with an iron bolt, cutting open the lip and causing blood to flow. Through interpreters, Liqua denied the charge and accused the station owner, Arnold Weinholt, one of the Pure Merinos of the Downs, of having fastened him to a tree and flogged him with a stock whip, of riding after him with a drawn sword and cutting him on the shoulder, and for this "his master charged him £2 10s. to get the wounds cured by a surgeon."[41] Liqua, the court reported noted, "dwelt a good deal upon the subject of wages said to be due to him." As in Bertelsen's case, the court was so shocked by the demonstrably true accusations that a verdict of not guilty was immediately returned and the prisoner was discharged. There is no record of redress of wages, let alone punishment of the powerful squatter for his torture of Liqua.

Direct action was usually the only reliable way for these men to find justice. Apart from absconding, refusing to shepherd and feigning sickness were the most common charges brought against the Chinese indentured labourers. "That men flouted their commitments," historian Michael Roe notes with regard to all the experiments with coloured labour on the colonial runs, "suggests an affinity with other assertive migrants."[42] On the big stations of the Burnett where the Chinese constituted a sizeable proportion of the workforce, they had at least the capacity to organize. As noted already, there were upwards of forty of them on Burrandowan, about thirty on Eidsvold, sixteen on Mondure, at least fifteen on Boonara, and the same or more at Dalgangal, Boondooma, Wetheron, Ideraway, Booubyjan, and Hawkwood, all of them vast, rich runs ruled over by their squatters like petty fiefdoms.

Withdrawing Labour

For about a year, between March 1852 and February 1853, when European labourers were deserting the woolsheds and stations of the Burnett for the southern goldfields despite the escalating rate of wages offered them, there was a spike in the frequency of charges brought against the Chinese labourers before the Gayndah Bench and other courts of law in Moreton Bay. The cases of absconding continued as before, but there was a new element of defiance in the action the men were taking. Whereas employers had previously charged the men with feigning illness or making other excuses for being absent from work, now the charge was "refusing to work," and sometimes the word "revolt" entered the reports about these indentured workers who were more usually regarded as mere nuisances.

Towards the end of March 1852, the Native Police arrested four of the so-called ringleaders in a revolt on Burrandowan and persuaded the others to go back to work.[43] The Chinese shepherds on the station had allegedly left twenty-eight thousand sheep in the hurdles and fled. Gordon Sandeman, the agent for lessee Philip Friell, had found the leaders a day later twelve miles from the head station. The four, Cheen, Keack, Loe and Cheat were charged in the Gayndah Police Office with "absconding from Burrandowan and the hired service of Mr Philip Friell" and committed to the Brisbane Assizes where they were sentenced to two months in Sydney Gaol.[44]

Six months later, the press reported, "Mr Gordon Sandeman's station, where thirty-seven of these people are employed, has again been in a state of rebellion."[45] A mysterious "white man" had been travelling from hut to hut, from one out-station on Burrandowan to another, telling the men that they were foolish to shepherd for four dollars a month when Europeans were receiving one pound a week. The men struck work, leaving the sheep in the hurdles for a whole day. Unfortunately for the strikers, Sergeant Kerr of the Native Police happened to call at the station and through his "co-operation" the shepherds were persuaded to take their flocks out. The Native Police patrol spent three days on this vast station—"forty miles in one direction and sixty in another"—and, it was reported,

> By his presence and demeanour, [Sergeant Kerr] succeeded in restoring order and confidence thus rendering essential service to Mr Sandeman at a most critical juncture; for having been engaged in the late Chinese war, Sergeant Kerr was immediately recognized by some of them, and respected accordingly.[46]

It is possible that the same labour activist had visited other stations as well. One month after the incident on Burrandowan, two shepherds, possibly brothers, on Booubyjan station, Dem Chi and Dem Whan were brought before the Gayndah Bench charged with refusing to do their duty and were given seven days in the local watch-house.[47] In December, it was reported, "Mr Ivory's Chinamen [on Eidsvold] have all bolted in a body in the midst of shearing and that gentleman has been left with only the blacks for shepherds."[48] Almost at the same time, two labourers on Dalgangal, Ti Koe and Lau Khe, went to the head station and declared that they were going to Gayndah to obtain higher wages.[49] They convinced seven of their compatriots to accompany them, abandoning about ten thousand sheep. On January 23, 1853, eighteen Chinese labourers absconded from Yandilla station, near Drayton, again in the middle of shearing.[50]

That seemed to bring the spate of strikes to an end. In the middle of all that strife, the riot on Boonara in July sparked by the shocking cruelty of Bertelsen remains like a beacon of abuse of this type of labour. In fact, while the strikes may have been motivated by demands for higher wages, for the most part, the Chinese shepherd withdrew his labour when cruel and blatantly unjust treatment left him without alternatives. There was always a chance that when called before the magistrates or a judge, he would have the opportunity to demonstrate his grievances, as in the case of Liqua who was flogged and slashed with a sword, or Dim Cheong who was left crippled when the overseer shot him in the arm. There were numerous instances of physical cruelty. On April 25, 1855, Sam Que charged William Humphreys with unlawful assault "with a stirrup leather, having the stirrup iron attached to it".[51] Sam Que, of course, was a Chinese shepherd; William Humphreys was the wealthy squatter of Wetheron and a magistrate of the Crown. Humphreys admitted the charge and was fined two pounds. Sometimes the violence was more cynical than that. On more than one occasion, men absconded and when charged said they had done so because the overseer had killed their dog.

On the other hand, as in the Bertelsen case, when violence and cruelty by the squatters or their deputies against the Chinese labourers was proved, the charges were either quickly dismissed or the prisoners were acquitted. There is little evidence that the victims were ever compensated for their suffering but at least some small justice was served. Overall, the Chinese labourers were treated harshly by the courts and the legal system. Sometimes the injustice led them to desperate ends, flight or even death.

Toe, Pang and Tan Siang had already completed their indentures when they were engaged, under order of the overseer, as day labourers at Dalgangal station to wash the whole flock prior to shearing.[52] They were denied permission to stop work for lunch, so they refused to continue despite threats concerning pay. When called before the Gayndah Bench at the end of January 1856, they were sentenced to two months in Sydney Gaol, an extremely harsh punishment. Two weeks after sentencing, while the three were being escorted to Maryborough and the steamer that would take them to Sydney, Pang slipped the handcuffs and escaped. The constable gave chase, but Pang remained at large until May 1 when the same constable discovered him in Gayndah and he was re-arrested. In his own defence before the magistrates there on June 16, Pang said, "I am a well-behaved Chinaman and have not done anything to deserve to be sent to Sydney Gaol for two months. I did not refuse to wash sheep…"[53]

In an unusual case, four men attempted to enter into proper negotiations with their employer over their contracts. How Koon, Law Choon, Tan Lauck and Go Hock had arrived in Sydney on the first voyage of the *Spartan*, in April 1852. The following month, they were engaged by Burnett squatter, Philip Button, for five years and transferred to Wide Bay by steamer. Three years into their indentures, according to the record of the Gayndah Bench, on May 3, 1855, they took the sheep to the head station at Broreenia (Brovinia) and refused to take them out again.[54] Button proposed cancelling the agreements after the next shearing provided they remained until then. The men instead offered to buy their way out of the contracts. Button refused, and the men were sent to Gayndah where they were charged with disobedience of the orders of their employer and remanded in lock-up until June 4.

Two days before the bench was set to rule on the case, Law Choon drowned in the Burnett River. That morning, the prisoners had been accompanied by a constable to the river to wash their clothes. The constable had left the men unattended while he returned to the lock-up to admit another prisoner, and when he went back to the river he found "three Chinamen sitting on a log crying."[55] Law Choon had been standing at waist-height in the river washing himself when he had suddenly fallen back into the water. It was believed he had fallen into a deep hole and drowned. The constable was charged with negligence, suspended and eventually dismissed from the force on July 2. When the bench heard the charges against the three remaining men, Button admitted that his overseer, Rogers, had struck one of the men, How Koon, when he refused to return to the out-station. Law Choon had gone to help his countryman, and Rogers had knocked him down "two or three times." It was the violence that had caused the men to refuse to take out their sheep and, although not stated, it may have been the violence that belatedly caused Law Choon's death. After the admission of cruelty by the overseer, the court dismissed the case, recording that "the charge cannot be sustained." But one man was dead and no charge was brought against the overseer.

Cui Bono?

The press reporting on the experiment with Chinese indentured labour throughout the 1850s amounts to a litany of complaints from the squatters who had purchased these Amoy men through agents like Robert Towns because their labour was cheap. It must be remembered that the importation of Chinese labourers was not a response to the real and severe shortage of pastoral labour in the Northern Districts that was caused by the major gold discoveries in the south. All arrangements for the sixteen shipments of men from Amoy had been made before the gold rushes began late in 1851. The squatters demanded inexpensive, docile, and subservient labour and they believed that the men from Amoy would satisfy those requirements. They had further believed that the importation of cheap labour from China would force down the rate of wages they had to pay Europeans. When the results of their experiment failed to meet their unrealistic expectations, they used their power and influence—as magistrates on the bench, as owners of the over-priced station store, by withholding wages or deciding how wages would be paid, by manipulating public opinion through their newspapers, and even by torture and cruelty—to force those men into submission. Admittedly, there were employers who did not fit this mould of men but they were the exception rather than the rule. Many of the big squatters of the Burnett, their agents and overseers, unfortunately, tended to fit the mould only too well.

The experiment with Chinese indentured labour was judged to be a failure at that time although later, nostalgically perhaps and when the media hysteria over the use of coloured labour had temporarily eased, as a success. Arthur Hodgson, "King Arthur," the first squatter on the northern Darling Downs, first justice of the peace, and leader of the Pure Merino squatters there recollected "his" Chinese shepherds in 1878 from the comfortable vantage of his estate near Stratford-on-Avon where he had retired to enjoy the life of a country squire:

> I employed eighteen for upwards of five years as shepherds, and I feel bound to say that the sheep were never better tended. They proved to be honest, sober and intelligent, and had they been accompanied by their wives, they would have proved themselves excellent colonists.[56]

There were several reasons why the trade in labour from Amoy ceased in 1852. Some of those reasons have already been noted. Maxine Darnell provides a summary of the main factors:

> Over-supply of labourers and the declining profits of the trade in combination with other factors operated to suspend the importation of indentured Chinese labourers from Amoy after the rush of 1852. Increasing competition in Amoy for labourers, dissent in Amoy towards the trade, the negative impact that these factors had on the carriage of labourers to the colony, increasing public dissent in the colony, the influx of labour that the gold rushes induced and the misbehaviour and flight to the goldfields of some of the Chinese were all factors.[57]

Most of the squatters, however, would have had the general public and the legislators believe that the fault lay squarely with the incompetence and intransigence of the Chinese labourers themselves. The fact remains that because the squatters' runs in the Northern Districts were so large and so over-stocked when Hargreaves' gold discovery started the rush to the south, the pastoral industry there could not have survived without the assistance of the

Chinese labourers. Along with the desertion by white labour, the escalating war of resistance being waged by the indigenous peoples of the Burnett and the Dawson River regions would have forced out many squatters or at least greatly delayed the northwards advance of the pastoral industry. In short, the history of colonisation in what is now Queensland would have been very different if the experiment with Chinese indentured labour had not been undertaken.

The pastoral industry continued to prosper throughout the transformative decade of the 1850s. Economic historian, T. A. Coghlan is adamant that although "for a time the rural industries were crippled by the desertion of the labourers, ... on the whole the colony did not at any time lose by the gold discoveries."[58] The Wide Bay and Burnett districts, for some years, suffered severe population dislocation as did the entire colony of New South Wales. The figures speak for themselves: at the census of March 1851, the population of New South Wales was 197,186 or more than twice that of Victoria where the major gold fields were located; by 1853, the populations were roughly equal, but by 1861, New South Wales had only two-thirds of Victoria's population.[59] The local correspondents described the scene in the Wide Bay and Burnett districts in 1852 in graphic terms:

> Then came the gold fever, and the coasting captains ever ready to fill their boats, told such marvellous tales of the big lumps of gold that were to be picked up at the diggings with the point of a pocket dover, that Wide Bay was depopulated of its three hundred inhabitants in a few weeks, and now two inns, with as many stores, together with a stray Californian widow for a laundress, and a constable or two, complete the number of its half dozen inhabitants.
>
> But though Wide Bay is not rich in bees, the hives are not entirely deserted, for every house is full of wool waiting in vain for vessels to fetch it away... crammed full of the Burnett squatters' golden fleeces. [The wool] is from the country on the other side of the Wide Bay range, the rivers Burnett, Auburn, the Boyne, and Dawson, better known as the Burnett district, where the majority of wool shipped at Wide Bay is grown....[60]

The author even admitted the provenance of that wealth:

> Those persons in search of runs for the increase of their
> stock will do well to turn their attention to this splendid
> pastoral country, so open that a Chinaman can shepherd
> three thousand sheep in a flock; so healthy, that disease
> among sheep is unknown; and so fertile that ninety-five per
> cent is the average weaning with an open, almost downs,
> county, and a climate somewhat resembling the Wellington
> and Macquarie River country, but more grassy...[61]

History does not record that any of the Chinamen responsible for so
carefully tending those huge healthy flocks that he referred to managed to
abscond along with much of the European workforce to seek their fortunes
and liberty on the goldfields of the south. It would have been most unlikely
if they had. The strict conditions of their indentures, enforced by the Masters
and Servants Act and the improper assistance given by Native Police patrols
to the squatters kept most of the Chinese labourers at work on the runs until
1857, by which time the main gold rush was over.

For their part in maintaining the industry in the north, however, the
Chinese pastoral workers received nothing but execration. By clever spin, the
squatters and their allies in the media were even able to convince the public
and the legislators that the system of imported Chinese labour had failed
"even in a pecuniary point of view."[62] Below is an example of this kind of
reporting by an Ipswich correspondent:

> [T]he "Celestials" have now proved themselves to be the
> most troublesome and ... most expensive menials with
> whom any unfortunate employer could ever be visited...
> Subject as they were to the bamboo despotism of their own
> country, from which they were glad to escape, and being
> suddenly transferred from such, as well as from comparative
> starvation, they ... cannot bear prosperity and consequently
> play such "fantastic tricks" before the Bench as causes no
> small additional expense to our revenue as well as to the
> employers not mentioning the great inconvenience and
> expense these latter must suffer from having to travel several

hundred miles leaving their flocks without shepherds and their huts without keepers.[63]

The final word on the experiment came from Henry Parkes, Chairman of the Select Committee on Asiatic Labor of the Legislative Council of New South Wales that in August 1854 investigated the issues surrounding Indian and Chinese indentured labourers to the colony. In the report issued on November 27 that year, he stated:

> Your Committee are of opinion, however, that, with the prospect of a continuous stream of population from the mother country, all ideas of a renewal of Asiatic immigration, at private expense, will be abandoned. It is admitted on all hands that the experiment of Chinese has disappointed the expectations of those who at one time strongly advocated their introduction and, with respect to the Coolies of India, advices have been received from the agents in charge of the ships dispatched from Sydney, informing the principals in the business that, owing to the restrictions of the law of India, they cannot be obtained.[64]

Thus, the considerable contribution of the Chinese labourers, and the Hill Coolies before them, to the pastoral industry in particular and to the future economic development of Queensland was erased from history. With clever twists of the truth, it was the northern squatter who habitually portrayed himself as the one who was sorely abused, if not by his servants then by the plagues of nature and the democrats of Sydney.

CHAPTER 8

Masters and Servants

In Moreton Bay and the Northern Districts generally, the Chinese indentured labourers appeared often and in considerable numbers before the local benches of magistrates, the police courts and later the district courts of the colony. A couple of cases involving them rose to the Supreme Court, and even to the full bench. It is mainly through their court appearances and the subsequent reporting in the press of the time that we are able to locate the men after their arrival in the colony of New South Wales and to understand their experiences under indenture and later simply as Queensland pioneers. So frequent, in fact, were their court appearances that it is not difficult to find the names of around two hundred of them, all Burnett residents of the Gayndah and Mount Perry police districts during the period 1850 to 1880.

The names under which many of the men appeared in court are, for the most part, untraceable. Sometimes, the Chinese names proved to be beyond the capacity of recorders to comprehend, and entries read peremptorily as "three Chinamen with unpronounceable names" or simply "Ivory's Chinamen", without any attempt to give the men an identity beyond that of their master.[1] At other times, the same name appeared in several guises so that only close reading allows us to assume that names Ung, Yung and Ang refer to the same person, and that Ke Tiam might be Ki Tiam, Te Keean or even Ker Tung. Among the Burnett Chinese, however, the diminutive "Ah" was not frequently used, at least for formal purposes, and men under charge were usually given their full names to the best ability of the transcribers. It was also uncommon for them to be given nicknames, as the indigenous workers were.

Only Bunjaban station seems to have done this, adopting names like Knight and Dick, no doubt for the convenience of European overseers.

Just as the experiment with Chinese indentured labour had coincided with the major transitional episode in the colony's economy, it also overlapped with important changes taking place in the colonial judicial system. When the Chinese labourers commenced work in the Northern Districts at the end of 1848, frontier justice was delivered by unpaid magistrates, justices of the peace, who were friends and acquaintances of their own masters who may have been magistrates themselves. Apart from the local bench or the police court in Brisbane, until 1850, the only genuinely professional court was in Sydney, more than five hundred miles away. Distance was both a blessing and a curse for the accused. The inconvenience and expense of sending witnesses of serious crimes to Sydney meant that many crimes went unpunished; on the other hand, it was also a long way to go to appeal for justice. The uncomprehending indentured Chinese shepherd charged with an offence by his master before the Gayndah Bench, therefore, could have expected to receive no more justice than might have been given to him by the county yamen in Fujian province.

This is not to say that the Chinese labourer on the frontier who was charged, convicted and punished before the law was a hapless victim of an unfair judicial system. For the most part, the system operated according to established rules and the law was applied according to the statutes, as far as they were known and understood. Whether it was applied evenly and equally to men of all colours and classes is not for this history to judge. In the course of their work, however, and in the course of their lives generally, it has been recorded that many of these Chinese men broke the law, and this brought them into direct contact with the British imperial justice system at a particular stage of its evolution in colonial New South Wales.

This chapter aims to examine the Chinese experience of the colonial justice system in the Northern Districts of colonial New South Wales between 1850 and 1880 specifically with relation to the labour law enshrined in the successive Master and Servant Acts.

The Judicial System in the Burnett District to 1880

Government administration, the law, the implementation of government statutes and the policing of the rules all arrived in the Burnett district in September 1849 in the person of the commissioner for crown lands, Maurice

Charles O'Connell, commonly referred to as Captain O'Connell in order to distinguish him from his father, the leading nominated member of the New South Wales Legislative Council and acting governor of the colony during the brief interval between governors in 1846. Given his family connections, this appointment, gazetted on November 7, 1848, was obviously a political one and his relations with the like-minded conservative Burnett squatters appear to have been generally cordial until the end of his term of office there in 1854. One of his earliest decisions was to deputise a band of armed squatters acting as vigilantes in two terrible reprisal raids on the Aboriginal tribes they blamed for the murders first of two servants of Gregory Blaxland of Tirroan (later Gin Gin) station that was, in fact, an illegal squattage outside the boundary of O'Connell's jurisdiction, and then of Blaxland himself in mid-winter of 1850. O'Connell was reprimanded by the governor for this abuse of his power and serious infringement of British colonial policy towards the indigenous peoples, and this may have been the reason why O'Connell features so little in reports of the administration of the district during his term of his office in Gayndah.[2]

The commissioners for crown lands were appointed in 1836 by Governor Richard Bourke to arbitrate in land disputes, to supervise crown lands outside the settled districts of the colony, and to police the Act that provided for licences to be issued to pastoralists there.[3] Until a chief commissioner of crown lands was appointed in 1849, they were responsible to the colonial secretary in Sydney. The chief commissioner's office lapsed in 1870 and that of the local commissioners was eventually abolished in 1880. Clause 9 of "An Act further to restrain the unauthorized Occupation of Crown Lands and to provide the means of defraying the Expense of a Border Police" (2 Vic., No. 27) that took effect from July 1, 1839 made provision for the enforcement of the local commissioner's powers in the unsettled districts:

[A]nd for each of such districts there shall be duly appointed by the Governor for the time being some fit and proper person being a Justice of the Peace who shall be called the Commissioner of such district and so many men mounted armed and accoutred in such manner as shall be appointed by the Governor as and for a Border Police Force to be under the orders of and attached to the said Commissioner …

The return of the Department of the Chief Commissioner dated October 1, 1851 shows that Captain O'Connell received an annual salary of £365, while each of his four mounted troopers was paid 2s. 6d. per day.[4] In neighbouring Wide Bay district, Commissioner Bidwell received similar remuneration and support. In return for this, the commissioner was required to remain constantly within his district, to keep the peace "and protect all persons being therein in their persons and properties and in their just rights and privileges …".[5] To that end, he had to visit the stations, hear complaints and resolve disputes between squatters concerning boundaries and stock, and also "hear and determine on all complaints between masters and persons hired or employed by them." Salaries and costs of maintaining the commissioners and the border police were defrayed by half-yearly assessments levied on the sheep, cattle and horses of the lessees within the district that were paid to the colonial treasurer in Sydney. Appeals against an assessment could be made at the nearest bench of magistrates sitting in petty sessions.

It is clear from the Act of 1839 that the position of local commissioner for crown lands was intended to be only an interim administrative measure. Certainly, his powers were wide-ranging in a large, remote and sparsely populated district like the Burnett in the late 1840s and early 1850s but given the restrictions placed on the exercise of those powers, his authority was not likely to become entrenched. As John Hirst observes, the local commissioners were carefully monitored and scrutinised:

> In the administration of their office and staff, the commissioners were very closely tied to Sydney. All except very minor expenditure had to be approved by the colonial treasurer in advance and explained to the auditor-general at the end of the year. A commissioner could not put new shingles on his hut without asking Sydney first. He had to send a form each month to the auditor-general to receive pay for himself and his men. He had to give a regular account of all the stores and equipment in his possession to the colonial storekeeper. The cooking pots of the commissioners and their men were numbered in Sydney. Red tape seems to have had an effortless conquest over the bush.[6]

The commissioners, therefore, were agents for Sydney where the real decision-making power remained. Hirst notes that the commissioners made recommendations about applicants for licences for runs, "but the licence itself was issued by the colonial treasurer after he had received payment in

Sydney. The squatter's Sydney agent made the payment and collected the licence for him."[7] In the case of Captain O'Connell, the prestige of the position derived more from who he was than what his powers actually allowed him to do. Like any other squatter, however, he could apply for the licence of a run he selected for himself. In November 1854, shortly before he was transferred to Port Curtis district where he is said to have acquired several squatting properties, he charged his servant, Liu Teo, with absconding from his services.[8] In the Burnett, however, his name was not attached to any of the biggest or wealthiest runs.

When a squatting (unsettled) district was declared a police district, any areas not comprised in the police district remained under the administration of the commissioner of crown lands as commissioner's districts for some matters including census-taking; however, the local commissioner no longer enjoyed the services of his own enforcement agency.[9] The border police were abolished in 1850 when a constabulary was established and placed under an inspector-general of police.[10] Gayndah, Maryborough and Surat in the Burnett, Wide Bay, and Maranoa districts respectively were gazetted as new police districts on June 17, 1851. In practice, a chief constable had already taken up his duties in the Gayndah police district in 1850, in preparation for the holding of the first court of petty sessions there on October 30 that year.[11] The district, however, had to wait until 1856 for the arrival of its first police magistrate, and during those six years policing and the administration of justice in general can at best be described as ad hoc.

Despite the institution of an inspector-general, there was no unified police force in the colony and no standard regulations concerning police recruitment and conduct until 1863, in Queensland's case. In the Northern Districts in 1842 when civil administration began, beyond Brisbane and Ipswich, there were no regular police at all. Lesley McGregor notes that as the colony of New South Wales developed, the police magistrate in each district had the power to swear in police for his district, but where no police magistrate was yet stationed, under the Police Act Amendment Act of 1848 (11 Vic., No. 44), this power was extended to a resident justice of the peace.[12] Police were thus appointed and dismissed by local magistrates and primarily responsible to them. This gave substantial power to the magistrates. For example, in December 1849, pioneer Downs squatter, Patrick Leslie, wrote to the colonial secretary on behalf of the Warwick Bench of Magistrates, requesting information about the punishment of Pentonville exiles employed in his district.[13] He quoted regulations that prescribed corporal punishment for some offences, but he wanted to know if, in the absence of a flogger, the punishment should be administered by the chief constable or an ordinary constable. The response of the colonial secretary was swift and adamant. His notes for reply were:

> Certainly not! Degrading office for Chief Constable—
> inform Bench to the above effect and also that it forms no
> part of the duty of an ordinary constable.

As previously noted, some of the northern squatters were not above doing the job of flogging themselves. Before the arrival of the police magistrates in the Wide Bay and Burnett districts, it was the justices of the peace who, sitting in pairs, constituted the courts of petty sessions held in Maryborough and Gayndah and who ruled summarily without the encumbrance of a jury on minor matters, both civil and criminal, that infringed the law and disturbed the peace in their districts. Although they were amateur magistrates in that they were both unpaid and untrained in legal affairs, their punitive powers, as the enquiry from the Warwick Bench suggests, were considerable. The honorary position of magistrate gave a gentleman status and prestige among his peers, apart from power and the other benefits that might accrue from the job itself, so it was a highly coveted commission that was awarded by the governor who alone had the power of appointment and dismissal. According to Bruce Kercher:

> Although the magistrates heard complaints by both sides,
> there was nothing neutral about their use of the law. Even
> if they were unable to hear complaints against their own
> servants, magistrates were themselves masters who heard
> complaints by members of their own class.[14]

Some magistrates were known to grease the wheels of justice to the mutual advantage of members of their class. In February 1853, the Brisbane press reported that some warrants of committal issued by the Drayton Bench on the Darling Downs had been "very questionable," even "defective."[15] The newspaper editor noted that some country magistrates possessed more vigour than legal lore and suggested that they consult "the Colonial Statues, which have been published by Mr Callaghan and in the *New South Wales Government Gazette*." "King" Arthur Hodgson replied promptly to the allegation, denying that the warrant in question had emanated from the Drayton Bench. With obvious delight, the editor responded:

> It is a remarkable coincidence that the warrant to which we alluded, and which committed some Chinamen to hard labour, bore the signature of "Arthur Hodgson, J. P."! There must be some mistake in the matter. It is said that two magistrates on Darling Downs were formerly in the habit of obliging each other with a regular supply of warrants, signed, but not filled up, so as to be used when wanted. Can this be one of those old documents come to light, and maliciously filled up by some foe to Kow Ching, Kong Foo, etc., etc., or whatever the names of the Celestials may have been?

Complaints about the magistrates who sat on the Gayndah Bench were usually of a more mundane nature. In 1854, a Burnett district correspondent, "Justicia", wrote at length to the editor of the *Moreton Bay Courier* criticizing magistrates who he considered were unfit for their duties. Whereas in the 1840s, he argued, the appointment of a magistrate was made only on the strongest recommendation, ten years later one simply had to apply; where once the jurisdiction of a magistrate was constrained by law, now the indemnity legislation, he railed, had provided impenetrable shields for his protection.[16] "In this position of matters," he continued, "it is no wonder that we are constantly hearing of the most wrongful acts of oppression: that prisoners are frequently acquitted at our Assizes through the folly of magistrates in not procuring evidence: and that others are discharged who ought never to have been committed, and who have been so committed upon almost no evidence at all."

By way of illustration, he referred to the incident recounted previously that had occurred on Boondooma station in June 1854, when a quarrel erupted among some of the Chinese labourers there and shots were fired by two of the men who were identified, warrants were issued, and they were apprehended. What happened after that, in Justicia's opinion, was a travesty:

> It would appear that the usual [Gayndah] Court day occurs but once a fortnight. On the first court day after the men's apprehension there was no Bench. On the second court day the superintendent [of Boondooma station] attended,

although it was quite uncertain whether Justice would sit that day. However, his Worship Mr "Justice Shallow" did make his appearance and required the case to be proceeded with. The deposition of the superintendent was taken and his evidence proved both the facts and the identity of the prisoners; and he also stated that the Chinaman who was prepared to corroborate his testimony would be sent at any time his Worship might name to take his deposition. Notwithstanding however that these prisoners were before the court on a charge of attempt at murder; notwithstanding that the gentleman in attendance swore positively to the facts and identified the men, besides offering other testimony, his Worship determined if only for once to display the enlightened Judge and erudite lawyer, proposed that the prisoners should be put on their oaths to clear themselves! Whether Mr Justice Shallow had ever been in the slave-holding states of America where between the white and black people such a system does prevail, I am not aware; but his Worship was only prevented establishing a precedent for this innovation upon our criminal jurisprudence by the intervention of the Chief Constable who informed his Worship that the course proposed was one which had not yet been introduced at that Bench. His Worship, however, was still determined to prove to the parties present that he was a "real Beak," and ordered the prisoners to be "bundled out," i.e., discharged.

It is therefore matter for little astonishment that many gentlemen who had been in the Commission for years have already been compelled to resign and that others positively refuse to act when they know that the parties with whom they are expected to meet and act are for the most part men whose want of social position and whose ignorance and coarseness can only be equalled by their gross presumption and over-weening self-importance.

The records of the Gayndah Bench suggest that the appointment in 1856 of the first police (stipendiary) magistrate, Arthur Halloran, brought some decorum to the regular courts of petty sessions in the district. Along with modifications of the Masters and Servants Act in 1857, the presence of a professional magistrate on the bench saw the number of appearances of Chinese labourers drop significantly, as well as the severity of the penalties they were given.

The Sydney Police Act (4 Will. IV, No. 7) of August 1833 had provided for the appointment by the governor of salaried police magistrates whose duties were those of ordinary justices of the peace with the additional ones of suppressing "all tumults riots affrays" and swearing in police. In 1847, they were given additional power to hear small civil cases. The appointment of a paid police magistrate, on transfer and thus without vested interests, in a remote northern district like the Burnett would no doubt have been deeply resented by the honorary magistrates accustomed to wielding power in their own class interests without anything like close supervision from what they liked to decry as the interfering "democrats" in Sydney.

In 1861, Michael Haynes was appointed police magistrate (P. M.) at Gayndah and Nanango, that is, for both the North and South Burnett. In the same year, the *Burnett Argus* newspaper began publishing, and the editor and the P. M. were soon at odds. Haynes appears to have been a seriously unpopular addition to Gayndah society, but the slurs against his character should not, perhaps, be taken at face value. In September, "An Observer" in Gayndah had the following letter published in the Wide Bay press:

> Sir,–You will be surprised to hear that Thomas White, the editor of the *Burnett Argus* has again been proceeded against by our police magistrate... Mr Haynes appears to be determined to crush the *Argus* if possible, and also injure Gayndah as much as lays in his power... If he carries on much farther it will become a perfect persecution; and for the peace and tranquillity of Gayndah and Mr Haynes, it would be advisable to have him removed.[17]

His rulings from the bench proved a far cry from those of the heyday of the squatter magistrates. In August 1862, in the Nanango court, in a wages suit under the Masters and Servants Act, the Bench ruled in favour of the defendant, declaring that "no employer was justified in making a stoppage from a shepherd's wages" despite the powerful squatter's complaint that eighteen sheep were lost and a kangaroo dog killed, and that the shepherd was "habitually a troublesome and negligent servant."[18] Rulings like this

Bottle tree in grounds of Gayndah Courthouse, 1929 (John Oxley Library, State Library of Queensland, Neg:APA-099-0001-0004)

and subsequent ones caused an outrage of letters to the editor about the failings of the police court system. In July 1863, Haynes was dismissed and replaced by W. H. Abbott Hirst who was much more to the locals' taste and popular for his "suavity of manners, legal knowledge and other high mental attainments ...".[19] Unfortunately for the denizens of Gayndah, after only six months, Hirst was transferred to Maryborough and replaced by John O'Connell Bligh, a former lieutenant of the Native Police Force and nephew of the first Burnett commissioner for crown lands, Captain O'Connell. The *Argus* editor waded into the fray:

> They want to place here in his [Hirst's] stead Mr Bligh, late officer of a few blackfellows. Good heavens—let us but ask, would the Government dare attempt to foist such a creature as this, as police magistrate, upon any other community in the colony! For shame, for shame, such an appointment stinks of corruption, and we shall not tolerate it.[20]

In fact, Bligh proved to be a highly competent administrator and a fair-minded magistrate, although he was almost constantly embroiled in controversy of one kind or another. Due to a misjudgement on his own part or perjury by one of his constables in a scandal that became known as the Tim Shea affair, Bligh was to be transferred to Clermont far west of Rockhampton in 1867, but the government changed its mind, "through the influence of Mr Bligh's relatives in Brisbane," according to the *Maryborough Chronicle*, referring to Captain O'Connell, who had risen to be president of the Queensland Legislative Council.[21] When in 1869 the government threatened to withdraw the post of police magistrate from Gayndah altogether, however, the citizens rallied to keep Bligh, or at least to keep the office he held. As Thomas White thundered,

> Every old resident knows that, when we were dependent upon "unpaids", we frequently suffered grievous wrong and inconvenience in Police Court matters—that the Petty Debts Court more especially was frequently postponed from month to month, owing to non-attendance of magistrates, while drunkards and other disturbers of the public peace went scot free from the same cause. We have pointed out again and again that the list of magistrates for Gayndah

and the Burnett is entirely fallacious—that it includes many dead men, many men who have long since left the district—and many who never attend the court, unless when questions bearing on their own interests are concerned. Our town magistrates are two—the Messrs Connolly, both storekeepers, both aldermen, both interested in nearly every petty debts or publicans case, directly or indirectly, and one of them, at any rate, as much averse to sitting on any such cases as the public could be to his doing so. Our local magistrates, the only ones who could be depended on at all, are the Hon. Messrs. Moreton (two brothers), Mr Thomas, and Mr Okeden—all squatters, and all, of course, not only liable to the imputation of the same class prejudices, but also liable to be all engaged at the same time in the lambing, weaning, shearing, mustering, and branding operations which are necessary parts of their profession. Can these gentlemen be expected to cast all motives of private interest to the winds, and come in, in the midst of such vital operations as shearing and lambing, to decide whether Can Chow owes Ah King the sum of 5s. 6d. or whether Mrs Cutler or Mrs Rauhe have exceeded the bounds of feminine delicacy, or public convenience, in their mutual recriminatory amenities? It is an open question whether any of these gentlemen would act at all, if the police magistracy were abolished—and we have heard rumours that every one of them would thereupon resign. Without going into this question we may fairly point out to our legislators that a great wrong will be inflicted upon us by the abolishment of the office of P. M., or by filling the office with an incompetent representative. A police magistrate is a necessity in Gayndah, and a reference to the statistical account of cases tried at our Police Court will show that we are amply justified in saying so.[22]

Maryborough lost its police magistrate in April 1869 and in mid-May, the government announced its intention to abolish the office in Gayndah on June 30. Thomas White lamented the decision but he was fatalistic. After all, he wrote, within the past two or three years, of all the police magistrates in the colony, one had been dismissed, one hanged, two or three suspended, and one arrested for embezzlement.[23] John O'Connell Bligh and his family were farewelled in style by the citizens of Gayndah in June.

In August, however, the justices of the peace in Gayndah, as threatened, resigned in a body in protest, and demanded that a stipendiary magistrate be re-instated. They were successful, and the following month Benjamin Cribb was appointed clerk of petty sessions and (acting) police magistrate in Gayndah; he was succeeded in the post by Alfred Compigne and in 1872, by John Rankin. By then, however, the role had changed with the formal separation of judiciary and police. As Lesley McGregor notes, the majority of police magistrates were removed as inspectors of police in Queensland in 1867 and their appointments were finally cancelled in June 1870, following a period of resistance.[24]

While matters relating to the administration of justice appear to have remained much the same in the Burnett, in fact, from 1850 and especially after the formal separation of Queensland as an autonomous colony from New South Wales in December 1859, there were fundamental changes to the justice system, and considerable progress was made.

On Monday, May 13, 1850, the New South Wales Supreme Court judge, Roger Therry, swore in the first jury and presided over the first circuit court in Brisbane. This was an important milestone for a civil society that had so recently housed one of the cruellest convict prisons in New South Wales, or anywhere.[25] The circuit courts were held in May and November each year between 1850 and 1855, and in 1856 there were three sessions. In the fifteen courts during that period, 347 prisoners were committed for trial, thirty-four of them sent by the Gayndah Bench. In all, there were 254 trials, resulting in 166 sentencings.[26] The highest number of appearances, by far, occurred at the May 1851 sittings and, as Raymond Evans notes, Chinese workers represented around half of those incarcerated in 1851 for incidents of industrial struggle. He states further that a significant number of Chinese also conducted campaigns of civil disobedience while in prison, which again, like their acts of organized labour resistance, were the first such protests by non-convict workers in what was to become Queensland.[27]

In 1857, Moreton Bay district was granted its own Supreme Court of civil and criminal jurisdiction with its own resident judge.[28] The bill for this reform had been tabled in the Legislative Council almost two years before. At that time, the Brisbane press had pointed out,

> The strongest argument in our opinion in its favor is the length of time men are liable to be kept under the present system immured in prison without being brought to trial. This is an evil which ought to outweigh, and we hope will outweigh in the minds of honorable members, all considerations of mere expense.[29]

After Separation, an Act of 1861 established the Supreme Court of Queensland as a court of record with civil and criminal jurisdiction, and the subsequent Supreme Court Act of 1863 (27 Vic., No. 14) declared it to have all the jurisdiction formerly exercised by the Supreme Court of New South Wales within the territory of the new colony of Queensland. Provision for circuit court districts and the holding of circuit courts by Supreme Court judges there, with both criminal and civil jurisdiction, was made in 1867. Maryborough was such a district; Gayndah, meanwhile, was happy to make do with a district court, the first of which opened in February 1866, Judge Innes presiding.[30] There were no criminal cases for trial on that occasion and while one application had been made for a civil court summons, the seals of the court had not arrived in time for a hearing. The judge explained that the court would sit twice a year, but it was abolished only three years later. Gayndah residents were not too concerned about the loss:

> We believe that District Courts cost the colony something like £30,000 per annum—and we have no hesitation in saying that they are not worth that amount. As far as Gayndah is concerned their worth is almost infinitesimally small—for, as so many of our Police Court cases have to be relegated to Maryborough, it would be only a trifling additional hardship to send them all thither for trial. It is only in civil cases that the staunchest supporters of District Courts have a word to say in their favour—at least as far as Gayndah is concerned...[31]

The Queensland Police Force, including the Native Police Force, was finally brought under the single command of a commissioner of police, himself under the direction of the colonial secretary, in 1863.[32] The Native Police Force, organized in 1848, had done the squatters' bidding of quashing Aboriginal resistance to European settlement in the Burnett and Wide Bay districts in the 1850s, but largely as a consequence of the squatters' own foolish pride, the force was much reduced in discipline and leadership by the early 1860s.[33] These districts were then no longer classified as "unsettled" for policing purposes and the native troopers were no longer welcome on the pastoral runs where Aboriginal labour was widely employed. Gilbert Eliott, who entered Queensland's first parliament in 1860 as the member for Wide Bay and was voted speaker of the lower chamber, used debate on the proposed police bill at the August 1863 parliamentary sittings to further his argument that the Native Police Force should be abolished altogether in the settled districts. Instead of doing the slightest good in the settled districts, he said, the presence of the native police was "not only a nuisance to the settlers but an outrage upon humanity". [34] Because some racial tension remained, however, by the end of 1864, in addition to the regular police force for the Wide Bay (a sub-inspector and six men), Sergeant Brown with two black trackers, "in reality troopers", were appointed to protect the district.

Therefore, by 1880, the elements of justice and administration had formed a whole that served all Burnett and Wide Bay residents, including, at that stage, the indigenous inhabitants of the region, with reasonable satisfaction. No longer squatters on the frontier, they were now all imperial citizens under the law.

Masters and Servants

Paradoxically, it is when labour shortages are most acute that those who sell their labour can expect to meet the most severe formal restrictions on their power to bargain with employers. It is generally agreed that it was the crisis of the Black Death in the mid-fourteenth century, when between one-third and a half of the population of England died, leading to a rapid rise in wages, that provoked the first spate of statutes and ordinances to regulate labour and its cost.[35] By the time the Amoy men arrived in the Northern Districts of New South Wales, at the height of the southern gold rushes when pastoral workers had largely deserted the runs on the frontier, five hundred years' worth of master and servant regulations and legislation had entered the British legal canon that circled the globe in colonial statutes and that would survive even the end of empire.[36]

This egregious legislation criminalized worker behaviour in breach of private contract with the overwhelming aim of subordinating the servant to the master's command in order to make labour more reliable, and, certainly in the use of migrant labour, non-competitive in terms of wages. It was, Douglas Hay and Paul Craven argue, along with land law and vagrancy law, the crucial legal instrument for making colonies profitable:

> It was law, more exactly legislation, for dealing with poor people, for recalcitrant serfs or labourers or artisans, and then for ex-slaves, "native" workers, and indentured "Coolies"... [I]t was speedy, cheap, shorn of doctrinal formality and procedural complexity, administered by magistrates, usually lay justices.[37]

As far as indentured workers were concerned, their freedom of contract, these authors remind us, did not mean freedom to break the contract, and the provision of summary justice by amateur magistrates with wide-ranging powers to impose punishment, meant that workers in breach were not only subject to fines and the forfeiture of wages earned, but to flogging, forced labour, and imprisonment.[38]

Because convicts had dominated the New South Wales workforce until 1840, employers or their agents, superintendents, and overseers had developed a mindset of repression and control towards their servants. Several of the Burnett squatters, including experienced bushmen like Bertelsen, had moved north from Bathurst and other areas around Sydney where assigned convicts and ticket-of-leave men had constituted the pastoral workforce, and where the lay magistrates who were themselves landholders, squatters, and military men had freely ordered the lash for "crimes" such as insubordination, insolence, and uttering obscene language. In the early days of the colony, especially in the outlying districts, we may assume that there was little real distinction made between the free worker and the assigned convict who shared the same status of servant in relation to their master. Immigration and the increasing use of non-convict labour, however, saw the need for formal local legislation, beginning with the 1828 Act.

The first labour laws in the colony were short and simply worded statues that granted sweeping powers to employers and little redress to servants.[39] Before Queensland separated from New South Wales in 1859, workers in the Northern Districts were controlled by five successive Acts that differed little in essence from each other; when social and economic circumstances changed, adjustments were made to suit the needs of employers. Australia's first industrial legislation, "An Act for the better regulation of Servants Laborers and Work People" (Servants and Laborers Act, 9 Geo. IV, No. 9), given assent on July 17, 1828, was harsh in its penalties, reflecting working conditions in a largely convict society. It imposed up to six months' imprisonment (or three months with hard labour in a house of correction) for absenteeism, refusing or neglecting to work, or desertion. With the end of transportation in 1840 and the need to encourage immigrants, the new Act that year (4 Vic., No. 23) was less oppressive. The prison sentence was halved and workers had the right to claim for wages up to £30, paid within fourteen days.

This Act was repealed by a new Act in 1845 (9 Vic., No. 27) that followed the financial crisis that had flowed to the colony from Europe. In the light of the collapse of banks and the rash of insolvencies in New South Wales, the new law was more conciliatory towards workers. The imprisonment term remained as before at three months, but in lieu the worker could suffer "the abatement of the whole or part of wages and discharge, provided it is the desire of such master, employer or manager that such servant shall be so discharged". In cases where workers were owed wages not exceeding £30, justices could examine and make order for payment, with costs incurred by the servant in prosecuting the claim. If the prosecuting servant happened to be successful, his employer could be sent to gaol for three months but "discharged out of custody so soon as his estate shall have been placed under sequestration." Prison was obviously not for the master class. The 1845 Act also provided for short hire work like sheepwashing or shearing. The penalty for not finishing the task was imprisonment but if these task workers suffered misusage, refusal of provisions, non-payment of wages, cruelty, or other ill-treatment, then magistrates could order that payment of wages and amends be made "as they shall think fair and reasonable."

The 1845 Act introduced the compulsory discharge certificate system that remained in force until 1857. This harsh regulation was intended to restrict worker mobility, or, from the employer's point of view, to prevent absconding. As can be imagined, the system was open to terrible abuse, although the law allowed that a certificate might be given by any justice of the peace where the master or agent refused to give it without reasonable cause. Successful prosecution by the worker, in the circumstances, was highly unlikely given the class interest of those appointed to be justices. Michael Quinlan suggests, however, that there was widespread evasion by both employers and workers and that the certificate system was a failure.[40]

Indentured labour was first referred to in the 1845 Act, where justices were given powers to punish "any wilful violation of the provisions of such indentures" with up to three months' imprisonment on condition that complaints be made within six months from the time the offence was committed. The subsequent Act of 1847 (11 Vic., No. 9), made in preparation for the importation of coloured labour, ensured that indenture agreements made outside New South Wales had the same jurisdiction and penalties "as if made within the colony," providing the contracting period did not exceed five years. A special clause, however, undoubtedly in retaliation for the failure of Ben Boyd's enterprise involving the recruitment of pastoral labour from the South Sea Islands, excluded "natives of savage or uncivilised tribes inhabiting any island in the Pacific Ocean."

The 1845 and 1847 Acts were continued and extended until they were repealed by the more moderate Act of 1857. These acts, in conjunction with the Hard Labor Act (17 Vic., No. 15, assented to on August 24, 1853), constituted the laws that were applied with rigour, if little legal lore, by the Gayndah Bench of Magistrates and those elsewhere in the Northern Districts to the one and a half thousand or so Chinese labourers under indenture on their runs and who were brought before them, on arrest warrants and in the custody of their own police constables who not infrequently enjoyed the quasi-military assistance of the Native Police officers and their troopers.

Master and servant legislation was used extensively in the eastern colonies of Australia in the nineteenth century, especially prior to 1860. According to Adrian Merritt's research, between 1845 and 1880, there were at least 115,000 such cases in New South Wales, more than half of them in the fifteen years to 1860.[41] This is an extraordinary rate of litigation considering the size of the European population that was only around one million by 1860, and much of that demographic increase was attributable to the gold discoveries after 1851.[42] Absconding accounted for forty per cent of all cases during those fifteen years and of those cases, around the same percentage of those convicted were punished with imprisonment.[43]

In the Burnett district, between 1851 and 1856, the six years when most of the Amoy men were still under indenture there, sixty-nine Chinese labourers appeared before the Gayndah Bench on a charge under the Masters and Servants Act, only three of them more than once. Given that the 1856 census of New South Wales counted only 142 China-born residents in the Gayndah police district, and even allowing that this was probably an under-estimate of the actual number in the district at that time, it is surely a harsh indictment of the frontier justice system that about one-half of this particular body of men were charged in court with breach of contract.

These were the years when the squatter magistrates ruled summarily in the absence of competent interpreters or even, apparently, with the aid of a legal handbook. Gui, for instance, was charged with absconding from Ideraway station in July 1851.[44] His defence was deemed "perfectly unintelligible" and he was sentenced to two months in Brisbane Gaol. Charged with negligence and absconding from Eidsvold, Tan Yin, Ninh Ny, Ong Hing, and Tan Sing were all bundled out of court in February 1852 and sent to Sydney (Darlinghurst) Gaol for two months and then their agreements would be cancelled; they had no defence because their interpreter was ruled incompetent.

In all, twenty-seven of those indicted by the Gayndah Bench during those six years were sent to Sydney Gaol: sixteen of them for the maximum term of three months and the rest for two months. A further four received prison sentences in Brisbane: two for three months, one for two months, and another for six weeks. Their "crimes" were absconding, disobeying orders, refusing to shepherd, mixing sheep, malingering, and insolence. Sometimes, the prison sentence was accompanied by a heavy fine. Lim Hein, for instance, employed on Burrandowan, received a fine of £4 10s., in addition to the maximum prison term, for disobeying orders and mixing sheep.[45] He had admittedly been involved in a stone-throwing affray involving the overseer, McLean, which no doubt exacerbated both the crime and the punishment, but when the fine amounted to eight months' wages, a further two months' imprisonment in lieu of the fine might have seemed a bargain.

Although the law did not change during this period, the penalties delivered by the Gayndah Bench progressively increased in severity, to the extent that some employers preferred to withdraw charges rather than lose valuable labour time. When Angee, Aming, Fooksee, Angteen, and Cham were all charged with absconding from Ideraway in July 1851, Angee went to Brisbane Gaol for six weeks because it was his second appearance for the same offence but the charges were withdrawn against his compatriots on condition of their returning to service. Two Chinese shepherds who absconded from Hawkwood in September that year similarly had the charges against them withdrawn. Maxine Darnell suggests that the high incidence of charges for absconding that occurred throughout the Northern Districts owed more to deliberate intimidation of the workers by their masters than a desire to punish them, and that the court appearance itself was used as a form of discipline by the squatters who then withdrew the charges because they were reluctant to lose labour through prison terms.[46] She doubts that most of the men charged were genuine absconders at all, as it was unlikely that a highly visible Chinese runaway would get far in small, remote communities that made up the Northern Districts in the 1850s.

Nevertheless, between October 1850 and October 1851, there were forty Chinese in Brisbane Gaol for breaches of the Masters and Servants Act, particularly for absconding.[47] The local press calculated the cost of imprisoning them, as well as the expense of police escorts to take them to Brisbane, their confinement before trial and the prospective cost of long prison sentences imposed by the circuit court for some of them, and arrived at the figure of about £500, or half the estimated cost of the Brisbane Gaol establishment for one year.[48] The editor argued that if the importation of Chinese labour was continued, then "those who require it should be called upon to pay the cost and be no longer allowed to levy so heavy a rate on the general revenue of the colony."

Given the unusually high rate of absconding from frontier runs that were so far from anywhere that might provide useful shelter and alternative employment, it seems more likely that these regular absences from the job—termed "absconding" or "neglect of duty" by their bosses—were due to visits with compatriots on other runs, even those in neighbouring districts. Because the European masters and overseers could not communicate with their Chinese servants, they seem to have assumed that the Chinese were not communicating with each other. The outbreak of civil disobedience that ranged from the Western Darling Downs to the North Burnett, especially during a roughly twelve-month period between 1851 and 1852, followed by a pattern of organized passive resistance among them once in prison, suggests careful planning on their part. In April 1852, for instance, the *Moreton Bay Courier* reported that there were then forty-eight prisoners in Brisbane Gaol, twenty-one of them Chinese, "and these men have lately been so insubordinate that three of the ringleaders have been sentenced by the Visiting Magistrate to periods of solitary confinement."[49] In European eyes, the Chinese preferred prison to honest labour, but as we know from the case of Pang, the self-proclaimed "well-behaved Chinaman" who escaped from custody rather than face imprisonment for something he had not done, this was not so. "Their willingness to go to gaol," Jan Walker notes, "frustrated the workings of the legal system, and, by flooding the courts with their number, they almost rendered the system inoperative."[50]

In 1852, on the big Burnett runs, including Eidsvold, Burrandowan, Boonara, and Booubyjan, the Chinese labourers defiantly walked off the job, not singly but in groups of up to seven or eight, or committed acts of open rebellion.[51] The two-month prison sentence was liberally applied to the offenders, except for the men on Boonara where torture was proved and Bertelsen either withdrew the charges or did not press charges against the eight men who appeared before the bench between July and September. Fortunately for Tan Tan, Tan Lau, Dem Chi, Dem Whan and Tin Tai who were all charged with absconding from Booubyjan, however, because a full bench of magistrates could not be found for a whole month between September and October that year, their master eventually declined to press charges against the men remanded in the lock-up.

After 1853, almost all the Chinese labourers who appeared before the Gayndah magistrates received three-month prison sentences in Sydney. This was surely indicative of the high degree of animosity that existed by then between the squatters who had once so eagerly sought the cheap labour of the Amoy men, and the Chinese themselves who were now fully aware of the extent to which they had been cheated by their contractors and employers and who were deeply resentful of the cruelty and injustice meted out to them.

For four short years between 1857 and 1861, servants in the Northern Districts employed under the Act enjoyed a moderation of the harsh penalties that had existed since 1845. The 1857 Masters' and Servants' Act (20 Vic., No. 28) took account of the ebbing labour shortage as gold fever abated, as well as the growing opposition of workers to the strictures of the earlier acts. The three-month imprisonment penalty was reduced to fourteen days, except in those cases where an advance had been paid, in which case the old penalty remained. Justices could cancel indentures or work agreements if they thought fit.

During its first legislature, in 1861, the Queensland parliament introduced the new colony's first master and servant legislation (25 Vic., No. 11). This Act repealed the 1857 law and re-instated the harsher penalties of the previous laws. Servants not entering into service, absenting themselves or neglecting to fulfil their duty were liable to a £20 fine (twice that under the former Act), in default, three months in prison, or forfeiture of the whole or part of wages due as the magistrate thought fit. For spoiling or losing property, the servant could spend three months in prison with or without hard labour. Prison time, of course, was not counted as part of the contract agreement time, and still had to be served after release. This harsh prison term was six times more stringent than that for offending servants in New South Wales.

The 1861 Queensland Act was a severe blow to the more liberal-minded, typically urban residents who had welcomed Separation in 1859. Although Queensland would be among the first of the new Australian federated states to repeal the Masters and Servants Act, which it did under the Ryan government in 1916, resistance to this early legislation marked the beginning of the intense struggle for workers' rights and highlighted the gulf that already existed between political factions, right- and left-leaning, conservative and radical, rural and urban, in the new colony. The *Courier*, in 1861, was scathing in its denunciation of the new Act. It warned:

> It is well known to those acquainted with the history of the colony, although possibly it may not be known to Mr Herbert (the very young English-born premier and colonial secretary), the country benches have occasionally queer notions of awarding justice, more especially in cases brought under the Masters and Servants Act... [T]here is a class of magistrates and employers in the interior vulgarly termed "nippers"; men not only avaricious and exacting, but also imbued with tyrannical and despotic notions, imbibed in days when society in the colony was somewhat different than at present... We sincerely trust that the house, in committee, will reduce the maximum term of imprisonment for some of the offences named in the bill by at least one-half. The bill in its present shape may be made the means of inflicting great injustice upon servants in the interior, - injustice which it is possible may never reach the ear of those who could enquire into it.[52]

Fortunately for servants in the Burnett district, as already noted, the police magistrates on the Gayndah Bench generally ruled judiciously and dared to challenge the authority of the squatter magistrates in many of the cases brought before them concerning breaches of the new master and servant legislation.

From December 1867 until October 1868, several Burnett runs made another experiment with imported coloured labour. This was the era when men and some women from the South Sea Islands were recruited to work not only on the sugar plantations of the Wide Bay district and elsewhere on the Queensland coast, but also on pastoral runs in the interior. The first piece of protective legislation was enacted some months after this experiment began, and eventually, the South Sea Islanders were virtually cocooned by acts of parliament that were supplemented with official permits, licences and strict regulations concerning registers and bonds, rations and clothing. Special government agents were appointed to accompany recruiting vessels and so-called Polynesian inspectors, responsible to the colonial secretary, addressed regular reports to Brisbane on the management of this new indentured workforce. In the Burnett, the police magistrate, John O'Connell Bligh, in addition to his regular duties, was such an inspector. In the meantime, however, there was much frustration and abuse that was not dissimilar to the first experiment undertaken by Ben Boyd twenty years previously.

When the Kanaka labour trade to Queensland began with the introduction of sixty-seven indentured servants from the New Hebrides and Loyalty Islands in August 1863, their hire should have been subject to the Masters and Servants Act of 1861 (25 Vic., No. 11).[53] As Kay Saunders notes, however, before 1868, many of the Melanesians were introduced without any formal contract with an employer and because the law only recognized those servants who had been engaged in foreign countries "by indenture or other written agreement," even the meagre protection of the Masters and Servants Act did not extend to them.[54] The first piece of protective legislation, the Polynesian Laborers Act (31 Vic., No. 47), given assent in March 1868, made late provision for "Polynesian labourers already in the colony or to arrive" to be subject to Queensland's Masters and Servants Act. The Act was thus both tardy and retrospective. Furthermore, in the view of the *Burnett Argus* editor, it was "an Act which being retrospective must almost necessarily be unjust, and which moreover seems framed for the especial purpose of puzzling the intellects of any but the most legal-minded of country justices of the peace."[55]

The South Sea Islanders were obviously confused and miserable in their work as shepherds, even when they could be induced to go to and remain on the out-stations. Their ill-defined legal status caused further confusion in local police courts where they sought assistance. No one in authority in the Burnett seemed to know whether Clause 25 of the Polynesian Laborers Act had retrospectively brought them all within the Masters and Servants Act, or only those with a formal written contract. Almost six months after the law was given assent, the *Argus* editor referred to what appeared to be a dangerous shortcoming in it,

> Already the Legislature have passed one Act to protect these
> men, but surely it would be very impolitic to allow any class
> of labour to be employed at all which could not, so far as
> the relations of employer and employee are concerned, be
> brought under the general Master and Servants Act.[56]

This year of experimentation with Melanesian labour on the Burnett
runs and elsewhere in the Queensland interior represented the lowest point
of industrial relations in the colony's brief history. The new law caused
consternation and regrettable injustice. In a classic case that was heard in
the Gayndah police court in September 1868, George Bolawa sued and
was sued by Messrs Okeden and Stuart of Mount Debateable for breaches
of the Masters and Servants Act. However, because the employers had not
engaged the man under a legal transfer and bond strictly in accordance with
the (retrospective) Polynesian Laborers Act, their complaint was dismissed;
at the same time, while it was argued that Bolawa could not be punished
under the Masters and Servants Act, neither could he recover wages from
those who hired him. The only remedy was in the Petty Debts Court which
was held so infrequently in Gayndah that Bolawa would have faced perhaps a
month's starvation before his suit was heard. The Polynesian Act Amendment
Act of 1877 attempted to remedy these legal shortcomings, and as an extra
safeguard, restrictions were placed on the men's hire that was to be for tropical
agriculture only and not to be employed more than thirty miles from the
coast; but some commentators in the Wide Bay and Burnett agreed that the
new law was "a feeble production".[57]

The experiment with Melanesian labour in the Burnett allowed Thomas
White to make comparisons with that of Chinese indentured labour, now part
of district history. The *Argus* editor said that he did not want to believe some
of the "scandalous reports" of coercion being used against the Melanesian
men, "but everyone must admit that there is a possibility (perhaps even a
probability) that the stockwhip may contribute a good deal to the 'satisfactory
working' of these immigrants on outlying stations".[58] He continued,

> When the Chinese were first imported by Captain Towns,
> we have heard strange stories of the means taken by
> squatters, supers, and overseers to induce them to work
> satisfactorily. Even with an educated race like the Chinamen,
> much cruelty was practised until they found the Masters

and Servants Act... We sincerely trust that a traffic which is already making our name a byword among the nations may be summarily stopped, and that the anomaly of our destroying the aboriginal race of savages, and at the same time importing another may not continue longer.

CHAPTER 9

Vagrants, Criminals and Dangerous Lunatics

The laws that the indentured Chinese men contravened were mainly those enshrined in the Acts relating to masters and servants, vagrants, and dangerous lunatics. Other studies have shown that the number of charges brought against Chinese immigrants in Australia before federation was vastly out of proportion to the size of their population in the colonies, and that their detention in lock-ups, gaols, and later in asylums for the insane was similarly disproportionate. In 1872, for example, sixteen per cent of those at hard labour in Darlinghurst Gaol were Chinese, although the Chinese comprised only 0.3 per cent of Sydney's population and less than 1.5 per cent of the entire population of New South Wales.[1] This was also certainly the case in the Northern Districts during the period when Chinese men were still under contract on the runs. At least part of the explanation for this high rate of incarceration lay in their inability to plead their case in court due to the failings of those called to interpret for them.

Nevertheless, the Burnett Chinese did commit crimes that ranged in severity all the way from petty theft to murder, and they were later also involved in civil suits which they brought themselves or which were brought against them. There were vagrants among them and occasionally others who showed genuine symptoms of insanity. The British courts had to adapt to the special circumstances of delivering justice to men who could not be sworn in the customary way and whose own language was incomprehensible to the judges and juries. In time, however, the Chinese also learnt the ways of the court and understood something of the laws under which they were charged, and they were able to manipulate some of those complexities and shortcomings to their own advantage.

The cases relating to criminal law in this chapter have been chosen for their special significance. Only nine Chinese men were ever executed in Queensland; three of them were indentured labourers and two of those three were connected with the Wide Bay and Burnett districts. Another criminal case from the Burnett district went all the way to the Supreme Court in banco, allowing us to trace the whole process of the law in frontier times.

Court Interpreters

The absence of Chinese interpreters, or when they were present in the court, their incompetence and failure to be impartial, was a constant source of irritation to the judges and magistrates, of amusement to spectators and reporters, and sometimes of concern to civil libertarians who feared injustice was being practised in the courts. In a very early case involving the imported Chinese labourers, Tieck appeared before the Brisbane Bench in March 1849 charged with neglect of duty and absenting himself from the hired service of William Thornton. Thornton told the court that he had no desire to have any punishment inflicted, "but that he wished the prisoner to understand that he must obey orders".[2] The Moreton Bay press reported the exchange of that information in the following way:

> Bench (to the interpreter): Will you have the kindness to tell the prisoner that he may go home; but caution him against any misconduct for the future. Interpreter: Now now cutchus tick, maw cum jolh row. Not bring water water, u go chokee chokee. Prisoner: So sum womqua, fol laul iddi iddi jiggi jiggi mop sop tinka tinka pol pol. - All parties seemed perfectly satisfied with this explanation and the prisoner was accordingly discharged.

Given the extraordinarily high rate of litigation involving Chinese servants in the Northern Districts, especially during 1851 and 1852, the services of a paid and impartial court interpreter were essential for the proper delivery of justice, and the failure to provide that basic service should have ruled charges against them out of court. Some citizens were concerned that these men were being "condemned unheard" which was a serious abuse of British justice.[3]

Furthermore, these critics reasoned, the penalties awarded by what were essentially kangaroo courts were far out of proportion to the offence itself and also to the capacity of the men to pay, given their very low wages. It was not uncommon, they argued, for a Chinese labourer to be charged the equivalent of almost two years' earnings for neglect of duty, when it appeared from the circumstances, although not explained in court, that the non-payment of wages due was the main cause of their misconduct in the first place. They alluded to the highly sensitive moral argument that it was the law and the individual's claim to its protection that represented the fine line between this sort of imported indentured labour and slavery.

The *Moreton Bay Courier* did not like what it called "this system of Chinese immigration, conducive as it must be to an unnatural condition of society, and to the degradation of the British labourer."[4] At the same time, however, it recognized the right of the Chinese labourers to "the most watchful care of the Government." To this end, it proposed a compromise:

> We conceive that in those districts where Chinese labour is largely employed, interpreters should be maintained, by means of a small rate, to be levied on the employers; and all employers of such labour should be bound to furnish to the nearest Bench periodical returns of the Chinese labourers on their stations, noting from time to time the removal of any of them by expiry of agreement or otherwise. Such a regulation ... would certainly be ... an act of justice to the employed.

None of this eventuated, of course. It was, however, a lesson that was learnt and later applied to the importation of South Sea Island labourers into Queensland after the passage of the Polynesian Labourers Act of 1868, although it can be argued that it was their greater numbers and the oversight of prominent advocacy groups that forced the government to adopt measures to protect them. This protection given to the South Sea Islanders was motivated by paternalism, or some sense of "a binding moral duty" on the part of the white man as the editor termed it, rather than by the more high-minded "democratic domestic compulsion" that Lord Olivier preferred, but even paternalistic justice was denied the Chinese.

From time to time, the Ipswich or Drayton Bench, and even the Gayndah Bench, begged the colonial authorities to provide a paid interpreter, but there is no evidence that this ever happened. Frequent interpreters in the Brisbane police court were Gan Som and Murray Prior's servant, Tinko, neither of them reliable or necessarily trustworthy. On one occasion, Prior himself decided to act as co-interpreter in the court as he believed that he communicated perfectly well with the Chinese men who worked for him and, with reference to the interpreter, Isim/Isam, on that occasion, he assured the judge, "I can make him perfectly understand the necessity of speaking the truth, as well as the difference between truth and falsehood."[5] In late 1852, Li, a servant employed on the Logan River, prosecuted a fellow servant, a German cook, for assault with injury. The interpreter was Gan Som who himself required interpretation, according to the press; the witness was an Irishman who made "confusion more confounded."[6] The editor believed that under these conditions, justice was made a mockery and its dispensation a farce:

> If the Government is too poor or too stingy to pay for the services of a proper interpreter, we would suggest the use of a pair of dice or (still simpler), the smallest coin of the realm to decide all cases in which Chinamen are concerned.

Vagrants and Dangerous Lunatics

Although the justice system worked poorly for strong and healthy men who had their wages mulcted and who lost valuable working weeks and months in the lock-up or prison, they would, conceivably, have recovered their losses in time. For the most vulnerable among the imported Chinese labourers, however, the unwanted and the mentally ill, their situation was almost hopeless.

Vagrancy was a crime and "idle and disorderly persons, Rogues and Vagabonds and incorrigible Rogues" were punished in the colony of New South Wales according to the law that effectively supplemented the master and servant legislation to maintain social control by the ruling class.[7] In colonial society, one was a master or a servant; otherwise, one was considered to be a real or potential threat to law and order. A vagrant was a person without visible lawful means of support, or insufficient lawful means: he might be found wandering in company with any of the Aboriginal natives of the colony; she might be a common prostitute; they could be habitual drunkards, beggars, or holders of a house frequented by thieves. The punishment, if found guilty, was a maximum of two years' detention with hard labour. There is no record that any of the Chinese indentured labourers in the Northern District were ever found to be rogues and vagabonds, but several of them were certainly found guilty of vagrancy.

Logically, an indentured labourer, imported from China at considerable expense and under contract to work for five years in the colony, could not be a vagrant. In the years between 1850 and 1857 when most of the men were still bound by their agreements, however, a handful of them appeared in the Brisbane police court or before the Gayndah Bench (and no doubt before benches elsewhere in the Northern Districts) on the charge. They included, Sai/Sui of Logan River who, in 1852, had been wandering about Brisbane without any settled occupation, and Hong Kong who had similarly been wandering around the Gayndah neighbourhood for eight or nine months before he was taken into custody. The same year, Seikh/See-eth, who told the court that he had no master, was charged for the first time and sentenced to one month in Brisbane Gaol. Two months after being released, he was charged again with wandering about the streets of South Brisbane and having no place of abode or any visible means of subsistence. Residents of the area had complained that he had intruded on their premises. He was given three months' imprisonment with hard labour on public works of the colony.[8]

Sai/Sui had been employed by Captain Collins of Logan River, and Hong Kong, to have reached the Burnett district at all, must have been contracted to work on a pastoral run there. It is possible, however, that Seikh/See-eth was part of the speculative stage of the labour import venture and, overlooked by potential employers after he landed in Brisbane, he was unable to return to China or to find employment in Brisbane. Rather than being guilty of vagrancy, these were abandoned and unwanted men. They had no master but the magistrate, and no home but Brisbane Gaol. The Gayndah Bench of Magistrates suggested that Hong Kong was of "unsound mind" when they sent him to Brisbane Gaol for six months. Because there were no institutions anywhere in the Northern Districts at the time to handle cases of mental illness, and because the Chinese men were without family or other means of support, imprisonment under a vagrancy charge was the only recourse available to the court.

After 1857, unsurprisingly perhaps, there was another cluster of vagrancy charges brought against the Chinese men. Having finished their indentures, their employers were no longer responsible for those of "unsound" mind. Dingo had been sleeping on the porch of St John's Church in Brisbane when he was arrested and charged with stealing a sheepskin in the winter of 1857.[9] Although he did not comprehend the charge and seemed "half-witted" when he appeared in the Brisbane police court, he was indicted under the Vagrancy Act and given one week in gaol.[10] The same year, Ban appeared on a similar charge and was punished with two weeks in prison, but the magistrate suggested that his was a case for a medical examination. In 1860, Hong Soon got three months' imprisonment with hard labour for being idle and disorderly and having no settled place of abode.[11]

In April 1857, there were three Chinese men in Brisbane Gaol, all on vagrancy charges and all obviously suffering from severe mental illness. Two of these men, Hong Lien/Lian and one simply called John/Yon, had their ordeals recorded in the Brisbane papers in some detail. In March, Hong Lien appeared in court on his second charge:

> [A] half-witted celestial was charged with wandering about in a state of semi-nudity in the neighbourhood of Eagle Farm and with consorting with a tribe of blacks in that locality… [He] had for some time been a constant source of annoyance to the settlers there … had even wandered on the public road with scarcely any clothing about him. The poor fellow was evidently half-witted and declared in the vilest possible broken English that the blacks had taken all the clothes from him.[12]

He was sentenced to gaol for three months with hard labour, and soon after release, in July, he was arrested again for vagrancy and for having assaulted the policeman who went to remove him from where he was lying in the middle of Russell Street, South Brisbane. He was committed for a further three months with hard labour.[13]

Hong Lien shared prison with John, or Yon. John had been free for only one day when he re-appeared before the Brisbane police magistrate in April 1857, looking more like "an animated mummy than a human being".[14] The court reporter noted,

> Not a word could be got out of him, and he stood in the dock as dumb as a statue, with his bleared eyes fixed upon the ground. It appeared that the fellow had only come out of gaol on the previous morning, and that he had been found

lying in the streets by a constable at 11 o'clock last night. After his arrival at the lock-up, food was offered to him but he showed no symptoms of an inclination to eat, and maintained an obstinate silence. The presiding magistrate said that the visiting surgeon to the gaol had called his attention to this man's case while he was in the gaol. He, with two others of the same nation, obstinately refused to speak, and John had even abstained from food for a week with the most dogged obstinacy, taking care, however, to make up for it during the next week by eating everything that came in his way.

John was sent to gaol for another month, and was again almost immediately re-arrested. The magistrates were at a loss to know to how to deal with him. The gaoler told the court that he was quite impassive, "and in whatever position he was put, there he would remain till he was removed."[15] On the previous day, when he was discharged from gaol, the gaoler said, "John stood outside the gate like a statue. He had to be taken away some little distance and was set down on the ground, where he remained until he was picked up by the police who took him in charge out of pity." On this occasion, the court ruled, there was no doubt that the man was insane, and committed John to gaol for a further week in order to allow him to be medically examined.

The trouble for the court was that neither Hong Lien nor John, or any of the other Chinese who were judged to be of unsound mind, was a "dangerous lunatic." In the parlance of the day, they may have been lunatics, but unless they were also dangerous, they had to be charged repeatedly as vagrants. Consequently, John was brought before the bench again in June. On release from prison, he had gone to Eagle Farm Wharf and settled down until he was arrested once again. He was sent to prison for two months for his protection and application was made for his admission to an asylum near Sydney, the Tarban Creek Lunatic Asylum that had commenced operations in 1838.[16]

Insanity, like vagrancy, was a threat to law and order. The Dangerous Lunatics Act (7 Vic., No. 14, 1843) was "An Act to make provision for the safe custody of and prevention of offences by persons dangerously Insane and for the care and maintenance of persons of unsound mind." While the public and the courts had sympathy for the mentally ill, and the 1843 Act was essentially humane, the priority was to guard against the threats their illness posed to the wider community, not threats to their own welfare.

In the case of a Chinese indentured servant named variously Champoo, Kim or Kimboo, the threat to society from a truly dangerous lunatic was very real indeed. It is most likely that this man, Kimboo, the name under which he was sentenced to death and later committed to Woogaroo Lunatic Asylum, had served his indenture on the Darling Downs, possibly at Yandilla or Clifton station where he was well-known. By early 1857, he was living in Brisbane and perhaps his compatriots were already alerted to his psychotic tendencies because what is striking about his residence in the city is his terrible social isolation. In February that year, he charged South Brisbane businessman James Orr with having assaulted him. In this bizarre case heard in the Brisbane police court, the charges were reversed mid-hearing, and Kimboo was charged instead with having pursued Orr with a knife. The bench dismissed Kimboo's complaint, and as Orr swore that he was in fear for his life, the Chinese man was bound over with sureties to keep the peace for three months, in lieu three months in Brisbane Gaol. Kimboo could not procure the sureties and went to prison instead.[17]

Almost immediately after his release, Kimboo was in court again, this time on a charge of disputed possession and being illegally on unoccupied premises. Once again, James Orr was involved, this time confirming the plaintiff's statement that Kimboo was in illegal possession. The chief constable, however, supported Kimboo's argument and because Kimboo could not explain his case clearly and because the owners of the property could not come forward, the bench dismissed the case.[18]

Exactly one year after this, Kimboo was charged again, this time in the Moreton Bay Supreme Court, with the stabbing of Charles Owen, the superintendent at Yandilla station, with intent to do him grievous bodily harm. Hired by Owen, Kimboo had refused to obey orders and was ordered off the run. He seemed to believe that the wages owed him would not be paid and he had refused to accept a cheque. When Owen tried to push him out of the kitchen, Kimboo had attacked him with a knife, stabbing him in the face and the thigh. The Chinese interpreter at the trial had hinted to the prosecutor that the prisoner was "cranky," that is, insane. The prosecutor considered this defence a "useless dodge," the jury found Kimboo guilty, and in light of his previous conviction for the stabbing of James Orr, he was sentenced to two years' hard labour on the roads.[19]

On 30 June 1860, the Queensland newspapers reported "a dreadful murder" at Drayton, near Toowoomba. Kim/Kimboo was charged with the murder of Garrick Burns, a shepherd, near Clifton station six days previously.

The body of this man, aged in his mid-forties, had been found on the bank of a creek two miles from the station "completely covered with wounds, and his clothing saturated with blood. His two faithful dogs lay by his side, and kept a jealous watch over the murdered remains of their late master."[20] Kimboo appeared before the Supreme Court in August.

The chief constable at Drayton where Kimboo was held before transfer to Brisbane, said that he had known Kimboo on and off for more than four years. He told the court that Champoo, as he knew the man, had complained about not having sufficient meat in his cell while he was detained there. The constable recalled their conversation:

> "Champoo, you are going cranky, I think." The prisoner said, "Me no cranky, Englishman cranky like it Clifton." I said, "What for that fellow Englishman cranky?" He said, "Because me no give it Englishman blanket." I said, "What for no give it?" He answered, "Englishman been got stick and beat me on the back of the head." He then turned up the sleeve of his left arm and said he got a knife and cut all about the Englishman. The stains on the trousers which he wore are from the blood; they were much fresher then than now. I examined his head and found no bruises but saw scratches on each side below the ears.[21]

The jury returned a guilty verdict with a strong recommendation for mercy. The judge then passed sentence of death on the prisoner, and Kimboo was escorted under guard to the gaol.

Kimboo's death sentence was never executed. His name appears on the list of those admitted to Queensland's first lunatic asylum, Woogaroo that opened in 1865.[22] The arrest and trial of Kimboo coincided with debate in the new Queensland parliament concerning the institution of a lunatic asylum, an orphan institute, and a benevolent asylum in the colony.[23] The colonial secretary and premier, R. G. W. Herbert, believed that the subject was not of sufficient urgency as to merit immediate attention. He considered that the number of lunatics and cases calling for benevolent assistance was still very small, "so small indeed that the provision made in the gaol had been found sufficient." Fortunately, the lower chamber had the support of the Legislative Council where a motion was passed the following month for a return of all the lunatics imprisoned in Brisbane Gaol for the five years, 1855 to 1859, "in order that the matter may be more clearly understood."[24] At the time, although there was no separate institution for the protection of lunatics, according to Judy Webster, psychiatric patients were treated at the old convict hospital.[25] Prior to separation from New South Wales, extreme cases, such as that of John/Yon referred to above, were sent to the lunatic asylum at Tarban Creek near Sydney.

Queensland issued its own Lunacy Act (33 Vic., No. 12) in 1869. The old practice of first committing "a dangerous lunatic or dangerous idiot" to gaol was discontinued. Any two or more justices of the peace, with proof on oath by one or more legally qualified medical practitioners could commit such a person to a lunatic reception house for one month. The person would then be discharged unless two doctors judged that he or she was not in a fit state to be at liberty, and the person would then be committed to the lunatic asylum at Woogaroo. The Maryborough police court applied the Lunacy Act to its ruling on the case of Ah Sam, charged with having attempted suicide at Tiaro in May 1873. He was judged a dangerous lunatic and committed to Woogaroo.[26]

Many Chinese men were admitted to this institution, later known as the Goodna Asylum, and they may have later been transferred to asylums at Toowoomba or Ipswich. As is so often the case, it is almost impossible to trace the Chinese inmates, given such scant information about their proper names. However, the list of admissions contains some familiar names: Ah Sam, the attempted suicide noted already, Kimboo who murdered Garrick Burns, and Hawk, from the mail steamer. Hong Soon, charged in Brisbane with vagrancy in 1860, is on the list.[27] It is likely that Hong Kong who wandered around Gayndah for many months is the same person as the inmate listed as Hong Chong, but whether the "animated mummy" John/Yon is the same as John (Chinese coolie) on the list, is purely speculation. It is hoped that he reached the asylum at Tarban Creek long before the one at Woogaroo was established.

Criminals

Compared to the many court appearances by Chinese for breaches of the Masters and Servants Act, those for criminal offences were relatively few. In the Northern Districts, up to 1880, apart from horse stealing and receiving, they were responsible for only petty crimes. The serious crimes they committed were generally associated with violence.

White overseers figure prominently among the victims of these outbursts of murderous rage. In June 1851, Ah Hung appeared in the Brisbane Circuit Court charged with assaulting Edward Kelly, David Archer's overseer on Coonambula and was given fourteen days in prison.[28] The following year, Tong Pean escaped from custody while in transit from Drayton to Brisbane to stand trial for stabbing with intent to murder an overseer at Callandoon. Weeks later, his body was found suspended from a tree about a mile from "The Old Man's Water Hole."[29] On Burrandowan, relations between overseers and the forty or so Chinese labourers employed there were constantly hostile. In November 1855, the Brisbane Circuit Court sentenced a man known only as Tan to five years' hard labour on the roads for wounding, with intent to do grievous bodily harm, Alexander McLean, the principal overseer on that vast station. Tan was so overcome with rage during an altercation with McLean that he hurled stones at the hut where McLean had taken refuge, then entered it and hit the overseer over the head with an iron bar.[30] Alan Dwight notices the same pattern among the crimes of violence the Chinese men committed elsewhere in colonial New South Wales during their indenture period. He suggests that European hostility towards them, acted out by stockwhip-wielding overseers, may have tried what patience and docility the Chinese had, and notes that in court cases, the Chinese usually appear as the assailants and any provocation usually passed unmentioned.[31] This would seem to be true also in Kimboo's case. The violence and even contempt inherent in the reactions of James Orr, Charles Owen and poor Garrick Burns to Kimboo's strange behaviour resulted in tragedy for all of them.

Pleading mitigating circumstances such as provocation, however, could mean the difference between life and death. At the November 1850 sittings of the Brisbane Circuit Court, a shepherd named Eu from Mondure station in the South Burnett was found guilty of the capital crime of shooting with intent to kill but, "recommended to mercy on account of great provocation and excitement under which he was labouring," he received a reduced sentence of seven years with hard labour.[32] Eu had been watering his flock on the run when the sheep strayed within two hundred metres of a pub run by a man named Kavenagh who had permission from the Mondure licence-holder, Richard Jones, to locate his business there. Kavenagh had ordered Eu away and when Eu refused to go, Kavenagh had assaulted Eu with a stick, "tripped him up a few times" and bloodied his nose. Eu had gone to his hut, grabbed his gun and returned to the pub where Kavenagh remained hidden and sent out Moran, possibly a customer, who was also armed. Shots were exchanged and Moran was wounded slightly in the hip. So slight was the injury that he easily overpowered Eu who was then taken into custody.

Eu barely spoke during his trial. In arrangements for the defence, Jones had retained the services of a counsel for his servant, and the overseer on Mondure was sworn as an interpreter. Henry Hockings had volunteered the services of his servant who was undoubtedly the now well-practised Gan Som who was sworn by kneeling on a saucer and breaking it. Through these interpreters, it was reported, Eu was asked if he was satisfied to leave his cause in the hands of his counsel and he was understood to give his assent. The counsel applied to the court for a jury to be composed of equal numbers of Chinese and Europeans but this was denied with reference to the Colonial Jury Act that restricted juries to persons being natural-born subjects of the Queen.[33] In the course of the proceedings, the jury heard that Kavenagh was a quarrelsome man; meanwhile, Richard Jones, his overseer and another European shepherd on Mondure all testified that Eu was quiet in his habits and of mild disposition. The overseer clearly stated that the waterholes where Eu was watering the sheep were on Jones's run and that no person had any right to send the sheep away.

Despite the recommendation for mercy, Eu was delivered a very harsh sentence. In his summing up for the jury, the prosecutor deliberately stirred racist sentiments in what the press reported was "a powerful address" and Eu's counsel reminded the jury that while "much complaint had been made of ill-treatment of British subjects in China" in a direct reference to events during the Opium Wars, he implored them not to let "a similar stain rest upon the administration of justice in a British colony." The irony that a poor Chinese shepherd on a lonely run at the very edge of empire should be associated in any way with these grand international affairs was wasted on the court.

One year later, in the same court, Angee/Anjie/Anghee, another shepherd from another Burnett run was found guilty of the murder of an overseer and sentenced to death. He was executed in Brisbane Gaol on January 6, 1852.[34]

Angee had been employed on James Blair Reid's run, Ideraway, since early 1849.[35] He first appeared before the Gayndah Bench in May 1851 on a charge of absconding. In fact, he had come to the head station and declared that he would no longer shepherd because he was afraid that one of his hut-mates would shoot him. After a week in the Gayndah lock-up, he returned to work, but in July he was before the bench again, for the same offence. This time he complained of ill-treatment by the overseer, but his complaint was dismissed and he was sentenced to six weeks in Brisbane Gaol. Immediately after his release from prison, he returned to Ideraway and, three nights later, he killed Halbert/Holbert, the overseer.[36]

On November 12, 1851, Angee was taken before Justice Therry in the Brisbane Circuit Court and indicted for wilful murder. For the first time, the accused's Chinese compatriots were called as witnesses. One of the witnesses to the murder, Fooksee, who had given clear evidence to James Reid on the night that Halbert died, had been so afraid of going to Brisbane to bear witness against Angee that he had hanged himself. Another witness, Ameen, who was sworn by breaking a saucer, had problems with interpretation. He told the court that he was from Canton so the trial was adjourned to the following day while a Cantonese interpreter was found. On that day, Murray Prior, a wealthy squatter on the Logan River and a magistrate of the territory, along with his servant Isam/Isim were sworn as interpreters for Ameen. To prove his credentials for the job, Prior boasted,

> I have had Chinamen in my employment for the last three years. I am able to converse with them by signs and broken English, I give them necessary instructions, and have never failed to make them understand...[37]

Ameen told the court that he had seen Angee shoot Halbert in the back as he was counting sheep around sunset. Angee then dropped the gun and fled. Ameen helped the overseer to a bed and then went to another station about three miles away to get help. Konee, the remaining witness, needed a Hokkien-speaking interpreter so Tinko, another of Prior's servants, was summoned and took a Christian oath. Through his interpretation, Konee confirmed Ameen's account, and said that he had left Fooksee with the dying overseer while he had gone to take care of the sheep. Apart from their fear and confusion about the strange proceedings of the court where they spoke openly and honestly, what is striking about this case is the calm and practical way the men dealt with a crisis of monumental proportions. Instead of taking flight after one of them had murdered a European, a natural instinct in the circumstances, they had stayed to take care of the victim, to seek help for him and even to ensure that the flocks were kept safe. Angee was obviously guilty of the crime. No evidence was given that Halbert had mistreated him although Angee obviously bore a grudge. He had murdered a man with "malice aforethought," as charged, and he suffered the terrible consequences.

At the November 1852 sittings, the Brisbane Circuit Court heard the charge of an assault by two Chinese servants, Tan Choo and Ke Tiam, on their master, Bertel J. Bertelsen of Boonara station, that dated back to July. This was a complex case and one that was carefully scrutinized by the colonial press because the sensational circumstances surrounding it bore resemblance to conditions of slavery and torture, highly sensitive issues in an ex-penal colony now experimenting with imported coloured labour.[38]

On July 11, the Native Police took six Chinese servants, including Tan Choo and Ke Tiam, to the Gayndah lock-up on the complaint of overseer Henry Walker that they had absconded, a common occurrence on Burnett runs that year. About two weeks later, however, the complaint against the men was withdrawn and they returned to work. Again, this was not unusual. On September 14, four more of them were brought before the Gayndah Bench for breaches of the Masters and Servants Act and again they were discharged as Bertelsen said he did not wish to press the charge.

Near the end of September, however, Bertelsen charged four men, including the two named above, with assaulting him on the night of July 6. The assault had obviously precipitated the first case of absconding when the Native Police had become involved. The six men had gone to Bertelsen's residence to complain, he said, about their rations, that there was no cook at one of the huts, and that one of their dogs had been deliberately shot. Bertelsen said he called for a candle, but Ke Tiam immediately extinguished the flame and struck him in the face with an iron bar. Tan Choo beat him with a garden hoe and then declared to the others, strangely in the colonial patois rather than his own language, "He's bong." Thinking they had killed Bertelsen, the six men then absconded.

None of these events, however, was made public at the time. The six men had returned to work on Boonara where the discontent festered. We do not know what prompted Bertelsen to bring the assault charge two months after the crime had occurred but perhaps he realized by September that the situation had spiralled out of his control. In the Gayndah courthouse on that occasion, the magistrate challenged Bertelsen to admit that at the time the assault was committed, he had a Chinese servant tied by the throat, arms and legs and left without food or water for two or three days and nights. The same magistrate commented that he had seen another of Bertelsen's Chinese servants come to his own neighbouring run bearing the cut marks of a stockwhip all over his body. Bertelsen admitted all this, saying that he understood that this was "an efficacious mode of discipline upon stations where Chinese are employed."

Despite the admission of torture by their employer, Tan Choo and Ke Tiam were detained and committed for trial in Brisbane.

At the Brisbane Circuit Court, the only evidence was given by Bertelsen who was himself the prosecutor. Bertelsen told the judge that the prisoners could understand English "very well." A court interpreter had already been sworn but because the judge believed that the prisoners could understand the proceedings, he dispensed with the interpreter's services. When asked if they had anything to say to the jury, one of the prisoners simply showed them his coat for which he said he had been charged one pound, and the other produced two "IOUs" which he said he had received in payment of his wages. The jury deliberated for about one hour and returned a guilty verdict, adding a complaint about the want of an efficient interpreter. The judge took into consideration the fact that the two men had already spent two months in prison and sentenced them to four months in Brisbane Gaol.

One Brisbane newspaper cried foul. Given the glaring deficiencies in the court process, the editor wrote,

> We pretend not to know what the law may be on this matter, but we are assured that neither equity nor common sense will warrant this most extraordinary decision. And it is a riddle to us, how a judge so able, honest, and clear-headed as the one that tried the case, could sanction such a monstrous injustice. Is there no law on our statute roll which provides that every man shall know the nature of the offence he is charged with and comprehend the process of his trial? If there is, then were Tong Chou and Ke Tiam, barbarians though they be, most unjustly and unfairly used.[39]

The editor considered that the safety of a few employers of Chinamen was not to be balanced with "the world-renowned purity of British law." He was in no doubt at all that the men were "totally and grossly ignorant of what was going on... [W]e could see nothing in the two frightened faces in the dock but utter ignorance and blank despair," he wrote. His counterpart at the *Moreton Bay Courier* was far less sympathetic, arguing that it was the men's assumed ignorance of the law and consideration of that which had saved them from a deserved and more severe penalty.[40] But, his opponent retaliated, if any imprisonment is unjust, how could four months be considered a mercy?

This was also the rationale of the three judges of the New South Wales Supreme Court in Sydney sitting in banco on January 7, 1853 on this special case sent from the Brisbane Circuit Court. The judges ruled that the defence of the prisoners should have been laid properly before the jury through the intervention of a sworn interpreter, and because this was not done, the prisoners were recommended for a pardon.[41]

The Chinese interpreters in court did improve their skills with time. In the 1855 case of Tan, the Burrandowan shepherd who hit the overseer, McLean, with an iron bar, the interpreter named simply "Johnny" impressed the judge so much that he declared Johnny to be the cleverest interpreter he had met in the course of his experiences. He had cross-examined the witnesses in a manner which would have done credit to a gentleman of the long robe, he said.[42] Therefore, when Deong was tried in the Supreme Court in Brisbane in 1861 for the murder in a Gayndah boarding-house of his long-time friend known to the European community as Johnny and to his compatriots as Chow, there was no good reason why the case should have collapsed as it did, due to the incompetence of the interpreter and his failure to proceed.

Once again, this was a case that the press reported in fine detail.[43] The Gayndah police were alerted to the murder in July by James Chiam, formerly a shepherd on Boondooma station and now, several years after the end of his indenture, a butcher and an alderman on the Maryborough City Council. He had been informed by a compatriot in Gayndah that Deong had murdered Johnny about eight weeks previously and that it was supposed the body had been buried in Ang/Ung/Ong Hoo's vegetable garden. With the aid of two Aboriginal men who thrust their spears into the ground at various places in the garden, the Gayndah constable located the carefully interred body. Following the inquest, four Chinese men were examined and a charge of wilful murder was laid against Deong who was believed to be in Sydney. A warrant was issued for his arrest. From what the four men told the inquest, it seems that Johnny and Deong had quarrelled over a gambling debt. Deong had fatally stabbed his friend in the stomach. He warned the others that if they told the police, he would take his own life. Then he fled.

At the trial before Justice Lutwyche in November, the interpreter quickly proved to be highly incompetent and the evidence he managed to convey to the court was full of contradictions. It was obvious to the judge that the interpreter was unable to understand the questions put by the attorney-general as prosecutor and that he had been asking the witness questions that were different from those posed. In the circumstances, the attorney-general said he would withdraw from the case. The judge agreed and gave directions to the jury who returned a verdict of not guilty. Yeo and Ang, charged with being accessories after the fact, were also discharged.

The *Courier* suggested that the interpreter had feigned incompetence.[44] The prosecuting team had taken sensible precautions and had brought an interpreter judged to be competent, from Sydney, but the trial had not proceeded far before he had had to be replaced; his substitute was no better. The editor put it all down to the fact that the Chinese in the colony were "inveterate gamblers" and then proceeded to lecture the readers on the need for a capitation tax on these "undesirable immigrants," ignoring the fact that Deong, Johnny and the others had been living in the colony and contributing to the local economy for more than ten years, far longer than most Queenslanders of 1861 had. This was poor justice for the victim, but only James Chiam seemed to care about the result. He tried to address the jury directly but was cut short by the judge who threatened to put him in custody for a month if he offended again.[45]

Whose Justice?

The Chinese labourer was liable to the same laws as any European free worker on the northern pastoral frontier. Apart from the clause included in the 1847 Masters and Servants Act that assured the employer that written agreements made outside the colony would have the same force and effect as those made in New South Wales itself, no special legal provisions were made for their employment. Unlike the Indian Hill Coolies who preceded them, their own government showed no concern about their welfare or treatment in a foreign land. On the contrary, the men believed that they had broken Chinese law by emigrating, and by cutting off their queues, they had also severed their relations with the past. Unlike the South Sea Islanders who arrived on the Burnett runs in 1867, there were no humanitarian and religious groups to lobby the colonial government on their behalf and to buffer them with protective legislation.

In New South Wales, all three experiments with imported labour were judged to be failures. The colonial newspapers, the employers, and the legislative chambers that held formal commissions of inquiry into the labour trades all considered that these indentured labourers were more trouble than they were worth, even in a pecuniary sense. This was demonstrably untrue.

If the experiments failed at all, then the failure lay with the employers' attitudes towards justice, especially in areas involving equity and common sense, as the editor of the *Moreton Bay Free Press* pointed out in 1852 in relation to the Bertelsen case. So great was some squatters' greed to maximize their profits, they believed they could simply intimidate the Chinese into working harder, while cheating them of the tiny wages promised in the contract, by wielding a stockwhip, and using the local bench as a form of discipline.

The failure to provide competent interpreters threatened the integrity of the justice system in New South Wales and then Queensland. At the same time, however, as the case studies demonstrate, on many occasions, wise legal heads did prevail in spite of the language problems, and good justice was usually delivered. It seems that it was only when juries were swayed by comments about Chinese behaviour elsewhere, say on the goldfields of Victoria or even in China during the Opium Wars, that they made poor decisions.

The absence of protective legislation made life difficult for the Amoy men while they were under contract and at the mercy of cruel overseers, but the lack of special legislation proved to be a boon for many of the Chinese men once their indentures were completed. Equal under the law and therefore inconspicuous in its presence, at least until the late 1870s, like other Australian pioneers with origins outside the Empire, they were eligible to become naturalized subjects of the Crown, and then property owners, respected citizens, and even, in a couple of cases, elected local officials.

PART III

Love and Fortune

From one point of view, only the slave trade from Africa was more tragic than the fates of the thousands of Coolies who were transported around the world. From another, emigration offered life and hope. These Chinese met the challenge with a fortitude and enterprise that confounded everyone, even their own governments and elites back in China. To understand this, we need to link their story to the nature of Chinese culture and history, but the heart of the story lies with the varied responses the sojourners made to the conditions they found abroad. In particular, the experiences they had that led many of them to decide to settle and not return to China shaped the kind of communities they established. This in turn determined the future they hoped their descendants would have in their adopted countries.

Migration involves multiple responses to alien stimuli, and the way Chinese sojourners and migrants managed new environments deserves closer attention than we have given it so far... It is not enough to say that Chinese immigrants are industrious, practise thrift and make sacrifices for their families, value education and social mobility, and organize themselves for effective defence and action. Many others do the same. How the Chinese have sustained what they do, however, does reflect their cultural origins and their uniquely structured history.

Wang Gungwu[1]

CHAPTER 10

Post-Indenture Challenges and Opportunities

When the Chinese labourers completed their indentures in the Burnett district, at different times between late 1853 and 1858, they were still young men with many years of active economic life ahead of them. The end of contract confronted them with important decisions about their future. Their importers were not bound to provide them with return passage, their savings, if any, were small, and every Chinese newcomer's report, as well as information passed on to them from the colonial newspapers about the deteriorating conditions in their homeland, would all have discouraged any plans they might have had for a return to China, at least for the time being. Census figures suggest that they responded to the next most obvious choice, whether to remain in the district they knew or to move away to what might have seemed the greener pastures of the southern goldfields, to Sydney or the burgeoning towns of Ipswich and Brisbane, with an overwhelming decision to stay where they were. In the northern half of the Burnett, at least, they remained a remarkably stable proportion of the district population right up to 1880.

For the most part, the newly independent Chinese labourers joined the resident pastoral workforce in taking advantage of the flow-on effects of the southern gold bonanza. Throughout their five years of indenture, they had acquired valuable and readily marketable skills. They were experienced in many aspects of the pastoral industry, not only in shepherding, but also in shearing, slaughtering and droving. There are many recorded instances of their passion for horses, and some of them ventured into related industries such as carting and carrying. As is well-known, many also retained their skills in market-gardening and they earned a decent livelihood by supplying townspeople with fresh produce. To all these skills and occupations, as Wang Gungwu observes, they brought the traditional southern Chinese traits of industriousness, patience and thrift.

These are admirable and useful personal qualities, but they are not the sole preserve of Chinese immigrants; as Wang Gungwu rightly notes, they are typical of most immigrant communities. The early immigrants of European origin to what is now Queensland, however, were eagerly awaited and warmly welcomed into the small settler communities there. Newspaper editorials and column inches were devoted to outpourings of gratitude and commemorative name lists of passengers arriving in Moreton Bay and at Maryborough wharf on migrant ships from Britain. This was never the case with the 1,500 or so indentured Chinese labourers who had arrived in the Northern Districts under a cloud of only suspicion and public antipathy. Despite the crucial role they played in filling the labour gap on remote pastoral runs following the southern gold discoveries in 1851, their contribution to maintaining the viability and profitability of the industry was never publicly acknowledged, let alone appreciated. Even worse, by the time they had completed their contracts and were free to secure a stake in the future of the colony on their own terms, they had to contend with widespread racial intolerance and hostility that had spilled over from attitudes towards the Chinese miners who had joined the rush on the goldfields of Victoria and parts of New South Wales. Their individuality was lost altogether amidst the influx of Chinese miners to the northern goldfields that eventually stretched almost the full length of the new Queensland colony from Gympie in the south to the Palmer River in the distant north. Following the pattern already set on the southern goldfields, European digger behaviour towards the Chinese miners was typically bullying and contemptuous. Therefore, in what remained an essentially alien and occasionally hostile environment, their own habits of organization and mutual cooperation were vital to their own long-term economic aims.

These strengths, both personal and communal, allowed them to take advantage of the opportunities that presented themselves at that particular time in the colony's history when they completed their contracts. From time to time, there were discriminatory laws concerning naturalisation of aliens or property ownership. These barriers could be overcome, however, so it was important to maintain good relations with the wider Burnett society and especially with the local officials there. From what we can gather from newspaper reports, the Chinese men were well-liked in the Burnett, especially those who were resident in the towns of Gayndah and Mount Perry. Many of them chose to become naturalized British subjects; so many, in fact, that they must have received encouragement and support from the local colonial authorities to do so.

There were many obstacles and even threats to be faced and overcome. Like all ambitious young men throughout history, they would have assessed their chances of success and happiness in life in terms of access to women and access to property. With respect to the former, they were quite successful. Despite the large, lingering gender gap in the pastoral districts that persisted throughout the nineteenth century, not to mention the almost total absence of Chinese women, let alone unmarried Chinese women, a considerable number of the Burnett Chinese men found wives among the local European and Aboriginal female residents. As for capital and loans to start up small businesses, the situation is less clear, but given that several of them became well-respected traders and merchants, they obviously overcame that obstacle as well.

The main threat that remained beyond their power to overcome or even to manage was the growing political agitation against their presence in Queensland and, as plans for federation and nationhood advanced, throughout Australia itself. This politically motivated racial hatred would eventually lead to restrictive and discriminatory laws and their enforcement that would preclude the men's best efforts to assimilate. Ultimately, theirs was a vanishing act. In the meantime, however, during the period from the mid-1850s until 1880, most of the Burnett Chinese proved to be successful immigrants.

The Social Sphere

Assumptions have been made about the Chinese indentured labourers that do not fit the lived experience of the men who served their contracts in the Burnett district in the 1850s and who then entered the free labour force in what was soon to be the separate colony of Queensland. C. Y. Choi, for example, argues that "[a]ttempts to keep Chinese indentured labourers on their jobs was difficult because they also deserted their employers for the gold fields."[2] By way of explanation, he makes reference to an attempt by W. C. Wentworth to introduce a bill in 1852 that would withhold a mining licence from any Chinese not properly discharged from their employers. This may have been the case for some of those men from Amoy who were employed on pastoral runs in Victoria and southern New South Wales where the major gold discoveries were made in 1851, but there is no evidence that Chinese labourers on Burnett runs absconded from their assigned workplaces with the aim of reaching the Victorian gold fields, one thousand miles away. The story may have been different had the Queensland gold fields been discovered earlier, but no major deposits were found there before 1858, by which time most of the Burnett Chinese, perhaps all of them, were free to seek work and fortune where they pleased.

With reference to the impact of the Queensland gold discoveries from the late-1850s to the early 1870s on the existing Chinese population, James Jupp suggests, "These gold discoveries drew those already resident away from pastoral work and into mining."[3] Again, while this statement might seem reasonable in the light of the stereotype of the Chinese sojourner to Australia in the second half of the century as either miner or market-gardener driven solely by the desire for quick profits and a return to his homeland, it does not coincide with the lifestyle that the Burnett Chinese chose. In fact, for the population generally in the Burnett and Wide Bay districts, gold fever seems to have been regarded as an obsession among foreigners, and not one that was suitable for long-time locals who were already regularly employed and grateful for work at a time of worsening economic depression. In fact, when prospector James Nash discovered rich gold deposits on the banks of the Mary River in the Wide Bay district about one hundred miles north of Brisbane in late September 1867, he found it difficult to trade his nuggets for cash in the nearest town to the strike, Maryborough. Hector Holthouse recalls,

> Maryborough by this time was a town of about 1,500 people. It had grown up as a port for supplying the surrounding stations and shipping out wool, hides, and tallow. It also exported timber—mainly cedar for Victoria—and had lately become the centre of a growing sugar industry. But Maryborough had never been a gold town, and Nash had trouble trading his nuggets. "I tried two banks and several stores but could not sell the gold," he said. "Times were so bad that they hardly knew what gold was like. At last I tried Mr W. Southerden a second time and he allowed me three pounds for it – one pound in money, the rest in tools and

rations." Gold at that time was selling in Brisbane for about three pounds an ounce.[4]

The lukewarm reaction to Nash's find is interesting because his was not the first major gold discovery in Queensland. This had been at Canoona station, to the north of the Wide Bay and Burnett districts, on the Fitzroy River near what is now Rockhampton, and where Captain O'Connell was subsequently appointed gold commissioner in 1858. The Canoona rush was soon exhausted, but eight years later, in June 1866, good payable gold was discovered at Crocodile Creek to the south of Rockhampton. By the end of that year, there were more than three thousand diggers on the site, and it was estimated that one thousand of them were Chinese.[5] In early January the following year, tempers boiled over when a European digger tried to jump a Chinese claim and, according to the pattern of racial abuse already set down in Victoria and southern New South Wales at Buckland River and Lambing Flat in 1857 and 1860-61 respectively, Chinese tents, huts and small stores were burnt down and many Chinese miners were manhandled and injured.

It is possible that some of the Amoy men from the Burnett joined the rush to Crocodile Creek, but it was a largely Cantonese mining community there who, the *Maryborough Chronicle* claimed, represented "the commencement of a system of Chinese immigration, under the auspices of a China merchant residing in Sydney."[6] This scheme was possible because the restrictive immigration laws enacted earlier in Victoria and New South Wales to check the influx of Chinese goldminers had been repealed by 1867 and the first law to check the flow of Chinese migrants into Queensland was passed only in 1877.[7] Therefore, the Chinese miners at Crocodile Creek were newcomers, neither formerly indentured shepherds nor ex-Victorian diggers; they had been shipped directly from southern China to Rockhampton, and at the beginning of June 1869, the Maryborough newspaper reported that there were still seven hundred of them quietly at work on the flat where they had cut a race of a mile and a half.[8]

By this time, there were teams of other Chinese diggers on the Gympie goldfields where Nash had made the first big strike late in 1867. The alluvial gold had been largely worked out within the first year, and when news of other good strikes nearby at Kilkivan caused a distraction and the European miners moved away from their claims on the Mary River flats at Gympie, about six hundred Chinese miners were able to get a foothold there. Hector Holthouse claims that within a couple of months in 1868 the Chinese miners took out thousands of pounds worth of gold that impatient white diggers had overlooked.[9] When things went wrong for the European diggers, as they soon did at Kilkivan and other nearby sites, and they returned to their old claims at Gympie, the Chinese were the scapegoats. There were anti-Chinese riots on the Gympie goldfields as elsewhere but Holthouse believes the perseverance of the Chinese also won the grudging admiration of white diggers, as did the neatness and good organization of their camps.

The Crocodile Creek and Gympie rushes were followed in quick succession by others in the north of the colony in the districts of Kennedy and Cook: Gilbert River in 1869, Ravenswood in 1870, Etheridge and Charters Towers in 1872, and then major finds on the Palmer and Hodgkinson rivers in 1873 and 1876 respectively. After that, Holthouse records, "The trek out of Gympie became an exodus. Not only diggers, but storekeepers, publicans, shanty-keepers, and a whole horde of gold-town hangers-on sold out or walked out and took ship north to the Palmer."[10] Thousands of Chinese diggers arrived there by ship from Hong Kong.

Before the discovery of gold on the Palmer River near Cooktown on remote Cape York Peninsula, according to 1871 census figures, there were 3,305 Chinese in Queensland, including just one Chinese woman, out of a total population of 120,104.[11] By 1881, there were almost three and a half times that number of Chinese, or 11,229 of whom twenty-three were women, and the vast majority of them—about eight thousand—were on the Palmer goldfields. In raw figures, the size of the Chinese populations of the eastern mainland colonies of Queensland, New South Wales and Victoria was almost identical in 1881, although there were important differences in their numbers in proportion to the general population and, of course, their distribution. Nevertheless, the perception that "white" Australia was being over-run by hordes of Chinese immigrants was always false, although it was easy to whip up public hysteria in support of local legislation when it was reported that in June 1877 there were seventeen thousand Chinese on the Palmer goldfields, a number equal to the entire European population of North Queensland.[12]

As the census figures show, however, and as historians have always agreed, in the fifty years after the arrival of the first shipload of indentured labourers from Amoy in 1848, around one hundred thousand Chinese entered the Australian colonies, but in no single year, even at the height of the gold fever, did their aggregate number ever exceed thirty-nine thousand. According to James Jupp, the largest proportion of Chinese in the Australian population was 3.3 per cent in 1861, falling to 1.7 per cent by 1871 and 1881, and to only 1.1 per cent by 1891.[13] In that last-mentioned year, there were thirty-six thousand Chinese-born men, women and children left in Australia, and 8,500 of them were registered in Queensland.[14]

Throughout the drama and debate surrounding the number of Chinese diggers on Queensland goldfields, the Chinese population of the Burnett district remained almost steady and exclusively male. In the earliest census, taken in March 1851, eighty-eight individuals, or about ten per cent of the non-indigenous population of the Burnett were registered as "foreign," that is, born outside of Britain or the Dominions. Some of these eighty-eight foreign-born men, perhaps the majority of them, would have been Chinese. For the whole colony of New South Wales in that census year, only 1.4 per cent of the population was born in foreign countries, so the much higher percentage figure for the Burnett suggests the contribution was made by those "Mahomedans and Pagans" of whom there were then 588 in New South Wales, and regarded as "a most unpleasing item in our population" by the *Moreton Bay Courier*.[15]

By the 1856 census, the Burnett's colonial population had grown appreciably by more than fifty per cent and around half of that increase was due to the commencement of German indentured immigration to the district.[16] That census year, there were reportedly 142 Chinese, all men, who still represented roughly ten per cent of the population and they were living mainly in the rural portion of the district; only nineteen were registered in the town of Gayndah where most were probably residents at the Chinamen's Boarding House between bouts of itinerant work on the stations. Many others were still working under indenture on the district's runs, alongside the Germans. The scale of German immigration was remarkable. Some of these indentured German pastoral labourers arrived with wives and children, but most of them were single men. In fact, by 1856, there were almost as many German-born residents in the Burnett as there were English-born, and there were also more Chinese men in the district than there were either Irishmen or Scots.

By the time of the next census, 1861, Queensland was a separate colony with a total population of only 30,115 plus an estimated indigenous population of fifteen thousand. The number of Chinese in Queensland was 537 males and, finally, one female, a resident of Ipswich; almost three-quarters of them lived in the rural areas of the colony. The gender gap in the Burnett district was showing a slight improvement, although there were still twice as many men as women in the total non-indigenous population of 2,125, and the district was losing its raw frontier character. Almost one in five people of the district now lived in Gayndah town where only Englishmen outnumbered the Chinese residents. In fact, with its Chinese population of forty-eight men, Gayndah accounted for one-third of the total urban Chinese population in the whole colony. The second largest concentration was in the town of Dalby on the northern Darling Downs with twenty Chinese men, while there were only fourteen in Brisbane and one more than that in Ipswich. The Burnett's Chinese population had actually grown by twenty men between 1856 and 1861, to a total of 162, even though percentage-wise their presence in the district was actually diminishing. In 1868, the year of the Gympie gold rush, there were two hundred Chinese men in the Burnett, two-thirds of them in the rural portions of the district.

The small but steady increase in the number of Chinese men in the Burnett according to the census figures suggests that their work habits were becoming less itinerant. By 1868, their median age would have been around forty, which was surely time for them to settle down, and Gayndah, which was declared a municipality in 1866, seems to have become something of a community hub for the former shepherds once scattered far and wide over the remote parts of the Northern Districts. It was certainly the gathering-place for the Burnett Chinese, very few of whom remained in the South Burnett where the census counted only a small number of them among the Nanango police district and town populations.

While the 1868 census indicated that the population of the Burnett was still growing, the rate of growth for the district was actually declining. The economic depression of the mid-1860s took its toll. By the next census in 1871, the population had increased by only 169 people, a rate that was one-quarter what it had been in the previous interval between censuses. The big runs like Booubyjan, Boonara, Boondooma, and Eidsvold still supported populations of seventy-five or more, and there were 125 on the largest of the runs, Burrandowan, but economic change was coming inexorably to the pastoral life. In 1871, there was a gold strike at Cania and large copper deposits were found at Mount Perry, both in the North Burnett, which drew people into new occupational pursuits and towards new locations of residence. These job opportunities in and around the mining industry must also have accounted for the further rise in the Burnett district's Chinese population to 270 by 1871. This disproportionate increase of seventy men between 1868 and 1871 had nothing to do with the original Amoy indentured labourers;

for the first time, the Burnett and Maryborough newspapers were reporting names of Chinese that were not typically Hokkien.

It is more difficult to trace the progress of the Amoy men in Wide Bay, the adjoining district on the coast. The early figures, as discussed previously are unreliable, but it is safe to assume that there were not nearly as many indentured Chinese pastoral labourers in the Wide Bay district as there were in the Burnett, if only because the scale of the industry was smaller there. The 1868 Gympie gold rush brought hundreds of Chinese sojourners to the district, so the number of those still at work on the pastoral runs would have been either lost in the rush or absorbed into those communities of miners. Moreover, at the same time as the gold rush, the pastoral industry in the Wide Bay was rapidly making way for the cultivation and processing of sugar cane on the plantation model worked by coloured labour, including a new consignment of Chinese indentured labourers. This experiment was short-lived, but it was uncomfortably reminiscent of the earlier one and no doubt drew unfavourable attention to those much earlier Chinese immigrants who were attempting to assimilate into Maryborough society.

Maryborough and Mackay, on the central Queensland coast, were the main hubs for the importation of Kanaka labour that commenced in the 1860s and continued, with a brief hiatus in 1891, until federation of the Australian colonies and legislation enacted in October 1901 that prohibited their introduction after the beginning of April 1904. Mention has already been made of the relatively small number of these Melanesian men who were indentured to work on the pastoral runs of the Burnett in 1867 and 1868, but they were far more numerous on the coast where they were employed as labourers in the sugar industry. According to the 1871 census, there were 538 "Polynesians," including ten women, in Maryborough town and district. Peter Corris explains that they were employed on eight plantations and seventy-two other holdings in the Maryborough, Tiaro and Wide Bay districts.[17]

The largest sugar estates in Maryborough, totalling over one thousand acres, were owned by partners, Tooth and Cran, who had owned and operated the abattoir and boiling down works at Yengarie sheep station before it was converted to a sugar plantation and juice mill.[18] In 1880 there was a medical inspection of the Cran estates, prompted by reports of high mortality among its workforce of South Sea Islanders. Death rates among these indentured workers in the Maryborough district was high enough at 79/1000, Corris observes, but the rate on the Cran plantations for the five years prior to the end of March 1880 was 92/1000, and in the year before the inspection it

Early photograph of Maryborough, 1864 (John Oxley Library, State Library of Queensland, Neg:35111)

had reached an appalling rate of 107/1000.[19] At that time, there were more than three hundred Islander men at risk on those estates. The medical report concluded,

> We are of the opinion that the excessive mortality among the South Sea Islanders on Yengarie, Yarra Yarra (sic), and Irrowa, the sugar plantations of R. Cran and Co., is owing to poor feeding, bad water, over-work, and the absence of proper care when sick.[20]

It was a great misfortune, therefore, that the last experiment with Chinese indentured labour in the Wide Bay and Burnett districts should have taken place on Yengarie plantation. The international trade in indentured labour was prohibited by the Hong Kong authorities in May 1873 and at the end of the year, the governor of Macau also proclaimed that there would be no further legal Chinese emigration from that port after March 1874. The trade, however, simply transferred to Singapore where, Eric Rolls notes, it became "more or less legitimate."[21] The Chinese labour trade had never been subjected to supervision or scrutiny by the Australian colonial authorities, so the "more or less" nature of its legitimacy was irrelevant when, in 1874, the company of Tooth and Cran imported thirty-nine Chinese men, all experienced in sugar-growing in southern China. They were engaged in Singapore on three-year contracts with an advance but, according to Rolls, "When they found out how low the comparative pay was, they refused to work. So there was more parading through the courts."[22]

Between April 28 and October 8, 1874, no fewer than sixteen of the thirty-nine men appeared in the Maryborough Police Court, one of them on two occasions, charged under the draconian Queensland Masters and Servants Act with disobeying lawful orders, absenting themselves from hired service, and absconding. Efforts were made by the prosecutors to portray the men as malingerers, cheats, and opium addicts, and in a ploy familiar from the way their compatriots had been treated in local courts two decades earlier, some of those charged were singled out as ringleaders while others had charges against them paternalistically withdrawn or reduced in order to allow their employers to divide and rule.[23] They paid heavy fines, including the interpreter's fees, or faced weeks of imprisonment. Five of the prisoners were apprehended at Gladstone. When these absconders appeared before the bench, the court was told that the men had believed that they would earn

South Sea Island worker at Fairymead Sugar Mill near Bundaberg, c.1880 (Fairymead Mill Collection [FMC], Picture Bundaberg:bun01951)

Recruiting schooner *Locheil* moored at Fairymead wharf,
c.1880 (FMC, Picture Bundaberg:bun01971)

South Sea Island workers' grass houses at Fairymead, c.1880 (FMC Collection, Picture Bundaberg:bun01955)

more money by going to Rockhampton. It is more likely, however, that the men knew there was a community of southern Chinese in Rockhampton—the gold miners at Crocodile Creek—who might help them find passage home to China. The agent for Robert Tooth explained to the court that they had been fully paid up and nothing was due, but he would take them all back, he said. Apart from these five, he had nineteen other Chinese in his service at Yerra Yerra, part of the Yengarie plantation. This was all that was left of the original thirty-nine, the other fifteen having successfully absconded. He asked for them to be punished as a warning to the others and the court complied, handing down a hefty fine to the two men singled out as ringleaders, in lieu of three months' imprisonment with hard labour, with the condition that they return to employment at the expiration of their sentence. Despite this harsh warning, two more of them were charged with absconding before the end of the year.

As the horrific mortality rate among the Melanesian labourers on Yengarie plantation suggests, no lessons were learnt from this second failed experiment with indentured Chinese about proper labour management or proper provision of decent working conditions. The Chinese labourers enjoyed no legal protection other than the meagre provisions of the Masters and Servants Act, but the detailed Polynesian Laborers Act (31 Vic., No. 47) of 1868 with all its regulations and stipulations obviously did nothing to prevent the gross exploitation and death of so many Melanesians on Yengarie plantation between 1875 and 1880 either.

The Queensland gold rushes and the development of the mining industry, as well as that other major restructuring from a predominantly pastoral economy to one that was increasingly agricultural, would all eventually have an impact upon the small group of former Chinese indentured workers who regarded themselves as part of the Burnett society. Fencing of runs, along with the transition from sheep to cattle grazing that came in response to changed market conditions as much as to the constant battle with drought and pests, significantly reduced labour demand in the district by 1880 and people drifted away from Gayndah and the Burnett district towards nearby established coastal towns like Maryborough and newly settled but vigorously developing new ones, especially Bundaberg. Alone among the municipalities of Queensland, according to the 1876 census, Gayndah actually lost population; the loss was only forty-five people, but compared to demographic gains of almost sixty percent in Maryborough, the trend was obvious. However, there were 112 Chinese men still living in the Burnett that year, and a further sixty-eight of them were registered in the adjoining Leichhardt district to the west. Five years later, the 1881 census counted only seventy-one Chinese left in the Burnett, all adult men, which was exactly half their total number enumerated by the 1856 census, the one which should have counted all the original Amoy shepherds. During those twenty-five years, they seem to have lived the same interesting, if unremarkable lives of other decent citizens, with little of the drama that had marked the period of their indentured labour.

Their Stake in the Economy

The southern gold rushes transformed the Australian colonies. During the golden decade of the 1850s, the population trebled and Australians became very rich. According to R. V. Jackson, in 1860, real product and consumption per head were much higher than in Britain and probably higher than in the United States.[24] So sudden was the rise in export earnings after 1851 that the economy underwent what he termed an inflationary shock: wages, prices and imports all rose commensurately with exports. By the end of the decade, Jackson continues, the growth rate had stabilized at a high level; the rate was slower after 1860, but the growth itself had a different quality that was "sustained, large-scale and complex."[25] Over the next thirty years, the period that some economists have called "the long boom," the population continued to grow steadily, doubling again to over three million by 1891.[26] More than half of this growth was natural increase, and the age and sex structure of the Australian population gradually became more normal. Assisted migration policies were also vigorously pursued during this period, particularly in Queensland, although the colony found it difficult to persuade its new immigrants to go to the rural districts where their labour was most needed or even to retain them, many leaving for the southern colonies soon after their arrival.

During the 1850s, the volume of exported wool rose only slowly. Pastoralists found there was more profit to be made from supplying diggers with meat, and given the exponential growth in gold exports, wool's former near-monopoly share of total exports fell to only about twenty percent by the end of the decade.[27] Once the peak of gold extraction from the Victorian fields had passed, however, and despite ongoing gold rushes, especially in Queensland, wool resumed its role as economic mainstay. For the period of this study, up to 1880, it can truly be said that Australia rode on the sheep's back. In numbers of sheep alone, the increase in the industry was staggering. In 1861 there were sixteen million sheep on runs that stretched in a wide arc from the western districts of Victoria and beyond to the Tropic of Capricorn in Queensland; by the early 1890s, there were more than ninety million sheep on the continent.[28]

The boom in the pastoral industry that resumed once gold fever had abated, was different from the one that followed the passage of the 1846 Waste Lands Act when vast tracts of the best country, well-watered and free of pests and weeds, were made available for the adventurous squatter for low annual licence fees and with minimal competition or official surveillance. After 1860, there was significant capital investment in infrastructure and technology on the runs. The most expensive outlays were on fencing that allowed for new techniques of sheep farming with much reduced labour needs, especially shepherding. For the time being, however, the construction of fences, dams, wells, tanks, and so on, not to mention attempts at pasture improvement through large-scale land clearing projects, all created employment opportunities for gangs of itinerant rural labourers, including Chinese workers who had settled in many inland towns throughout New South Wales and Queensland. According to G. L. Buxton, "Few Australians objected to the widespread use of Chinese for [ring-barking], nor for the even more arduous years of scrub-cutting and sucker bashing which followed."[29] In the 1860s and the early years of the following decade, the high cost of this investment was borne by the industry itself. Australian sheep farmers were buoyed by good prices for their product and encouraged by improved ocean transport as well as the technical advances in the European textile industry that guaranteed continuing strong demand for Australian wool, as shown in the table:

Table 3: Australian Wool Exports to England 1859-70 and Prices Realised[30]

Year	Bales	Prices realised (d./lb.)
1859	170,082	23.5
1860	184,425	24
1861	208,833	21.5
1862	226,016	21
1863	302,177	22.5
1864	332,360	21.5

1865	348,628	21.75
1866	348,628	21.75
1867	412,641	18.5
1868	491,218	16.25
1869	499,610	15
1870	549,264	15.5

As the table indicates, wool prices began to fall towards the end of the 1860s, but the momentum of the great boom in the industry sustained it for a further decade, while increased production disguised the deep problems that the boom itself had created. Many of the new pastoral ventures were purely speculative and increasingly located on marginal lands in the interior of New South Wales and Queensland where climate conditions could not support intensive grazing. At the same time, the industry was coming under constant political pressure for land reform.

In the early years of responsible government for each of the three mainland colonies of eastern Australia, much of the legislatures' efforts were taken up with the stated objective of "unlocking the land," that is, of allowing small farmers and graziers access to the land already monopolized by the big squatters. There was a profusion of land laws during the decade; Queensland, desperate for immigrants and revenue alike, passed ten acts in the attempt to satisfy diverse interests. Around the major towns and along the coastal strip, small-scale farming made some progress but the pastoral character of inland Australia did not change much. Transport and other infrastructure facilities were limited and most of the land was not suitable for anything other than grazing.

By 1870, however, the growing population had created pressing demand for jobs and resources, including land for closer settlement by both agricultural farmers and small graziers. The outback was becoming more accessible thanks to the arrival of the telegraph, better roads and the construction of railways. Wages growth since the 1850s had allowed frugal pastoral workers to accumulate savings that they could invest in land. A farm labourer in Queensland in 1860 was paid, on average, £45 a year with board and lodging or six shillings per day without rations, and even shepherds earned £40 annually.[31] A Gayndah correspondent reported in October that year that shepherds in the Burnett were receiving £52 with rations.[32] In 1863, the high rate of savings among rural workers was used as an argument in favour of a bank in Gayndah, the editor of the local newspaper claiming that a shepherd in the district might have as much as two or three hundred pounds in deposits from settlements left with the employer.[33] High wages and high savings were proof positive of the prosperity and optimism of the squatters. During the decade 1856 to 1866, according to Duncan Waterson, the Darling Downs squatters "coined money."[34] This was the golden age of the Pure Merinos when sustained high prices for their meat, stock and wool allowed them to accumulate financial reserves, exercise their pre-emptive rights to buy their homestead land and invest in pastoral improvements that they could use to withstand both unfavourable economic circumstances and political obstacles to their traditional demand for security of tenure.

In 1866, there was a temporary halt to the boom when Queensland experienced a severe economic depression. Calls for separation from New South Wales had started in 1850, less than ten years after civil administration had commenced in the former penal colony. Even at that stage, the political scene was fractious and parochial, with animosity between the squatters and the merchants on the one hand, and between the squatting regions of the Burnett and the Downs on the other. At the end of 1854, a special meeting was held in Gayndah with the purpose of drawing up a petition to the Crown against fixing the seat of government of the proposed northern colony at Brisbane. William Forster told the Gayndah meeting he had believed that they did not have the means of forming a separate government, "[b]ut on reflection, when he came to consider the indifference shown towards their interests by the Sydney Government, he could not avoid the conclusion that it was necessary for them to have a government of their own."[35] Forster's doubts about the adequacy of means were well-founded. It is said that when the governor, Sir George Bowen and his staff arrived in Brisbane in December 1859 that the state treasury contained only 7s. 6d., stolen the same night, to serve the administrative needs of twenty-five thousand Europeans across 560,000 square miles (roughly 1.45 million square kilometres) of territory.[36] Financial difficulties were inherent in the establishment of the new colony. As Kay Cohen explains,

> Queensland was unique in that it was the only colony which started its political life with parliamentary government full-blown from the beginning, rather than first serving a period as a Crown colony. Moreover, it was obliged to be economically self-sufficient from its inception since, in

contrast to other colonies, it received no subsidies from Britain, and New South Wales had claimed any moneys held by the Moreton Bay settlement immediately prior to Separation.[37]

The new colony almost immediately commenced an ambitious public works programme funded by loans taken out in London, but when the London bank crashed in May 1866, all was confusion in Queensland, "cheques dishonoured to the extent, it is reported, of £150,000 whilst other enormous sums are owing by Government on contracts."[38] The press laid the blame for the disaster squarely with the government and its extravagant course to attract population and support them by commencing public works. "The style of expenditure adopted has been utterly beyond our means," the editor of the *Maryborough Chronicle* complained, adding,

> Well, the reckless game has been played—the bubble burst— and we are not astonished to find the Government without funds, without credit, and overwhelmed with debt.[39]

The debt was reported to be slightly more than three million pounds which was a lot for a population that had grown to around only one hundred thousand by the time of the crash. The Maryborough editor claimed that it made Queensland the most heavily indebted colony in the world.[40] Meanwhile, public meetings were held in that town to consider the level of destitution among its citizens and to devise some mode of relief. There were the first rumblings of discontent among organized labour:

> Your motto "Money for Labor" is no longer supportable; "Labour for Money" is the device on the banner of the employer and he it is who is to regulate the amount by aid of the imperial bushel found at relief camps.[41]

In Brisbane, the courts were inundated with insolvency cases and, it was said, any business where a "Wanted" sign was posted was literally besieged by job applicants.[42]

Even the invincibility of the squatters was questioned. The registrar-general's statistics for 1865 suggested there had been an increase in the colony's livestock, but almost all the livestock was mortgaged to Sydney capitalists; of the 6.8 million sheep in Queensland, more than 6.56 million of them were pledged as security. The minister for lands and works described the effects of this situation on the colony's prosperity as "a canker eating into its vitals, and reducing it to a bag of bones."[43]

Until the early 1870s, these warnings were ignored because very high prices for Australian wool comfortably covered the cost of the mortgage for most Queensland sheep farmers. The statistical register for Queensland for the year 1869 recorded 8.5 million sheep in the colony which was actually a small decline in numbers due to heavy losses caused by severe and prolonged drought then floods but despite the poor weather, the total value of Queensland's pastoral production increased by 6.25 per cent that year.[44] Overall, it seems, the prospects were good:

> The Pastoral Interest ... continues in a sound and healthy condition; ... it appears to have gathered strength through the limitations caused by the operation of the Crown Lands Alienation Act of 1868 and it is receiving and likely to receive an enormous impetus through the demand for preserved meat created by the war in Europe.[45]

On the other hand, as a less optimistic analyst pointed out, 890 runs had been abandoned in the three years since the implementation of the 1868 Act and there had been a decrease in the general revenue of more than £27,000 "at a time when the prosperity of Queensland is a vaunted theme in the home country."[46] He referred to over-production, the costs of production on remote stations, as well as the unsuitability of stock and mismanagement of stations in some cases. For him, however, the heaviest costs were those contingent on the speculative nature of the industry. He explained how most new runs were financed:

> [T]he usual mode of procedure is one-third or one-fourth cash and the residue in bills extending over a period of years, bearing interest from ten to twelve per cent, secured on the property; the whole of the wool and stock for sale having to pass through the hands of the mortgagee and chargeable with commission, the supply of rations and all other goods through the same channel, subject to a like commission,

and interest charged upon the cash advanced for current expenses.[47]

Sheep farming had to be a highly remunerative pursuit, he believed, to realize a profit on a purchase made according to those conditions.

The capital for these rash new squatting ventures came from Sydney where it was claimed "something like the value of £4,000,000 of Queensland mortgages [is] held ..., paying an annual return of something like £600,000 a year."[48] Given the acrimony left over from the separation debate, it should not be surprising that Sydney capitalists were blamed for the "speculative mania" in Queensland's pastoral industry. This rancour was expressed in colourful terms:

> To advance on a station in January and to give notice of foreclosure before the next December was common enough, and while buyers were forthcoming it paid well... The country, in fact, became a Sydney plantation with a few white niggers trying to make a living on it. There was more real power in the name of a Sydney firm than the Queensland Government possessed.[49]

While squatting may have been respectable as a pioneering operation, it was considered a poor model of development for a modern British colony. The Crown Lands Alienation Act of 1868 (31 Vic., No. 46) was Queensland's first serious attempt to establish a rural yeomanry that might eventually balance the power of big pastoral interests. In the settled districts of Queensland, the Act split large holdings in two, making one half available for subdivision into selections ranging between forty and 160 acres in size that could be bought on reasonable terms at cheap prices by Australian standards, while the other half could remain under a ten years' pastoral lease. The official designation, "settled", included more than fifty million acres of Queensland territory. Strictly speaking, the term did not refer to districts that had already been settled but rather to districts that could be made legally available for settlement. As the editor of the *Maryborough Chronicle* explained, this meant (the half of every squatter's run excepted) "all the country within thirty miles of the sea, and also the whole of the Moreton district, and portions of the Darling Downs, Wide Bay, and Port Curtis districts, which are at a greater distance from the sea than thirty miles."[50]

For classification purposes, the Burnett district remained an "unsettled district" until the 1876 Crown Lands Alienation Act redefined all crown lands as town, suburban or country lands. As such, throughout this period of study to 1880, apart from areas in the vicinity of towns like Gayndah, most of the district's runs avoided close settlement and selection for purposes of agriculture or small-grazing. Despite the many changes to land legislation during the second half of the nineteenth century in Queensland, until resumption of leases commenced in 1885, the established runs of the Burnett remained largely unaffected, unlike the pastoral holdings on the Darling Downs. The Crown Lands Act (48 Vic., No. 28) of 1884 divided runs under existing leases into two portions, one which remained available to the lessee for a further lease of ten to fifteen years with annual rent set by a land board, and the other half became crown land on which the former lessee had the right to graze stock until that land was selected.

Bad seasons, however, were as deleterious as unfavourable land laws for the squatter. The Burnett and Wide Bay districts experienced severe drought from 1866 to 1868, with "sheep and cattle dying in all directions."[51] In March 1870 there were cyclones and floods throughout Queensland; the Mary River exceeded by more than a metre the level it had reached in 1864, which was a flood level that the Aboriginal residents then said was unprecedented.[52] Throughout that year, the river overflowed its banks four times and eleven inquests were held into drownings. After a few good seasons, the summer of 1875 brought floods and cyclones of even greater intensity, leaving "swampy and boggy roads for miles, here and there tremendous landslips, portions of made roads swept clean away by the heavy rains, and streams running in all directions."[53] By 1877, however, drought had taken hold once again and stock perished in huge numbers. A newspaper correspondent described the scene at one station in the North Burnett:

At Rosslin Station, the drought has been so severe as to parch the life out of the very swamp oaks and tea trees in the beds of the creeks, hundreds of which may be seen sear and withered. In this part of the country no attempt is being made to save the lambs of the season, which are perishing by thousands, every effort being made to keep the parent ewes alive ...[54]

A boom once begun, takes time to brake despite the obvious warning signs. The pastoralist always had faith in better seasons and better prices as long as there was vacant land to occupy, and the colony's northern and western frontier seemed boundless. By 1891, there were almost twenty-one million sheep in Queensland, even though the cost to the land in terms of erosion, damaged watercourses, introduced pests and weeds, not to mention the destruction of the indigenous peoples, their culture, livelihood, society, and dignity, was unimaginable and irretrievable.[55] After 1870, Queensland increasingly also became cattle country, the number of head multiplying five-fold to 5.5 million by 1890.[56] Add to this scenario, the mining boom in gold, of course, but also in copper, tin and coal, and, ignoring the costs in human and environmental terms, one can hardly wonder that the prosperity of Queensland was a "vaunted theme" at home and abroad. The Chinese indentured labourers had been among the earliest pioneers of the colony, so they may have expected to share the benefits of a booming economy. The extent to which they were allowed to participate was measured by their political status, a measure that proved to be as unreliable as the Queensland weather.

Their Political Status

Another false assumption about the Chinese in colonial Australia, one that was actually a racial stereotype, was that they were alien and servile. This common grievance about them, John Rorke contends, was restated with increasing bitterness up to the time of Federation in 1901 and beyond:

> None seemed to have the slightest interest in establishing himself as a citizen and many were in various forms of servitude to masters in China. This servility of the Chinese was to be one of the strongest grounds for denunciation in the later years of radical nationalism when the merest contemplation of it aroused the *Bulletin* and William Lane's *Boomerang* to a sort of vehement horror.[57]

Apart from cutting their hair and donning the uniform of the Europeans in the bush, as the Amoy men had done from the commencement of their contracts in the Burnett, there was little more they could do to appear less alien in physical terms. In any case, their numbers alone should have rendered them anything but alien on the pastoral runs of the Northern Districts where between a quarter and one-half of all the shepherds were said to be Chinese in the 1850s. As for the charge of servility, the bitter experience of many squatters on the Burnett who had employed Amoy shepherds had proved that label to be simply ludicrous. Finally, the general criticism that they were uninterested in establishing themselves as citizens was demonstrably untrue; the historical records show that their eagerness to join the colonial society of British subjects was thwarted only by intermittent changes to the law, not by any inherent desire on their part to be forever alien.

The Aliens Act (11 Vic., No. 39) of 1847 contained no references to race at all. An alien resident in New South Wales was simply a person who was not a British subject and as long as that person was the subject of a "friendly State," he or she had the same rights to all property except "chattels real" as natural-born subjects. Although the unnaturalised subject could not own land in the colony, under the Aliens Act that came into force in 1849, that person could hold land for the purposes of residence, trade or manufacture under lease for twenty-one years. After residence of five successive years in the colony, an alien desiring to become a naturalised subject could present a memorial to the governor who would grant a certificate that was enrolled in the Supreme Court and within sixty days of enrolment, the applicant could take the oath of allegiance before a judge who then signed the certificate. Naturalisation granted all the same rights as a natural-born British subject except that of becoming a member of parliament. Even this disqualification was removed when the Electoral Act (22 Vic., No. 20) of 1858 gave naturalised subjects with five years' residence in the colony the right to be elected to the lower house.

This was the law when the first Chinese indentured labourers arrived in the colony and once they had completed their five-year contract, they should have been eligible for naturalisation. It was unfortunate for them, therefore, that vast quantities of payable gold were discovered during their term of indenture and that a major consequence of those discoveries was the influx of thousands of Chinese miners to the southern gold fields. The publicity given to new arrivals of Chinese miners and the occasional violent disturbances at the diggings put all the Chinese in Australia under intense political scrutiny. In 1854, a select committee of the Legislative Council of New South Wales investigated the issue of "Asiatic Labor" and concluded that "the experiment of Chinese has disappointed the expectations of those who at one time strongly advocated their introduction."[58] The seeming failure of Chinese labourers to fulfil the demands of their pastoral employers was conflated in the public mind with the media-stoked image of hordes of Chinese miners over-running the gold fields and extracting large amounts of the precious metal that were then destined for the coffers of China.

By 1858, the colony of New South Wales had responsible government and consequently more freedom to legislate while remaining within the parameters of British law. In July, a select committee was appointed to consider the provisions of a bill for the regulation of Chinese immigration. Returns to parliament showed that there had been a dramatic increase in the number of Chinese arriving in New South Wales that year; more than twelve thousand had arrived by July, compared to only 327 throughout the whole of the previous year.[59] Most of the Chinese diggers were in the southwestern districts of New South Wales, especially around the township of Sofala. The hostility between the European and the Chinese diggers there was said to be very strong but elsewhere the gold commissioners reported variously that the Chinese were "peaceable and submissive to all rules and regulations," "orderly observers of the law," "peaceably disposed," and "industrious, hard-working, and very orderly and quiet."[60]

The Chinese Immigration Bill of 1858 passed through the lower chamber but it was rejected by the Legislative Council and thus failed to become law. At the end of June 1861, however, violence erupted on the gold fields near the town of Yass at Lambing Flat, a field which had been discovered by Chinese, when a mob of around three thousand European diggers armed with bludgeons and pickhandles attacked the Chinese camp, robbing, looting, burning and cruelly assaulting the unarmed and unresisting Chinese.[61] The Sydney press was sympathetic towards the Chinese and blamed "the riff-raff of all the colonies" for the violence:

> It is not even alleged that the Chinese have committed any encroachment or injury, or, indeed, that they have done anything which, irrespective of their colour, their language, and their strange apparel, could arouse the enmity of a trueborn Englishman. In fact, we understand that, excepting a large sprinkling of thieves from the old penal establishments, the active parties in these disturbances are chiefly foreigners.[62]

While exonerating the Chinese diggers, the author of those remarks still believed that, given prevailing public opinion, some restriction on Chinese immigration could be expected in order to prevent what he called "a recurrence of these evils":

> Whether the Chinese should be permitted to come to this country, or upon what terms, must be, however, settled by law, and not by the caprice of individuals.[63]

This proved to be the case. The failed Chinese Immigration Bill of 1858 was revived, revised, and quickly passed through both chambers of parliament. It was given royal assent in November 1861. Meanwhile, at the Goulburn Assizes in September, those charged with leading the riot at Lambing Flat were acquitted by the jury. Under the circumstances, it was a harsh and shameful Act that marked the beginning of racial discrimination in New South Wales against a specific ethnic group other than the indigenous peoples of Australia. Perhaps its most shameful clause was the one denying naturalisation to Chinese immigrants.[64]

The Queensland law on aliens that repealed the 1847 Aliens Act in that colony was also given assent in 1861. Like the New South Wales Act, the new Aliens Act (25 Vic., No. 9) discriminated on the grounds of race. Europeans or North Americans simply had to take the oath of allegiance before a judge or a justice of the peace to become a naturalised British subject. Asians and Africans were not entitled to be naturalised unless they had been resident in the colony for three years and were married, the "wife" also being resident. The law was consolidated and amended by the Aliens Act of 1867 (31 Vic., No. 28).

The first of the former Amoy shepherds on the Burnett to be naturalised was James Chiam who had completed his indenture on Boondooma station in 1857. He took the oath of allegiance in Maryborough before the police magistrate, Arthur Halloran, in September 1858, just early enough to avoid the restrictions on Chinese naturalisation that debate in the New South Wales parliament was threatening to impose.[65] Six months later, three of his compatriots in Gayndah faced unforeseen obstacles when they attempted to do the same.

Three months before Queensland was created as a separate colony, while the Burnett and the other Northern Districts were still subject to the legislation of New South Wales, a Gayndah correspondent wrote about "Injustice to the Chinese" in his community:

> In our little town there are a great number of Chinese; and so far as I am aware they have always conducted themselves well; but the injustice I am about to comment on is applicable only to three of them, viz.: Leong (sic), who has resided on the Burnett eleven years, five of which has been passed in Gayndah, Pangsee, eight years' residence on the Burnett, two years of which has been passed in Gayndah, and Drian (sic), seven years' residence on the Burnett, two years of which has been passed in Gayndah. These three have purchased land at the public land sales, and paid in the case of Pangsee, £67 per acre, Drian £42 per acre, and Leong £32 per acre; which for the quantity is the highest average paid in Gayndah. Yet the Government refuse to naturalise, return their money, or give them any satisfaction. It may be well to stop a further increase of Chinese; but I think justice demands that such that have been known for years as really good men, should not now be debarred privileges they could have claimed four years ago. You will see from the return of land sale following, they are again purchasers, so that the Government has not instructed the land agent to refuse their bids. They are now petitioning, and will receive the support and signatures of many of our leading men.[66]

Petitioning to parliament by the leading men of Gayndah in support of the three men was successful. In 1860, Thomas Ashney, John Deian and David Deong re-submitted their memorials to the governor.[67] Their request for naturalisation was granted and they took their oaths of allegiance in the allotted time. John Connolly, Gayndah's leading citizen and most likely the shipping agent who had arranged John Deian's assignment to his employer after he arrived at South Brisbane Wharf in 1850 was one of the three witnesses to his signature on the naturalisation certificate.

It is impossible to give exact figures, but at least twenty of the Amoy shepherds who remained in the Wide Bay and Burnett districts became naturalised British subjects between 1858 and 1875, and approximately one-third of them took their oaths of allegiance before John O'Connell

Bligh during his term of office as Gayndah's police magistrate. After 1875, there was a hiatus of several years as Queensland introduced a series of laws similar to those previously enacted in Victoria and New South Wales aimed at restricting the entry of Chinese into the colony, specifically to the gold fields, although Queensland never legislated to deny naturalisation to Chinese immigrants. After 1880, however, Chinese residents throughout the colony continued submitting applications to secure their status as loyal subjects of the British Crown.

CHAPTER 11

Fortune

During the period from the end of 1853 when men from the first consignment of Chinese labourers to Moreton Bay finished their indentures to about 1880, there was sustained high demand for labour throughout a rapidly expanding pastoral frontier. New industries, especially mining and agriculture, offered alternative opportunities for fortune-seekers in the new colony of Queensland, while the growing population in towns and settlements along the coast and hinterland encouraged the diversification of labour into occupations allied to the provision of goods and services.

The studies that have been made of Chinese settlement and adaptation in regions of colonial Australia, including far north Queensland, the Riverina and western districts of New South Wales, as well as the detailed reports of a royal commission into the situation of Chinese residents of Sydney and of a British Foreign Office consul in relation to the Chinese miners on the Palmer River goldfields all point to the fact that, as far as possible, Chinese industry, commerce and labour did not enter into direct competition with that of Europeans.[1] Instead, Chinese workers and their headmen who were usually local merchants, developed niche markets in, for example, land-clearing, or banana cultivation, or, in the towns, in furniture and cabinet-making that did not pose a competitive threat to the established European trade. Even in mining, the Chinese diggers employed different methods, although it can be argued that this was forced on them by discriminatory legislation that excluded them from the major gold fields.

If it were the case that a kind of agreed upon race-based segregation operated in the labour market generally, then it is surely a contradiction to argue that it was the threat of reduced wages posed by cheap Asiatic labour in competition for jobs with white labour that underpinned the introduction of harsh discriminatory and restrictive laws against Chinese immigration and settlement at the end of this period of study. Contradiction, deception, and sham racism, however, had characterised the political debate surrounding the use of non-white labour in New South Wales all the way back to Ben Boyd's ventures with South Sea Islanders at Twofold Bay. It must be remembered that the introduction of Chinese labourers from Amoy and Hill Coolies from India had been a deliberate attempt by the squatters to force down the price of European labour and to maximise their profits. At the time, they even trumpeted this claim. Furthermore, they advised each other to keep their coloured workers apart from the other workers on the runs, not to avoid racial conflict, but in a vain effort to prevent their indentured servants from becoming aware of the real value of their labour. As previous chapters have illustrated, the Amoy men quickly realized that they had been cheated by their white contractors, and they took direct action to resist exploitation. They never willingly chose to work for less pay than their white counterparts. This remained their firm stance after the unequal contracts had expired and when they started to join the free labour market in late 1853. At that time, market conditions were overwhelmingly in the workers' favour.

An examination of the post-indenture careers of some of the Burnett Chinese shows that work and remuneration, success and failure, had less to do with ethnicity than with skill, hard work, and reputation. The scale of the Burnett economy was too small to allow for division of labour along racial lines, and the community was too closely knit to tolerate anonymity and exclusion. The societies that evolved in and around the Burnett townships of Gayndah and Mount Perry were certainly stratified but this was determined by class and property and had little to do with race; stratification eventually developed within the Chinese community also. There is sufficient evidence to suggest that racism and xenophobia ran deep within the European society, but there is even more evidence that Chinese and European labourers worked together on the runs and in the mines at near or equal rates of pay, that the Chinese stores and carrier services were patronised by the general populace, and that everyone apart from a handful of European competitors enjoyed the produce of their vegetable gardens. Shirley Fitzgerald reminds us in her study of the Chinese in Sydney that although "a cabbage is a cabbage, timeless and universal," Chinese success in European terms was confronting for many Europeans.[2] This was the case generally, and it was certainly so with the aphisfree, cannonball-like perfection of cabbages produced by Chinese market gardeners in Maryborough. Some members of the local horticultural society there considered this degree of success to be an affront to their own national pride and "a grave reflection on the intelligence and energy of Englishmen."[3]

Most of the former indentured labourers in the Burnett district earned their livelihood in occupations now commonly associated with other Chinese migrants in Australia in the second half of the nineteenth century: as itinerant rural labourers, miners or market-gardeners. Some of them did all of these jobs at different times in their post-indenture working lives; some did these jobs concurrently, such as working as a feeder in a mine while being regularly employed as a station hand on the property where the mine was located; some found that skills such as slaughtering that they had practised on the station transferred readily to the occupation of butcher in the town; and others ran boarding houses while tending gardens that supplied their own establishments and the townspeople with much needed fresh produce.

Itinerant Rural Labourers

In the pastoral industry, the formerly indentured Chinese labourers worked alongside European labourers in the woolsheds, the washpools, and on the runs of the Burnett district until at least the mid-1870s. Given the high level of demand for this sort of labour for most of the period under study, there was no genuine competition for jobs. Chinese pastoral workers, particularly the itinerant workers, did the same work for the same rates of pay as itinerant Europeans. On Yarrol station, due north of Gayndah, for example, Tan Yang and John Stewart were both hired in 1869, the former for fifteen weeks as a shepherd and the other for thirteen weeks as a "generally useful." Each was paid £1 a week. Tan Yang finished his job with £9 12s. in his pocket, while John Stewart spent three shillings more than he earned at the station store and on having his horse branded. Depending on personality traits and family commitments—Tan Yang was two years married by then—those earning outcomes could easily have been reversed.

From the wages books of three stations in the Burnett covering the period from 1854 to 1883, it is clear that there was no wage discrimination among labourers hired for pastoral jobs once they had completed their indentures.[4]

There is no evidence that Chinese men were ever employed as superintendents or overseers, and there are no examples of Chinese bullock-drivers but many of them were shearers, cooks, shepherds or watchers, lambers, washers, wool pressers and balers, and generally usefuls, and they were paid at the same rate as Europeans employed on the same run in the same occupation.

The first men to complete their contracts had arrived from the *Nimrod* in Moreton Bay on October 28, 1848.[5] Wages were due from that date, so we can assume that they were free to seek employment on the open market exactly five years later. In the Burnett district, the earliest recorded instance of a free Chinese labourer employed on a run was Gue Lack who was engaged by Boondooma station for two years in November 1853 at the annual wage rate of £24, which was the standard rate for shepherds and generally usefuls, if there were such a thing as a standard rate of pay at the height of the southern gold rushes.[6] Downs squatter, James Canning Pearce on Perseverance station had offered £35 to shepherds and £30 to hutkeepers that month but this was a late and desperate attempt to secure labour for the shearing season as he had already paid advances and expenses to seven men who never arrived on his station.[7] Thus the Lawson brothers who appear to have been scrupulously fair employers set the example for equal pay to free but coloured labour in the Burnett. As previously noted, Boondooma practised a rigorous policy of fair pay and incentives towards its largely indentured labour force in the 1850s that also included Germans and Pentonville exiles.

In 1853 and 1854, the first batch of Chinese labourers on Boondooma, those hired in the first quarter of 1851, who had already paid off their advances were receiving 18 shillings ($4.50) per month plus extras and rations, not the flat monthly rate of 12 shillings ($3) with rations that was stipulated in the contract. For example, in August that year, Goe Lit was paid for two months' watching at $2.25 per month and received his annual lambing bonus of £1 in addition to his regular quarterly wage calculated at $4.50 per month. In 1855, the same indentured men, now in the final year of contract, were paid at least £1 per month, so when the extras were taken into account, their annual earnings were not far below those of T. G. Mann, most probably an indentured German labourer, who was engaged for two years from 1 May that year at £20 per annum. Some of these Chinese men, even the recalcitrants, remained on the wages book and the store account at Boondooma for several years after the end of their indenture when they returned as itinerant labourers at lambing or shearing time, or shepherded at casual rates. Ong Seo, for instance, one of the two men charged in connection with the shooting incident in mid-1854, was paid the handsome sum of £23 19s. during the 1856 shearing season for his tally of 2,128 sheep. Tan Yang, from the first group of men off the *Duke of Roxburgh* who were released from contract in February 1856, was listed in the store accounts in 1857, and he was again paid for lambing in 1858.

By the end of 1855, the indenture process seems to have broken down as far as wages were concerned. The decade-long boom in the industry was underway and the pastoralists were so eager to procure labour that it was impracticable to hold a man to a fixed contract at below standard rates of pay. On Boondooma, even some of those "d–d scoundrels" who were discharged that year for allowing scabbed sheep to get mixed with healthy flocks were re-hired. Chew Han/Chan was one of those five discharged men, but in 1857 he was again shepherding on the run for £40 per annum. Ng What who had served six months in Sydney Gaol for attempting to rescue prisoners passing through the run under Native Police escort in 1854, returned to Boondooma in 1857 and was signed on as a shepherd at £50 a year.

Not all the indentured Chinese were as fortunate as those men. In mid-1855, on Broreenia/Brovinia station, north of Boondooma, four men, all shepherds whose contracts were set to expire in May 1857 tried to negotiate their way out of their contracts after the overseer, Rogers, had violently struck two of them. The squatter, Philip Button, proposed cancelling their agreements after the shearing but they offered instead to buy out their contracts. Button refused and the men were charged with disobeying orders and taken to Gayndah where, in custody, one of those who had been abused drowned in the river.[8] Early the following year, on Burrandowan and also at Wetheron station, Chinese labourers were charged under the Act with absenting themselves from hired service before the completion of agreement. It was obviously difficult to enforce working conditions that had been knowingly unfair from the start when rural wages and job rates were so high; it is equally difficult to imagine the spitefulness of a "master" like Bouverie, the manager at Wetheron who took Teang before the Bench for "unlawful absence since January 29, 1856" when his contract was set to expire on February 10.[9] For five years, Teang had obviously been keeping a careful eye on the Chinese calendar, not the Western one, which easily explains the discrepancy but he nevertheless agreed to serve out the time he had been absent.

In this golden decade before the slump of 1866, wages in the pastoral industry more than doubled compared to pre-gold rush rates of pay, partly because of demand and inflation, but also because the squatters had the capacity to pay, given the very high prices they were receiving for their wool

Jim Channer, eldest son of Tan Chan, c.1895

and stock. This prosperity was experienced throughout the whole country. The following account from the Lower Murrumbidgee in 1858 could just as easily have come from the South Burnett, except for the arrival of English immigrants, something that was long anticipated but longer in coming for the Northern Districts. Thousands of German migrants, brought out under contract to the squatters on the Darling Downs and the Burnett district runs between 1852 and 1866, however, made an invaluable contribution at this time:[10]

> The amount of labour lately present in this district has been far from equal to the demand—in fact, during the whole time of shearing there was a deficiency of men. There has been a demand for hutkeepers, cooks, and milkmen, which has not been supplied. Many families have been brought out, and are still arriving from England, under special engagements for employment in the bush... The present average rates are: Stockmen, £60 to £80; shepherds, £40 to £45; man and wife on station, £75 to £85; milkmen, £60, all by the year; hutkeepers, 15s. to 25s.; tailors, 15s.; labourers, 15s. to 20s., all by the week.[11]

Rates of pay varied, especially in relation to distance from close settlements, and while wages were comparatively high throughout the 1860s, they then remained almost unaltered for the following thirty years.[12] Prospective migrants in Britain in 1861 were advised to expect wages in the relatively modest range offered by the following table of averages taken from the evidence of employers and labourers to a select committee of the New South Wales parliament in 1859 but they could have earned much more in Queensland. In October 1860, the Brisbane press reported that shepherds in the colony earned £45 to £50 per annum and bullock drivers £50 to £55, all with rations equal to a further £25 a year along with houses and huts.[13] "Therefore, £75 per annum is the lowest sum at which the value of a man's labour can be calculated," the article claimed. Later that month, the Gayndah correspondent advised readers of the *Moreton Bay Courier* that Burnett shepherds could expect to receive £52 per annum with rations.

Table 4: Rate of Country Wages, Per Annum, with Rations, 1860[14]

Farm labourers	£30-40
Married couples	£40-50
Hutkeepers	£20-25
Shepherds	£25-30
Stockmen	£40-50
Bullock drivers	£40-50

In all the above cases, the rations for each individual comprised flour, 8-12 lbs; meat, 10-14 lbs; sugar, 2 lbs; tea, ¼ lb per week. Wages paid to pastoral workers in the Burnett peaked during the season prior to the 1866 slump. In the following table, annual wages only were supplemented with huts and rations:

Table 5: Burnett District Pastoral Workers' Wages, 1864–65 Season[15]

Occupation	Wage Rates, 1864-65 Season
Shearers	3s. 6d. to 4s. 3d. per score
Washers	6s. per day
Woolpressers	30s. to 35s. per week
Lambing hands	25s. to 30s. per week
Hutkeepers	£40-50 per annum
Shepherds	£45-70 per annum
Bullock-drivers	£65 per annum

Shearers, the aristocrats among Australian bushmen, were paid by the score of sheep shorn. According to Duncan Waterson, throughout the 1860s and the 1870s, the rate was 3s. 6d. per score but by 1888, the year after machines were first demonstrated at Toowoomba on the Darling Downs, pastoralists were offering only three shillings.[16] The vast scale on which the industry operated in 1870 was indicated by the fact that Jimbour station on the Downs engaged fifty-four shearers to shear 210,000 sheep that year, and they filled 1,409 bales in fifteen weeks during the season that started in early October and finished in mid-December.[17] Waterson does not specify if any of the shearers on Jimbour were Chinese. On another large, prestigious Downs station, Jondaryan, however, Jan Walker records that there were "a few Chinese who worked as burr cutters, cooks and rollers, a wool classer and a couple of shearers" throughout this period, but she adds, "Shearers particularly resented sharing the board with a Chinaman and feared that his presence would depress wages."[18] This attitude must have developed later in the period, instigated as much by the depression of real wages as by the political ferment over the question of Chinese immigration, because Boondooma and Booubyjan stations had no problems employing Chinese shearers throughout the 1850s, at least, the period for which their records are still available.

During two shearing seasons, in 1855 and 1856, a team of ten Chinese shearers was employed to take the wool off Booubyjan's flocks. These men: Harry, Hee, Tan Wan, Tan Zi, Loo Him, Hock, Hong, Tan Zoon, Toa/Tua, and Goh Ying/Guo Yin, were each paid four shillings per score and none of them had trouble paying Ju, the shearers' cook, one guinea each from his wages. On Boondooma, shearer Tsan Shan (Tan Chan) was also paid four shillings per score in 1858, and the following year Hong was paid at the rate of 3s. 9d. Twang, Chong and Chow were other identities among the Burnett's Chinese shearers. Some of the shearers were also paid between five and seven shillings a day for washing the sheep prior to shearing, so they earned a lot of money during the four months of the shearing season. Those who did not shear could earn twenty-five shillings a week in the Boondooma woolshed, perhaps as pressers and balers. In 1857, even abstemious shepherds and hutkeepers could save impressive amounts from their wages. Co Tiong, shepherd, and Ten/Tin Tai, his hut-keeper on a Booubyjan outstation earned £8 9s. a quarter, exclusive of extras and rations, and in that time, each spent less than £1 5s. at the station store.

Writing of Jondaryan station, Jan Walker notes that some squatters quite openly admitted that it was general practice to defray their wages bill by profits derived from the store. She explains,

On Jondaryan the ration issue was always flour, sugar and tea in the ratio of 4:1:1/8, although the quality might vary. A shepherd, for instance, would receive eight pounds of flour, two pounds of sugar and a quarter pound of tea... Sixteen pounds of meat was the usual allocation. Anthony Trollope estimated that receiving rations was worth 5s. 6d. a week [£14 6s. a year] to the washer. On Jondaryan, at Jondaryan store prices, it was worth 10s. 4d. per week [£26 18s. a year]. Jondaryan's management used the ration incentive to secure their labour force. Workers would not be placed on the ration list until they had signed on for the season.[19]

Stores were issued to resident employees and washers, but other contract and itinerant groups had to buy their own rations and, at least in the case of shearers, pay the cook. No doubt station store prices were as much affected by distance from settlement and ports as wages were, but close examination of a selection of prices at the Booubyjan station store, fifty or sixty miles from Maryborough by dray, at July 1, 1854, suggests that they were not grossly inflated:

Table 6: Booubyjan Station Store Prices at July 1, 1854[20]

Food Items	Price	Clothing Items	Price
Flour	6d./lb.	Moleskin Trowsers (sic)	12/-, 8/-
Rice	4d./lb.	Cord Trowsers	12/-, 8/-
Tea	3/-	Duck Trowsers	4/6, 3/-
Sugar	6d.	Blue Serge Shirt	7/-, 5/-
Tobacco	6/-, 4/-	Coats	20/-, 18/-
		Socks	1/-, 10d.
		Blankets (pair)	£1 12s. 6d.
		Boots	15/-, 10/-
		Belt	3/6, 2/6

In the last quarter of 1853, the New South Wales immigration agent advised prospective British migrants that they could expect wheat to cost nine shillings a bushel (a two pound loaf of bread cost seven pence), tea 4s. 4d. per pound, and sugar 3.5d. per pound.[21] Prices were not stable, however, and T. A. Coghlan notes that flour had reached £50 a ton in July 1854, and after it was shipped to Moreton Bay, the price was as much as £10 higher. Therefore, six pence per pound in the Booubyjan store was reasonable, given cartage costs, but the price of rice, the Chinese food staple, was high. In 1854, the Lawson brothers at Boondooma tried to dispose of rice they had ordered at £13 a ton and considered it was cheap at that price of roughly 1.5d. per pound; it usually sold in Sydney at 2.5d. per pound in 1871, according to Coghlan.[22] Rapid price inflation was a consequence of the gold discoveries in Victoria and New South Wales in the early 1850s, and Coghlan estimates that clothing prices reached their highest point in 1854 and 1855, and then fell back to 1851 prices, except for boots and shoes which still cost from twelve to sixteen shillings per pair, which was about the same as at Booubyjan. According to his calculations, moleskin trousers would have cost ten shillings in 1854, and a shepherd's coat around £1 4s., again more or less consistent with the Burnett station's store prices. A pair of blankets cost considerably more at Booubyjan than the 1851 price of fifteen shillings quoted by Coghlan, but in general, it cannot be said that the store was seriously over-charging on most items. According to the store accounts of Boondooma, Booubyjan and Yarrol, all the Chinese customers were inveterate smokers of tobacco. A twist of tobacco, matches and cheap clay pipes that cost a penny each appeared beside the name of every Chinese station hand. Imported tobacco cost three shillings per pound in 1871 in Sydney, and colonial tobacco just one shilling. Perhaps it was on this single item that the station stores made most of their profit. Given their passion for tobacco, it should not be surprising that it was originally a Chinese industry in Australia, according to Coghlan,

> The growth of the plant was mainly in the hands of Chinese, by whom the curing of tobacco was not properly understood. At its first introduction it was used almost entirely as a sheep-wash, but its use for smoking extended, although it may well be imagined that colonial tobacco was not exactly suited to a palate which was in any way delicate or refined.[23]

After the early 1860s, the available information concerning the employment of Chinese itinerants is less detailed. On Yarrol station, where the ledger extends to 1883, the last entries for Chinese pastoral labourers included £2 paid to both Har Sin and Har Coo for two weeks of shepherding in 1869. As the census figures show, the size of the population of Chinese men in the Burnett remained steady throughout the 1860s and into the early 1870s, so we can assume that Jan Walker's depiction of their employment at Jondaryan applies with fair measure to that on Burnett runs. She records that although they were quite an unstable supply of labour in the early 1860s, some staying only two to four months, there were some Chinese who worked on Jondaryan for years:

> One fellow worked on and off for thirty years, one shepherd
> worked from 1861 to 1863 and another from 1861 to 1869.
> Of the eighty who were recorded as having worked on
> Jondaryan, only one was ever discharged.[24]

In the Burnett district, the same pattern emerges that in the years post-indenture, the Amoy men returned to work on those runs where they had been treated fairly, and gave their loyalty to deserving employers. For instance, after fulfilling his indenture on Boondooma station in February 1854 and a few years of itinerant work, Tan Chan appears to have spent most of the next thirty years on Yarrol station in the upper Burnett, leaving there only after the death of the lessee, Robert Buffet Ridler.[25] During that time he was a stockman but he also worked in one of the several mining ventures undertaken on the station, and together with Tan Yang, probably a brother who was a regular itinerant labourer on Yarrol, ran a butcher shop in Gayndah. A naturalized citizen and married to an Irish-born domestic servant who was also employed at the station, he raised six of his children on Yarrol before moving the family to the new coastal settlement of Bundaberg in the early 1880s. He died there in 1920, aged "about ninety."

The financial crisis in Queensland in 1866, precipitated by rash borrowings to fund an extensive and populist public works programme, created massive unemployment that was compounded by the arrival of shiploads of assisted immigrants from Britain.[26] Many of the unemployed took to the track and, as Jan Walker observes, scores of men were going about the stations in search of work so that "[s]hepherds on Jondaryan had to carry their rations out on the run with them because their huts were frequently robbed."[27] The opportune discovery of a major goldfield at Gympie relieved this situation, but at the same time wool prices were falling and dropped below ten shillings a pound in 1870 which was almost half the price that squatters had received in 1862 and 1864.

By 1872, the wool price had rebounded and the industry recovered in terms of profits. Wage rates returned to the high level of the 1860s but did not increase beyond that. Labour, however, was beginning to transform itself. By the end of 1874, shearers were calling for the formation of a shearers' association, and from the first Intercolonial Trade Union Congress in 1879 there was continual reference to the labour movement's opposition to assisted white and non-European labour. At the fifth congress held in Brisbane in 1888, it was made quite clear that opposition to Chinese workers was both on a job-competitive and racial basis.[28] By 1891, there were only 148 Chinese pastoral workers left in the whole of Queensland.[29] By then, of course, the original Amoy men would have been at least sixty years old, and perhaps some of the lucky ones had already taken their shearers' wages back to China.

Miners and Gardeners

The gold digger and the market gardener are the stereotypes of the "Chinaman" in Australia's colonial history. The two roles are usually regarded as sequential: the Chinese digger supposedly quickly realized that greater profit was to be made from providing the European miners with fresh produce than could be gleaned from the goldfields after the Europeans had abandoned them. No doubt there is some truth in this as in other stereotypes about them. On the squatters' runs in the Northern Districts and early Queensland, however, some of the Amoy men had worked the homestead vegetable gardens for many years before the first gold discoveries in the colony. The indentured Chinese labourers were sometimes assigned to be cooks and domestic servants for the homesteads, so tending a garden was an obvious extension of their job. On Jondaryan station in September 1862, for instance, Jan Walker notes that the Chinese gardener, Whey, was busily laying out the garden and plants.[30] The previous year, in Gayndah, poor Chow's murdered body was reportedly found buried between the cabbages and eschalots in Ong Hoo's garden that supplied his Chinese board and lodging house in the town. To confound the stereotype further, Chinese miners in Queensland were not solely involved in gold mining; the mining of tin on the Downs, and galena in the Burnett also engaged Chinese labourers, but not on the same scale as gold.

As in other parts of Queensland, rewards were offered for the discovery of gold in the Burnett because it was seen as a way of attracting people, especially their labour, to the region. Gold was discovered in the Burnett, but compared to the finds made in Gympie to the south and the later strikes in the far north, the gold fields in the Burnett were judged to offer only moderate success. The first discovery of any significance was at Reid's Creek in the upper Burnett in late 1863. It was first reported that this find was capable of carrying "even as many as a thousand Chinaman diggers."[31] Within a year or two, however, the initial enthusiasm had been replaced by sheer drudgery, as the report from a correspondent on the diggings to the Gayndah press explained,

There are several parties, most of them Chinamen, working here, and none of them are at the present time making more than rations, for the creek on which we are at work is the only one in the neighbourhood where there is any water, and this creek has been thoroughly worked out... [I]n fact we have had no rain up in these regions for the last eighteen months save a passing thunderstorm. The washing dirt is too poor to pack and so we are just going on from hand to mouth.[32]

In 1868, the new Galatea field soon attracted at least six hundred men, and the nearby Cania and Kroombit gold fields also caused another moderate rush of between five hundred and six hundred diggers, both European and Chinese.[33] It is impossible to know if any of the Amoy men joined these rushes in the upper Burnett. These were the years of economic confusion and urban unemployment in the young colony and the European diggers tended to bring mayhem with them as the following extract from the report on the Burnett district gold field describes. Joining a rush, especially if you were Chinese, was not for the faint-hearted. The Gayndah publican mentioned in the extract was a former indentured labourer from the *Nimrod* and therefore was among the first Amoy men who arrived in New South Wales in 1848:

Some of the diggers at Gayndah have been rather rowdy, and a rush by about fifty New Zealanders, I hear, was made on the premises of Thomas Ashney, the Queensland Arms Hotel, on Wednesday night, and considerable damage done, besides the loss of liquors which I believe were carried off wholesale. The efforts of the police, of course, were unavailing under such circumstances. I have also heard of some instances of bounce and a good deal of petty thieving... [so] for the present I advise no one to come to the Burnett Diggings until fresh ground is opened.[34]

The gold rush brought a crime wave to the Burnett. Later that year, there were "outrages" (armed hold-ups) at Wetheron and Boondooma stations, Yarrol station was "shamefully stormed by a band of loafers from the Gympie goldfields" and a Gayndah publican was forced to close his house to prevent it being "sacked" by the mob.[35]

Yarrol station in the upper Burnett provided access to these fields from Gayndah.[36] It was on the same ore-bearing reef and payable deposits of gold were mined there, but there was more interest in the opportunities for silver, lead and copper mining on a larger and far more lucrative scale. A silver-lead mine opened there in January 1869 and for exactly one year it showed great promise. The Burnett Galena Mining Company was floated in Melbourne in June and active operations commenced at the end of the month.[37] No sooner had work started on extracting the silver-bearing ore than Robert Ridler, the lessee, advised one of the mine's proprietors that there was a copper lode in the ranges a few miles from the station. On inspection it was judged from the lumps of copper that lay along the surface for a distance of 340 yards that it was one of the richest copper lodes ever opened up in the colonies, consisting of "lumps of copper ore varying from 150 pounds weight downward, in such quantities as would enable the gentlemen to fill a dray in ten minutes without moving the dray."[38] An average sample of the ore was taken to Brisbane for testing where it was expected to show at least seventy-five per cent of copper.

In January 1870, however, after only one year of operations, it was reported that the Yarrol Silver and Lead Mining Company had totally collapsed and that the directors had called a meeting to wind up its affairs. The failure of foreign capital was one reason given but it was also reported that shareholders had been induced to invest "upon certain representations which were scarcely borne out by facts subsequently elicited."[39]

Fortunately for the workers who had made the long, arduous trek to the district, another rich copper field with very dense specimens had been discovered at Mount Perry, thirty or so miles from Yarrol and about the same distance from Gayndah. There were some lucky speculators who managed to exchange at par their shares in the Yarrol Silver Mine for those of the Mount Perry Copper Mine just five months before the collapse of the former company.

Undaunted by the collapse of the silver and copper mining ventures on Yarrol, Ridler and his associates formed the Beehive Gold Mining Company in September 1873 and with the usual optimistic flair, it was reported, "Yarrol bids fair to become one of the most important gold fields in the country. There are various reefs, for example Beehive, Bridgewater and Dolly Varden, all showing permanency and good payable gold."[40] By the middle of June the next year, a small mining community had evolved near the Beehive mine. The description of it that appeared in the press contained some alarming details:

The population of the place is between fifty and sixty adults. The business establishments consist of one public house; two stores, one of which combines butchering with storekeeping; two boarding houses, and one Chinese gardener and opium seller. This latter occupation is almost entirely confined to supplying Aboriginals. There really ought to be some law passed (if such does not already exist) prohibiting the sale of this poisonous drug to the blacks. It is killing them slowly, but surely; the use of it is more fascinating and deleterious than even that acme of a blackfellow's desires—rum, and the poor creatures in this neighbourhood have nearly all acquired the pernicious habit of opium-smoking. We are a peaceful and quiet population, and require, or at least have, no police, except on pay days (once a month), when some few pay amongst us their respects to Bacchus, and become noisy, not quarrelsome.[41]

Among those fifty or sixty men, according to the Yarrol ledger, was Tan Chan/Channa, who was paid £17 1s. 8d. for two months' labour in 1874 as a feeder at the mine. The standard wage for (shaft) miners, all Europeans, was £10 per month. Another Amoy man, Tin Kat, the gardener and opium supplier, was not on wages but in 1873 he was paid £4 10s. for supplying 180 sheets of bark to the mine.[42] There can be no doubt that this bark was collected by the Aboriginal people in the area, and it is most likely that payment was made to them in opium, or rather opium ash. Another former Amoy shepherd, long resident in the area, Sam Coey/Qui, was paid for charcoal and its cartage from Mount Perry to the Beehive mine.

The Mount Perry Copper Mine fared better than the one at Yarrol. Three separate assays of copper ore yielded an average of forty-five per cent copper, which was about the same quality as the test results had yielded on the Yarrol specimen.[43] The first miners arrived at the end of April 1871, the first Chinese market garden was established in July, and within a year the township of Mount Perry had a population of over one thousand.[44] Thomas White, editor of the *Burnett Argus*, moved his printing press there from Gayndah and renamed his newspaper the *Mount Perry Mail* in which he continued to lambast the local police magistrate and the squattocracy. In October 1872, he reported that the town's population had reached three thousand.[45]

In the late 1860s and early 1870s, there was mining mania throughout Queensland, and the largest mining venture of the era was located at Mount

Perry. Of thirty companies registered in Queensland, according to Mervyn Royle, only the National Bank and the Queensland Insurance Company had a larger nominal capital than the six companies formed to mine copper there.[46] This was despite the vast gold mining projects then underway from Gympie to the Palmer River, as well as the colony's many pastoral and agricultural activities. Given uncertain prices for copper and the very high cost of transport of ore to the coastal ports at least seventy miles away, only mania can explain the rush to form these copper mining companies. Except for one of them, the Normanby Copper Mining Company, which represented significant local squatter investment, the future of the town relied heavily on the major shareholder in all other five companies, Ebenezer Vickery.

The town's population rose and fell with the world price of copper, and by 1876 there were no returns on production. First, wages were reduced, then retrenchments followed. In July the following year, orders came from Sydney for the complete shutdown of the mine and tenders were called by the liquidators. By 1885, the population had dropped below four hundred residents.[47] Some of the miners who remained turned to gold prospecting and for the next decade, gold was of greater importance to the district than copper mining which only recovered at the turn of the century. By then, Mount Perry's population was very small, between two hundred and 250 residents. The town's Chinese population of market gardeners, general labourers, store keepers and carters seems to have fluctuated at the same overall rate. After the second great boom in copper-mining commenced, by 1904, there were twenty-five Chinese among the town's resurgent population of around two thousand, and when mining ceased again, finally, in 1913, there were only two Chinese gardeners left in the town's dwindling population of 1,428.[48]

Chinese market gardens were an established feature of Queensland country towns before the mining boom commenced; as elsewhere in eastern Australia, these gardens grew wherever people settled. Chinese cultivation methods intrigued some of their curious European neighbours, and won reluctant praise, as this account from Toowoomba, the main township for the Darling Downs explains,

> A party of Chinese have lately taken up some land in this town at the foot of Ruthven street, and are cultivating it after their peculiar fashion. They have taken advantage of the fall in the ground to bring the water by a drain of some two hundred yards long to their land, through which it can

be distributed by any required number of channels. These Chinese have thousands of cabbages growing of different ages, so as to meet the market, from the full-grown vegetable nearly as solid as a cannon-ball to the young seedling. The plants are all watered, when necessary, by hand, the channels through which the water runs having hollows sunk in them at every few yards distance for that purpose. Whether or no their system of irrigation be the best that could be devised, it has, at all events, this effect, that it answers the object for which it was intended. There are no cabbages in the district which look so healthy, and none which are so entirely uninfected by the aphis. The Chinamen are able to teach Europeans a lesson in, at all events, growing cabbages. They are considered semi-barbarians, and yet they are able to surpass us in an art the degree of perfection attained in which is usually considered to be the test of the degree of civilisation. We may pride ourselves on being a superior race, but in one respect we are certainly inferior to them. Both in this district and in other parts of Australia they have proved that by the means of artificial irrigation the soil may be cultivated with certainty of profit.[49]

The success that some praised provoked irate envy in others. Chinese achievements in what Englishmen had long regarded as the national pursuit at which they excelled was too confronting for the Maryborough Farmers Society to tolerate, as "A Member" wrote to the editor of the *Chronicle* in April 1869:

Sir,—At the meeting of the Farmers Society the other day, Mr Sheridan, in the course of some remarks anent the pleasures and profits of agri-cum-horticultural pursuits, referring to the Chinese, said "it was a grave reflection on the intelligence and energy of Englishmen that they allowed themselves to be surpassed in the matter of gardening by a tribe of semi-barbarians;" and Mr Howard assured the meeting that said semi-barbarians were making a "pile" by their horticultural speculation—that they had now about four acres under cultivation, from which they were deriving somewhere about £1000 a year! and that their expenses did not exceed £200.[50]

Chinese market gardener delivering vegetables, Bundaberg, c.1880 (FMC, Picture Bundaberg:bun01949)

The anonymous author argued that it was only the "grovelling habits" of the Chinese that enabled them to exist where an Englishman would starve and that if the situations were reversed and the Chinese were to attempt to cultivate a garden in England, "they would [not] be a whit more successful as gardeners there than the English have been and are here." He demanded to know how such a profit could be obtained from the cultivation of four acres of land that less than two years previously had been mere wasteland. A reply came promptly from George Howard who explained further that the Chinese gardeners, in fact, cultivated more than nine acres of land, the remainder worked in a rougher manner with sweet potatoes, corn, pumpkins, and so on. He continued:

> Now, Sir, as I live on the spot, and have an opportunity of observing the never-flagging industry of these peculiar people and considering they work from daybreak to dark, often by moonlight, never indulging in St Monday, the Thursday half-holiday, or eight hours movement, they work every day of the year, Sundays not excepted; moreover, they irrigate their land, having cut a race from a swamp which, if "A Member" had to do a similar job, would make him tremble; they have cut trenches all over the ground, in which the water is continually flowing; they have dug about sixty reservoirs for the purpose of watering their plants, which they do morning, noon and night; they also purchase Peruvian guano at Melbourne at £25 per ton, go miles to gather sheep dung, and make liquid manure; and when we consider that there are eight men in the company who by early and late work and no holidays make out of twelve months at least fifteen;—I must now say that when I made my statement I did not say positively they were taking £1000 worth off the ground, but that it was my firm opinion, and I drew my conclusions from the fact that they grow nearly everything in the shape of vegetables, having such a large market as Maryborough, together with the supply of all the steamers, and sending various vegetables to Gympie; I do not think it is overdrawn to say that they sell £3 worth per day. Now I allowed £200 for their expenses, such as tools, seed, rations, etc., which leaves every man in the company £100

per annum; and, according to the way they work, I do not think any one would say that is too (much)...[51]

It is not possible to know if any of these Chinese gardeners in Toowoomba or Maryborough were former Amoy men. In Mount Perry, however, thanks to Thomas White's fascination with the Chinese from his time recounting their crimes and misdemeanours as indentured pastoral labourers in the *Burnett Argus*, we are able to follow the histories of a few of them in Mount Perry, including Sam Coey/Qui, Peian and Tan Choo/Chew. As Mervyn Royle noted in his history of the shire, the first market garden was established there by 1871. The location of the earliest garden is not recorded, but it may have been on Sunday/Sandy Creek where another celestial gardener, Ah Sam, two years later produced a sweet potato that was "perfectly sound, weighing seventy-two pounds, and several others varying from twelve pounds to twenty-five pounds."[52] Far from the bitter rivalry provoked by Chinese success in the horticultural field in Maryborough, this remarkable vegetable aroused only wonder and amazement in Mount Perry where it was proudly reported, "We have not seen, nor have we heard of its equal in size in any part of the colonies."[53]

Chinese market gardening was a labour-intensive business that was usually carried out by groups of eight or so men, depending on the area they worked. They rented the land, preferably from a naturalized and successful Chinese merchant who had the right to own land, or from a European landlord, and they paid the rates, which gave them the right to vote, at least in municipal elections. It is surprising how uniform this pattern was from the Riverina in southern New South Wales to Cairns in far north Queensland, and towns and small rural communities in between. The 1891 royal commission in New South Wales noted that in the cultivation of vegetables in and around Sydney, the Chinese gardeners had few competitors:

It is apparently their custom to form themselves into syndicates for the leasing and working of suitable land, in some instances in an uncultivated state at the time they enter into possession. By dint of skill and industry they prepare it for planting and, in less than six months cart the first vegetables to market... [I]t is no uncommon thing for each partner, after paying expenses, to put by £50 or £60 a year as his share of the profits.[54]

At the time of that commission, in Sydney's Waterloo district, almost half of the 375 Chinese residents were gardeners; in North Botany, there were fifty-five separate assessments of Chinese gardens in the borough with about two hundred Chinese ratepayers from whom the borough earned £107 7s. in annual rates. One gardener at North Shore had cultivated eight acres for six years at the time of the commission and he paid £44 a year rent. He was assisted by six men whom he paid a weekly wage of £1 with food and board.

By then, the number of Chinese residents in Australia had started to decline markedly. Sub-Inspector Lawless told the 1891 commission that during the previous year, the number in his district of Waterloo had been reduced "something like seventy-five per cent; they have gone back to their own country." In New South Wales that year, almost four thousand of the 13,127 Chinese "breadwinners" in that colony gave their occupation as "market-gardener;" and if "other agriculture" and "greengrocer" were added to the figure, almost half, or 45.5 per cent of the total number were engaged in the cultivation and sale of agricultural produce.[55] In Queensland generally, a little over half, or 50.8 per cent of all Chinese adult males in the colony attributed their earnings to those sectors. There were more Chinese greengrocers than Chinese pastoral workers in Queensland by 1891. In the far north around Cairns, according to Cathie May, they dominated all classes of agriculture except cane-growing by 1886:

> In the district as a whole, they accounted for sixty per cent of all farmers and gardeners and ninety per cent of all indoor agricultural servants... [B]y 1891, they accounted for 73.9 per cent of all cultivators (excluding labourers) with a virtual monopoly in market gardening and fruit growing.[56]

Most Mount Perry townspeople welcomed the company of their Chinese gardeners, and, in turn for this support, the Chinese were generous in their contributions to civic improvements such as the cemetery fence. Therefore, when land agent and auctioneer Edward Stone attempted to purchase a five-acre block of land already occupied as a market garden, he was accused of "land-jobbing" and "jumping a Chinaman's claim" and a petition was drawn up in the town seeking redress for the Chinese gardener.[57] In retaliation, Stone threw back the charge of dummying, based on the frequently held suspicion that all Chinese were secretly under the command of a powerful, distant headman: "Ask any Chinaman who all these gardens in Queensland belong to and he will tell [you] a very rich Chinaman in Sydney, and all these men are in his pay."[58]

In the 1870s, there were two large Chinese gardens in the town worked by several men, and others that were worked individually with paid occasional help from a fellow Chinese labourer. The biggest garden was at Drummer's Creek and when valuations were completed in 1880, one of the first complaints was from Mah Coon protesting the annual rate of £7 10s. levied on the thirty-eight acre selection that his garden occupied.[59] The other garden was next to Martin's Sawmill. As the following paid notice in the local newspaper implies, the gardeners there observed a strict code of behaviour:

> Mrs Bah Goon who got married in Victoria about two years ago and who is now staying near the big Chinaman's Garden next to Martin's Sawmills, is hereby requested to leave off Smoking Opium and Drinking and to keep out of our Garden, and stop making use of bad language.
>
> [Signed] Ah Soy[60]

Mrs Bah Goon was definitely the European spouse of the absent Bah Goon, because there were no Chinese women registered in either the 1871 or the 1876 census for any part of the Wide Bay and Burnett districts. The Mount Perry market gardeners appear to have been confirmed bachelors who were not attracted by the charms of Mrs Bah Goon or the other charms of opium and alcohol.

The original tenants at Drummer's Creek were former Amoy men, Sam Coey/Qui and Tan Choo/Chew. In mid-July 1874, Ah Chew and Ah Qui advertised that they had sold "all our Right, Title and Interest … all the horses, spring cart, saddles, harness, tools, book debts, crops, trees, etc., therein and thereon" to Oy Hong for the sum of fifty pounds.[61] Sam Coey then started up a small wood and charcoal carting business, but the record tells us nothing further about Tan Choo, one of the shepherds who had gained notoriety for assaulting Bertelsen on the Boonara run more than twenty years previously. Oy Hong did not hold the gardening business for long, however, because in October the following year, Mah Coon was in charge at Drummer's Creek. That month, he and two of his helpers, the brothers Ah Poey/Fowey and Ah Walley, were all charged with assaulting Thomas Mason, a selector on the opposite side of the creek whose calves had been trampling their garden. In an altercation, Mason was hit once on the hip with a shovel. Mah Coon and

Ah Walley were fined and cautioned in the Mount Perry Police Court, but Ah Fowey was committed for trial in Maryborough. At the Central District Court in March 1876, he received a sentence of three months' hard labour for grievous bodily harm, a sentence that was said to be lenient in consideration of the "written character" signed by twenty well-known residents at Mount Perry that was handed to the court and the prosecutor's acknowledgement of Ah Fowey's "excellent character."[62]

There is good reason to believe that Pean/John Peang, another Mount Perry gardener, was also Peian, an Amoy man who had served his indenture on a Burnett run in the 1850s. His record is that of a likeable but hapless and perhaps simple-minded character who attracted strife. In September 1868, he was shepherding on Canindah station in the upper Burnett, not far from Yarrol, with Tan Choo. The station overseer had told Peian to change camps, and when he went to collect his swag he met the storekeeper, T. H. Lee, who ordered him to go back without it, then got off his horse, punched Peian in the face and brutally kicked him several times while down. When Tan Choo asked Lee why he had beaten Peian, the man replied that the overseer had told him to do so. He ignorantly repeated this defence in the Gayndah court where he declared that he was only doing his duty to his employer. Lee was fined £5 and court costs.[63] Thomas White of the *Argus* used this brutal attack on Peian to exemplify what he called "the truly British spirit of 'He's a furriner, Bill, 'eave 'alf a brick at um'".[64] At the time, the editor was arguing against the importation of South Sea Islander labour on the grounds that there would be many similar cases of oppression and brutality against them and no efficient protection offered. "Chinamen can take their own part," he reasoned, "Polynesians can't."

In Mount Perry, Peian had a vegetable garden next to Ah Qui's, and kind-hearted local people went out of their way to protect him from himself. In July 1875, he was charged with "having uttered a cheque with the intention to defraud" which in Peian's case meant that he had luckily found a cheque that someone had dropped and he innocently then tried to exchange it for a pair of boots.[65] The man who had drawn the cheque, a butcher, and an employee at the store where Peian had tried to use it in payment both stood sureties for his bail in the Mount Perry Police Court. When the case came up for hearing at the Maryborough District Court in October, the storekeeper was not prepared to swear that Peian ever tendered the cheque in payment. The judge argued that the case had to be founded on whether or not there was intention to defraud and the jury, after deliberating for twenty minutes, found Peian not guilty.[66]

Peian was back in the Mount Perry Police Court just four weeks later. This time he was charged by his neighbour, Ah Lac, a wood carter working for Ah Qui/Sam Coey, with assault. Ah Lac, however, could not speak or understand English and none of the other Chinese in the court would interpret for him. Sam Coey, when called as a witness, gave monosyllabic responses, and eventually the Bench had to dismiss the case because nobody would cooperate. Peian, in good English, then accused the three wood carters, Ah Lac, Sam Coey and Sing, of assaulting him. In his defence, Sing wrote a note that Mah Coon interpreted for the Bench to say that Peian was lying. Peian had said that if he could get £50 for his garden, he would leave Mount Perry and go to the Palmer goldfields. This had led to claim and counter-claim over who owed money to whom until Peian took another beating, this time at the hands of his thoroughly frustrated fellow countrymen.[67] The case was dismissed and all were cautioned about taking the law into their own hands.

CHAPTER 12

Success

The regional studies of Chinese immigrants or long-term sojourners in the self-governing British colonies of eastern Australia during the second half of the nineteenth century, especially those by Cathie May and Shirley Fitzgerald, portray a typical overseas Chinese settlement pattern, commencing with a vanguard of young, mobile, single males, the few most commercially enterprising and successful of whom were later joined by wives from China or married local women and became permanent residents.[1] By dint of tireless effort and sound organization, most managed to carve out a niche for themselves in an alien society while not intruding too closely into competition with the racially dominant white population. In the case of New South Wales and Queensland, this migration pattern was overwhelmingly rural in its location.

The lives of the Amoy men who arrived in the Wide Bay and Burnett districts under contract to European masters fit well with that general description but in many ways their settlement experience was significantly different from that of most other Chinese immigrants before Federation in 1901. Most Chinese in the Australian colonies in the latter half of the nineteenth century, for instance, never worked for Europeans. Dundas Crawford noted this fact in his report to the Foreign Office in 1877:

> In many bizarre branches of trade Chinese are found, as butchers, bakers, hands on back-country stations, cooks on tripang boats, furniture makers, and sometimes as

> contract road labourers; but their employment by masters other than their own countrymen is quite inappreciable, and quite inappreciable their employment, even in tropical Queensland, in any domestic capacity. No Australian capitalist employs Chinese in any manufacture or in any agricultural industry.[2]

He later reiterated this point, stressing that "[t]he employment of Chinese by Australian colonists is limited to a very few instances."[3] Moreover, because of the nature of their trades and businesses, or the way they organized themselves to conduct these occupations, most Chinese never worked alongside Europeans either.

The indentured labourers from Amoy, on the other hand, were employed solely by European masters in Australia, in what for them was a most bizarre industry that was concentrated on one animal, the sheep. Although the social sphere that the Amoy men entered in the mid-nineteenth century may not have been large, and they may not always have been welcome within it, they were indisputably part of the general life on the station where they were indentured for five years. Therefore, when they moved to town after they had completed their contracts, they felt no compulsion to create a separate "Chinatown," as occurred in far north Queensland settlements such as Innisfail and Cairns, or to live as fringe-dwellers in camps consisting of their own countrymen, as they did in the Riverina and western New South Wales.[4] Unlike in other parts of the colonies where the Chinese congregated, there is no evidence that they even built a temple or a meeting hall of their own in the rural towns of Gayndah and Mount Perry. The editor of the *Burnett Argus* welcomed the first Chinese-owned hotel in Gayndah in 1867 because he believed it would give the Chinese residents there a comfortable place to meet, relax, converse in their own language, transact business, and so on, presumably because there was no other place already set aside for those purposes.[5]

Gayndah, in particular, offered opportunity for ambitious Amoy men, once free of their indentures, to follow successful careers in diverse fields of business. As within the wider society, it was up to the legislators and opinion-makers, in this case the notable citizens of the town, who were also the justices of the peace and aldermen, and the editor of the local newspaper to take the lead in admitting the Chinese men as full and active members of the community—or excluding them from it.

Merchants and Townsmen

The Chinese general store was as much a feature of early rural Australian towns as was the Chinese market garden. In Mount Perry, there were four Chinese storekeepers in mid-1875 when continual flooding left the roads in such a bad state that it took drays five weeks to arrive from Bundaberg, the nearest port.[6] In Maryborough's main streets, there were grocery and fruit businesses, cabinet-makers, carpenters and upholsterers, all with Cantonese names on their doors. A Maryborough chemist advertised fresh dugong oil for sale in early 1874, produced by Mr Ching of Ching's Dugong Fishery at Hervey's Bay where he employed Aboriginal labour. "Every portion of the dugong is valuable," the *Maryborough Chronicle* reported,

> The head, when boiled makes a magnificent dish, without any extraneous aid; the flesh, either fresh, salted, or smoked, is preferable to any other description of meat; the bones are equal to African ivory and will readily secure a market, whilst the tusks are pure ivory and very valuable. The entrails are much relished by the blacks and would probably make excellent sausage skins.[7]

Mr Ching's business was a novelty in the Wide Bay district that was not replicated by others, and the trades and businesses in Maryborough town that were run by merchants such as Sun Hop and William Yee, Cantonese attracted to the region by the presence of Chinese diggers on the Mary River goldfields, were already recognizably Chinese enterprises that were, but at the same time were not in direct competition with European equivalents. The British consul, Dundas Crawford observed,

> The daily increasing popularity of their stores for cheap necessaries is viewed with some disfavour by the retail trade; but agents for wholesale firms appreciate the custom engendered by distrust, which obliges the Chinese shopkeeper to pay for his goods on delivery in hard cash; and the public displays little national feeling in the purchase of groceries.[8]

When the Amoy men in the Wide Bay and Burnett districts entered the commercial arena, however, they did so in the expectation that they would be regarded as full equals with others in the existing trade. In Gayndah, with a settled population and an established social order based on squatting interests, two of the former indentured Chinese labourers emerged as leading businessmen. In Maryborough, with a greater social mix and a regular turnover of population, and where some elements such as the cedar-getters had a reputation for rowdy and racist behaviour, the situation for the early Chinese pioneers was a little different, but the personality of the actors was also a factor in winning success and public esteem.

Thomas Ashney arrived in Sydney on the *Nimrod* on October 2, 1848. This was the first ship to bring a cargo of indentured labourers directly from Amoy to New South Wales and Ho Seah was among the sixty-four out of the total consignment of 120 men and boys who were then sent on to Moreton Bay. Ah Seah (the name easily converts to Ashney) never appeared in court, which was the usual way for these men to have their names recorded in history, and it is not known where he completed his indenture but during those five years he seems to have given a lot of thought to his future. Within one year of the completion of his contract, in 1854, he married a Scottish woman, Jemima Wood, in Sydney. The birth of his first child was registered in Gayndah four years later when he gave his occupation as a cook.[9]

On October 16, 1860, he successfully applied for naturalisation. In his memorial to the Governor, he described himself as "a native of China, aged 35, a shearer at Gayndah."[10] He took the oath of allegiance and obtained his certificate of naturalisation on December 29, 1860.[11] For the next six years, little is known of his career but in April 1867, it was reported that he was to be the proprietor of The Mechanic's Arms Hotel in Gayndah. The *Argus* editor believed that this was the first instance of a Chinese publican in Queensland.[12] He gave the "pros and cons" concerning this application, reminding the readers that Chinese public houses in Victoria had been found "very troublesome" to the police on account of gambling, rows, occasional stabbings and a want of cleanliness, but he felt it was

> ... hard to deny to a class, almost equally sober, and quite as industrious as our German fellow-colonists, the right of having a house of call which may be considered a national one, and in which they can unreservedly converse and transact business, without subjecting themselves to the sneers, or open insults, of the lower class of our own

countrymen—ever ready to quarrel with aliens of any kind, and more especially with the Chinese.[13]

In fact, however, it was rowdy New Zealand diggers, not any of the *"mauvais sujets* of the Celestial Empire" or even "the lower class of our own countrymen" about whom Thomas White had warned his readers who raided Ashney's hotel in March the following year, causing considerable damage and robbing the hotel of its liquor supply.[14]

At the end of 1868, the same year as the raid on his hotel, Ashney's wife died, leaving him with the care of his own four small children and responsibility for another. That year, too, his hotel cook, fellow Amoy man, John Uhr also died.[15] Around this time, he seems to have sold his hotel because by early 1871, married once again, he had started a butcher's business in Gayndah and later extended the trade to include the purchase and sale of hides and other by-products of the growing cattle industry in the Burnett. This new venture was reported with praise in the *Maryborough Chronicle*:

> I am given to understand that Mr Thomas Ashney, butcher, of Gayndah, obtained a hawker's license, and that it is his intention to visit the different stations in the district, in the course of his business, and that he intends to purchase hides and other commodities, he having established an agency in Sydney for their sale. To the station holder this will be a great convenience, and to Mr Ashney, it is hoped it will prove remunerative, for he really deserves it. It would be well for this district if we had many humble yet enterprising men such as Mr Thomas Ashney.[16]

These good wishes must have borne fruit because in July 1875, Thomas Ashney advertised that he had much pleasure in informing his old friends and the public of the Burnett district generally that he had purchased the Queensland Hotel from Mr Michael Short which he intended to keep as a first class hotel and had supplied it with "a stack of the Best and Choicest Wines, Spirits, Ales, Porters, Liqueurs, etc., to be had in the colony, and also every other necessary to ensure the comfort of visitors and travellers. Special attention to the comforts and wants of visitors is guaranteed by the careful superintendence of Mrs Ashney. Moderate charges, civility and every attention is 'Tom's Motto.' Billiard Bagatelle Table on the premises."[17] Two years later, in 1877, Thomas Ashney was elected an alderman of the municipality of Gayndah. Between 1880 and 1885, he became a major property owner in Mount Perry with more than twenty town allotments registered in his name. He died in 1908, aged 76 (or 83 if measured by the age given on his naturalisation certificate), in Roma.

Another Amoy man, John Deian, married the half-sister of Thomas Ashney's first wife in Gayndah in August 1860.[18] The same month, he submitted his application for naturalisation. In his memorial, he described himself as a native of Amoy, aged 29 and a butcher in Gayndah. He had arrived in Moreton Bay among 108 indentured labourers on the *Favourite* (ex-*Cadet* from Amoy and Sydney) in May 1850 and, like Ashney, moved to the Gayndah district after he completed his contract. He must have made an early favourable impression in the town because his application for naturalisation was supported in those difficult times by some of the leading Gayndah citizens, including John Connolly and Doctor Stevenson. He took the oath of allegiance in Gayndah on October 1, 1860.

At the time of his death in August 1867, aged only 36, he owned several stores and other premises in the town, some of which he rented to fellow Amoy men, including the butchers Tan Chan and Tan Yang. His widow died the following year, leaving a young daughter whom Thomas Ashney promised to care for.[19] In the Northern District Court a year after Deian's death, Julop/Ju Lock claimed that he had lent Deian various sums of money in 1864, 1865, and 1867, totalling £220.[20] He had requested repayment from the executors but they had not refunded any portion of that debt. He argued that he had an account of the loans in his book which was kept on his behalf by Deian's Chinese clerk, James Tongo. Tongo's evidence, however, was not reliable because he had been dismissed by Deian for embezzlement—he was on bail when Deian died so the case did not proceed—and there was naturally suspicion of collusion between Julop and Tongo. The matter was resolved when Duncan McNee, an accountant, took the stand and verified that a document acknowledging the debt, signed by Deian and seen by the court had been prepared by him at the request of Mr and Mrs Deian and that on one occasion, Deian had admitted owing Julop "plenty money." He told the court that Deian was "a very respectable man—he was a Chinaman." The court ruled in Julop's favour, but the case dragged on until September 1873 when the Supreme Court of Queensland finally ruled on the sale of property from the estate.[21]

These cases are interesting because they reveal how enterprising former shepherds managed to succeed in an alien environment, where they found the start-up capital to build businesses with the same value as European businesses, how they were prepared to lower their status from publican to common hawker in order to rise to a higher level of prosperity, and how trust among compatriots could not always be relied upon. Their standing in the European community was vitally important to their success but of equal importance was their loyalty to the fraternity of Amoy men.

James (Con) Chiam was an entirely different sort of man from Ashney and Deian. While recognized by other Maryborough citizens as very intelligent and even charismatic, he was also impulsive, hot-headed, and more than a little obsessive. He arrived on one of Robert Towns' vessels, *Ganges*, that docked in Sydney with 213 men on January 26, 1852 and commenced his five-year contract on Boondooma station only three days later. Like Peian, he was saved from his own shortcomings by the intervention of both loyal compatriots and some tolerant Europeans. Chiam was arrested in May 1854 for firing a gun at other Chinese labourers on the run "with intent" and spent six weeks in the Gayndah lock-up before the matter was judged an old quarrel and the case was dismissed.[22] Greater harm was avoided on that occasion because Tan Chan, already an old hand with three years' experience of European ways, had warned the superintendent that there was going to be a "row" and together they took steps to prevent the matter from getting out of hand.[23] Chiam must have realized how fortunate he had been because once back on Boondooma, he took responsibility for a huge flock of more than two thousand sheep and quickly repaid his advance. From this first brush with the law, he seems to have developed a fascination with and a deep faith in the British justice system.

Given time spent in gaol that had to be made up, Chiam would have completed his indenture in March 1857. It seems that he moved to Maryborough soon after that because in December he was in custody there, this time for having assaulted a "respectable married woman" with the intent to commit a rape.[24] According to the press, "The charge of assault was fully made out, notwithstanding the prisoner's original style of cross-examination." John Jan/Tan Chan, the same former Amoy shepherd on Boondooma who had informed on him to the superintendent in 1854, was sworn as interpreter in this case that was judged in the Moreton Bay Supreme Court. Once again, Chiam proved to be lucky in court; he was found guilty of the lesser charge of common assault and was sentenced to four months' imprisonment

Ashney family grave, Gayndah Cemetery, and memorial to Thomas Ashney.

Mary Ann Sooti, née Channer, eldest child of Tan Chan, with
daughters Jessie Rowe Channer and Grace Sooti.

in Brisbane Gaol. Within a week of the end of that (second) gaol term, on September 6, 1858, James Chiam took the oath of allegiance in Maryborough as a naturalized citizen, the first of the Amoy men in the Burnett and Wide Bay districts to do so.

Maryborough held its first municipal elections in 1861. The decision to incorporate the town had been hotly debated and the atmosphere surrounding the elections was volatile. Four of the elected aldermen, including the mayor, resigned before the end of the year, the first of them within a month of being elected. James Chiam was present and outspoken at the first meeting to replace an alderman, and a few months later was himself nominated to fill a vacant seat on the council. Surprisingly, once again, his prison record was not held against him. One correspondent to the *Maryborough Chronicle* encouraged voters to elect him despite his nefarious past:

A comparison of my friend, the Chinaman's, past character with that of the present Municipal body will, I maintain, tell in his favour. True, he once in an unguarded moment acted the Lothario character, and for that trifling act of gallantry suffered durance. But his past career amongst us is free from those charges—unfortunately too well-founded—of plodding self-interest ...[25]

Another correspondent, however, advised caution:

I do not object to Mr James Chiam because he is a naturalized Chinaman, for I consider him superior in the social and intellectual scale to some of his supporters and to many among those who affect to be horrified at the possibility of contaminating the sang azul of that very mixed race, the Anglo-Saxon, with a Mongolian strain. But I do object to him because, as he understands but little of our language and still less of our institutions, he will find it very difficult to understand and assist in the deliberations of our councillors and to appreciate the details of duty which the position of an Alderman imposes.[26]

James Chiam was elected to the council by an overwhelming majority. His prepared speech was read for him because the one he addressed was delivered "in a dialect peculiarly his own," but it provides a rare insight into how the Amoy men regarded life in the colonies:[27]

> I am told by my friends that some are trying to make a tool of me. They tell you wrong. My reasons for coming before you were these:- I am now eleven years in the colonies; I found your Government good and, not like all my countrymen, I have spent my money in your land, built houses, and bought property from you, and have been duly recognized and granted the benefits of the Queen's subjects and cannot now go back to my own country; and as such subject I will do my best by attention, industry and honesty, to attend to the true wishes of the ratepayers of Maryborough... The working men—the true representatives of honesty and free labour have returned me, and they well may be proud for the honour is theirs, not mine; for by keeping together they can always have their own true man to represent them. Hurrah for the Queen!

Before a new council was elected in February the following year, James Chiam along with another alderman retired, by rotation, thus ending his brief political career.

Despite his success as a businessman and his election to local office, Chiam never earned the genuine respect from Europeans that his compatriots Ashney and Deian in Gayndah did. He seems to have been constantly in court, either in the Court of Requests, claiming payment for cartage or rent, or being prosecuted for loans of relatively small amounts of money that he, in turn, pleaded not indebted; he was even charged before the Bench with keeping a ferocious dog, and for carting without a licence. Many of these charges were petty and spiteful and most were dismissed. Two further charges of assault that were brought against him were also overturned. Overall, therefore, his record makes for uncomfortable reading. Despite his best efforts, his obviously high intelligence and his considerable commercial success, he never genuinely assimilated and was kept at arm's length by the general community of Maryborough. James Chiam died in January 1883, aged 51, and was buried in the Maryborough cemetery.

Organization

The suspicion that Chinese immigrants were organized according to the rules and rituals of secret societies was commonplace in late nineteenth century Australian society. The media enjoyed exploring the potential criminality of such associations and the imagined ulterior purposes of the joss house. At the height of anti-Chinese hysteria, in 1874, the New South Wales parliament established a select committee to investigate and make a report on common lodging-houses that, for years after its publication, according to Phil Griffiths, was used in parliamentary debates and public meetings to prove the immorality and viciousness of Chinese men.[28] The falsity of these lurid claims was proved by the 1891 report by a royal commission that was appointed to inquire into those issues surrounding alleged organized gambling and immorality among the Chinese communities in Sydney.[29] Although this latter report produced little positive effect on public opinion at the time, it provides historians with a many-sided view of the lifestyles of Chinese men in the city at the end of the nineteenth century from which details might be extrapolated to the long-established communities of Chinese men elsewhere in the country.

The Chinese labour recruits had survived the nightmare conditions on board ship from Amoy by assigning roles and duties to one another, and as indentured labourers on the Burnett runs, they had organized themselves effectively almost from the outset. The strikes and walk-outs they staged in 1851 and 1852, and their acts of civil disobedience once inside prison, demonstrated clever mobilization on their part; and all the events surrounding the murder of Johnny/Chow in the Gayndah boarding-house and Deong's subsequent trial further displayed their solidarity and efficient crisis management. In fact, it was their habit of organization bound by mateship, not membership of any specific society or clan association, which supported the Burnett Chinese throughout the thirty years from 1850 to 1880. Their numbers were too small and scattered, and the clan groupings on any one run were too insignificant to allow them to derive much benefit from traditional guilds and associations. The deeply-ingrained cultural habits of good organization and mutual support proved to be essential for their later well-being and success.

The indenture system left little room for organization along traditional southern Chinese lines. Clan loyalty was difficult to maintain when ten or so young men found themselves randomly allocated to an employer on a remote run, and then sent individually to an out-station with only one or two other countrymen for company. In such circumstances, they were fortunate to be partnered with someone who at least could communicate in the same or similar dialect, let alone one who shared the same clan identity. This did not mean that clan rivalry and vendettas were left behind in China. It is more than likely that the shooting incident involving James Chiam that occurred on Boondooma in 1854 was clan-related. Such matters would have been incomprehensible to any Gayndah bench of magistrates, but the fact that the case was judged to be an "old quarrel" suggests a cause deeper than merely a gambling dispute. Dundas Crawford believed that the Chinese in Australia kept these matters in check because of their "great respect for the local authorities and fear of the constabulary" despite the "rivalry of race between Hakka and Punti, and in spite of feuds maintained merely on the score of geographical position, chiefly between the Cantonese and the natives of Fuhkeen (Fujian), these last carrying their animosities further to their own provincials, village against village …".[30]

The difficulties they encountered during their indentures, especially problems related to work conditions, payment and punishment, cut across these traditionally-held animosities and instead fostered solidarity and fraternity that stood them in good stead once they were free to choose their own place of work. As James Chiam's speech to his constituents suggests, they also developed a working-class consciousness that may also have assisted their efforts to integrate with the broader community. Several examples have already been given of pairs of men who worked together for years on stations in the Burnett. The 1861 trial of Deong for the murder of his close friend and old work-partner, Chow/Johnny, also demonstrated how loyalty to each other and to old values was sometimes at odds with their new reality and their aim to conform. The special court interpreter brought from Sydney for the trial broke down and was found to be incapable of putting proper questions, so the trial was tainted with the suspicion of collusion among the key witnesses and deliberate confusion by the interpreter. In the general population, this sort of behaviour gave rise to genuine concern about the involvement of Chinese secret societies and protection of members from the due process of the law. On the other hand, it was James Chiam who first alerted the Gayndah police to the case, at the prompting of Tan Chan who had made a special trip to Maryborough for that purpose, and who objected so vociferously when a mistrial was called that he himself was threatened with imprisonment for contempt of court. It was Tan Chan who, back in 1854, had informed on James Chiam in relation to the shooting incident, which was an early break with a strong tradition that would normally have invited serious reprisals.

The 1891 royal commission in Sydney into alleged Chinese immorality and gambling made very clear how Chinese interpreters and informants to the police were regarded by other Chinese. These were potentially dangerous roles to play. Among the Burnett and Wide Bay Chinese, however, if anyone bore a grudge against a fellow Chinese complainant, there is no record that he acted upon it. When necessary, they charged one other with crimes like assault, theft and embezzlement and seem to have been satisfied with the court's rulings. The relationship between James Chiam and Tan Chan, however, must have been a deep one because, despite (or because of) the Boondooma incident, Chiam called on him to act as interpreter in court when he was charged with attempted rape in Maryborough in late 1857. The men were obviously from different clans, so that is not sufficient reason to explain the bond that persisted between them. One obvious bond that did tie them, however, was their shared Christian faith.[31]

Several of the Amoy men were, or professed to be Christian. Dundas Crawford regarded these conversions as purely pragmatic:

> Only about eight per cent of Chinese immigrants embrace Christianity, and these generally on account of unions with Christian women desirous of having their children baptized.[32]

Little is known of the interior life of the men who arrived in New South Wales from Amoy as indentured labourers, apart from that very brief electoral victory speech prepared by James Chiam. The same has to be said about the thousands of Chinese who arrived in search of gold, so Crawford's unfounded assumption about religious motives must be regarded simply as that. There are, however, some facts. In the court record, the source of most available information about the Amoy men, the manner of swearing the oath identified some of them as Christian many years before any of them could have married those "Christian women" referred to by Dundas Crawford. Most of the Chinese who appeared in court performed a strange ritual that seems to have been devised solely for practice in the Australian colonies: that is, they blew out a candle or a match, or broke a saucer by kneeling on it, supposedly to signify the extinction or destruction of the soul if they broke their word and lied to the court. The few who took the Christian oath were almost without exception the interpreters.

In most court cases, the interpreters were "regulars" or acquaintances of the accused. In the early years, the two Amoy men most frequently called to assist the Brisbane Bench or the Police Court were Gan Som and Tinko. In his first appearance in court, Gan Som charged his employer, Henry Hockings of South Brisbane, with assault.[33] Hockings had invited Gan Som to accompany him to a Sunday church service, but Gan Som said that he preferred going to chapel where he could understand the minister more clearly. On that court occasion, Gan Som took the Chinese "oath" but it is obvious from the circumstances of the case that he was, if not already Christian, then certainly interested in becoming one. Tinko was clearly identified in the colonial press as "a baptised Chinaman in Mr Prior's employ."[34] He assisted in the trial of Angee for the murder of the overseer Halbert, a capital offence.

Another Amoy interpreter for important court cases was Charles Dean.[35] He was called to interpret in the criminal sittings of the Supreme Court in Brisbane in August 1859 when the judge was not satisfied that the nominated interpreter, Teecne, "a very intelligent countryman of the prisoner," could understand English sufficiently and Charles Dean replaced him, satisfying His Honour "not only as to the language but the Christian Faith."[36] At the same sittings, Dean also interpreted for Loy who was charged with setting fire to the house in Ipswich of John Sim ("Christian for two years") that was used in part as a home for Chinese when sick. Sim and another Chinese had bought the property for "Chinese in the bush." It was judged at that trial that the prisoner was "cranky" and known to be so by a number of Chinese.[37] The most important case for which Dean was called upon to act as interpreter was that of the dangerously insane Kimboo/Champoo for the murder on the Downs of Garrick Burns.

It is probably no coincidence that those with most proficiency in English were also Christian converts, or, for that matter that these men married European women. Protestant missionaries who proselytised among the indigenous peoples of the Wide Bay and Burnett districts no doubt felt the same compulsion towards the Chinese indentured labourers, and they would undoubtedly have provided language training along with religious instruction. Those young men who reflected on their experience in the colonies and who saw opportunity as permanent residents were also the most likely to persevere with learning the language and to engage with other aspects of the target culture. Their willingness to behave as Europeans, however, did not isolate them from other Chinese, nor did it require them to abandon all their Chinese ways. On the contrary, their perceived better understanding of Europeans made them a valuable resource for those who retained old habits and past affiliations.

Some of the Burnett and Wide Bay Chinese were almost certainly members of the Heaven and Earth Society (*tiandihui*) known commonly as the Sheathed Sword or Small Sword Society, simply because the members were generally provided with knives or small swords. Young men from the Amoy region of Fujian province were practically born into this society. Dundas Crawford argued that no other association had the same preponderating influence of the sworn fraternity of the Sheathed Sword and he described its origins as religious:

> Its creed, founded on the correlation of heaven, earth, and man, and free from the idylls and idols of Buddist (sic) and Taoist superstition, gives expression to a simple faith in a triple bond between man, the dead below, and the life above. Its observances, like those of an Italian "confraternità," resolve themselves chiefly into a public regard for the rites of burial and revenue for the dead...[38]

For overseas Chinese, as those called to give evidence before the 1891 royal commission in Sydney maintained, the main purpose of this society was supporting the sick and elderly and returning the bones of the dead for burial in ancestral villages. In Fujian, however, when the young Amoy men were preparing to travel to Australia in the early 1850s, it was politically and actively committed to the overthrow of the Qing dynasty. An American missionary in Amoy who lived through an insurrection there in 1853 claimed that the whole populace for miles around Amoy appeared to sympathize with the movement.[39] Once they arrived in the Burnett district or elsewhere on the Australian frontier, however, the strictures placed on leaving the run to visit other indentured Chinese on neighbouring runs would no doubt have dampened efforts to sustain the driving force behind these associations, and time and other contingencies would have worn away their enthusiasm for a distant political cause. As researchers have noted, the Sheathed Sword Society eventually affiliated with the widespread Masonic Society in Australia which, in terms of ritual and the guiding principles of fraternity and solidarity, should have made for a comfortable union.

It is impossible to know if any of the secret societies were active among the Burnett and Wide Bay Chinese, if only for the purpose of mutual assistance.

There was the boarding house in Ipswich owned by John Sim and a partner that served as a kind of hospice for the elderly and infirm Chinese, and it is probably not a coincidence that for many years the sole Chinese woman counted in the Queensland census was a resident of Ipswich. Whether or not these associations existed, the absence of women must have affected their capacity to care for those unable to care for themselves. From the available evidence, it seems that they generally supported each other, but the vagrants and lunatics among their number were left to the services of the penal system, and several of the sick and impoverished older men committed or at least attempted suicide because they could no longer support themselves and presumably received no assistance from other Chinese. As for the separate function of returning the remains of the dead to China, there is only one recorded case in the Burnett district of human remains being exhumed for shipment to China; that was from the Mount Perry cemetery in 1911 and it was probably too late by then to have had any connection with the indentured labourers from Amoy.[40]

It is hard to imagine that the Amoy men did not celebrate the most important Chinese festivals and observe the most fundamental rituals. We know from Teang's error about the date his contract expired that they kept note of the days and the passage of time, but there is nothing in the record that suggests that they openly practised their culture. Above all, they should have observed the proper rites for the dead but apart from a few men who married European women and received a Christian burial in a Christian cemetery, the graves of the Amoy men are generally not marked.[41] Several of those indentured on runs in the Burnett and Wide Bay districts were killed in aboriginal attacks, one was executed in Brisbane Gaol, a couple drowned, more than one was murdered by a compatriot, a few "absconded" and were presumed lost in the bush, four or five committed suicide, and undoubtedly others died of accidents, snake bite, and illness but today there is little trace of where they were buried.

It seems that in relation to funerals at least, they were not alone in their neglect. Dundas Crawford found that the Funeral Associations' Hall, related to the Sheathed Sword Society in Cooktown, the town and port for the Palmer River gold rush, showed little zeal regarding funerals. "Usually these have been left to be arranged by the local hospital," he noted, "and the expenses defrayed by the coroner or the police, on the representation that deceased had no estate."[42] He believed that it was the case throughout Australia that the Chinese usually received a pauper burial. On Boondooma, however, there is still a memory of upright posts with Chinese symbols drawn on them to mark graves, and what are undoubtedly tall tales of Aboriginal people deliberately killing Chinese shepherds on the run in order to take advantage of the food offerings left for the spirits of the dead.[43]

The former indentured labourers from Amoy displayed strong characteristics of independence and individuality, which is seemingly at odds with the studies of Chinese men who came to the colonies of eastern Australia during the gold rushes and then joined the rural economy typically as members of work gangs that shared accommodation in camps on the outskirts of rural towns and performed local jobs contracted through resident Chinese merchants with landowners. In the Riverina and western districts of New South Wales, apart from market gardening which was also a communal occupation, several thousand Chinese men were employed in land clearing. Referring to the Brennan report, Barry McGowan notes that there were over one thousand Chinese labourers in the Riverina area alone.[44] Extensive land clearing work for the pastoral industry was conducted throughout the 1880s in western New South Wales by these teams of highly organized Chinese all the way from the Riverina to the Queensland border. Their equipment, supplies and transport were provided by Chinese merchants in the towns. In far north Queensland, in the Cairns district, the Chinese were also "in effect, a mobile land clearing machine."[45] Cathie May argues that the Chinese there were almost solely responsible for opening up the land and her description of their labour organization in tree-felling, cane-cutting, and the banana industry as well as the special economic relationship between storekeeper and contract commission agent bears strong similarities with that given by Barry McGowan. She notes, however, that while some aspects of traditional social organization were observed among the Chinese residents in the north, in other ways they were required to adapt to local circumstances:

> Despite enduring loyalty to China and its culture the immigrants were not able to completely replicate Chinese society overseas. Important components of everyday life, and indeed the whole framework of social organization, were absent anywhere outside the native village. Other unsettling factors were the artificial age and sex structure of the emigrant communities, the inter-mixture of diverse groups in one locality, and the economic exigencies of the host country.[46]

The size of the immigrant society was also an obvious determining factor in the extent to which they could maintain their traditions. In the Gayndah area, although the Chinese population there was large in proportion to the general European population, it was small in actual numbers, and too small to have allowed for economies of scale in labour organization along the lines described in those studies by Cathie May and Barry McGowan. There were, as already noted, the ten Chinese shearers on Booubyjan, but if even if they were organized as a regular team, it is impossible to imagine that they were organized externally. There is no evidence at all that the Amoy men ever attempted or even wanted to replicate Chinese society in the Burnett. Once they had overcome the hurdles involved in the early stages of adapting to the local culture, they seem to have relished the adventure, freedom and opportunity that frontier life offered them. In this respect, they were not essentially different from the other pioneers of the Burnett and Wide Bay districts who, like them, were for the most part also young, male, single, and enterprising.

Love

In the very personal business of finding a marriage partner, these young men who had been successful in organizing other aspects of their lives despite the obvious cultural difficulties, met their biggest challenge. Involved in the effort of attracting a potential spouse was a plethora of unforeseen and largely unknowable rules and sexual taboos of Victorian colonial society that they somehow had to overcome.

Given the demographic circumstances of rural Queensland around the time of Separation, the chances of a former indentured Chinese labourer finding himself a spouse were even more remote than his location. As late as the Queensland census of 1876, when even the youngest of the Amoy men would have been over forty years old, the number of males was still nearly double that of the females in those areas where the Amoy men were concentrated, namely the Darling Downs (North and East), the Leichhardt, Wide Bay, and Burnett districts; but the disproportion between the sexes was only among the adult population where the ratio was much higher. There were exactly thirteen Chinese women in Queensland that year, and not one of them was a resident in any of those districts where the Amoy men lived. Add to those almost insurmountable barriers, the others of language, custom, religion, and race, and it is clear that the chances of an Amoy man marrying were practically nil. The majority of them, like the market gardeners of Mount Perry, seemed content to accept the life of confirmed bachelors. The most ambitious and successful among them, however, did marry European women and, in Thomas Ashney's case, married again after the death of his first wife. The three men already discussed, Ashney, Deian and Chiam, along with David Deong were all naturalized just before changes to the Aliens Act in Queensland in 1861 (25 Vic., No. 9) made naturalisation, and thus the right to ownership of real property, contingent on marriage to a naturalized resident. After this date, marriage was essential to fulfilling ambitions for a conventionally successful life.

Marriage, admittedly, was not only for the purposes of naturalisation, property ownership, and dreamed-of prosperity. Nevertheless, after August 1861, for those Amoy men who had been in the colony for at least ten years and who wished to remain and to enjoy the privileges bestowed on British subjects, marriage was a pre-requisite for naturalisation. Between October 1861 and June 1867, a further (at least) thirteen Amoy men took the oath of allegiance before the police magistrates in Gayndah and Maryborough, the majority of them signing before John O'Connell Bligh who sometimes also stood as guardian and gave consent for their brides to be married if they happened to be under the age of majority.[47] Throughout the 1860s, campaigns to attract single female domestic servants from England, Scotland, and Ireland to rural Queensland were moderately successful and it was among these young women that most of the Chinese men found marriage partners. It is also a well-attested fact that Chinese men entered into informal married relationships with Aboriginal women. In the Burnett district, this history is recorded on the museum map of the former mission at Cherbourg on Barambah Creek with the area designated for what were colloquially termed "Chinarigines."[48] There is so far, however, insufficient research to trace specific Amoy men to descendants among the indigenous communities of the Burnett district. In the years before the "Aboriginals Protection and Restriction of the Sale of Opium Act 1897" (61 Vic., No. 17) made it illegal for Chinese men to cohabit with Aboriginal women and to employ Aboriginal labour, according to Guy Ramsay, the two cultures were drawn together by "their common experience of marginalisation from White society."[49]

Finding a partner among the dominant white society for these young Chinese men was fraught with unknown complications and risks. During the 1860s and until the mid-1870s attitudes towards race and cohabitation between races were still relatively liberal. From what has already been quoted from reports in the Burnett and Wide Bay presses, xenophobia—that "'eave 'alf a brick at 'um" reaction towards non-Europeans—was not uncommon, and successful foreigner competition in areas of business and expertise normally regarded as British preserves was resented. Miscegenation was frowned upon, but no doubt it was frowned upon more or less in equal measure by all races. All of these base instinctual responses to peoples of other ethnicities were complicated by class relations and, of course, by rumour, hearsay, and the sometimes sensationalist reports of violence and misdeeds committed by or against the Chinese that occurred elsewhere in the colonies. However, until these largely unconscious undercurrents within the white population were orchestrated and exaggerated for political purposes, starting from the mid-1870s and later institutionalised by the White Australia policy, the marriage of young European women to Chinese and Islander men was likely to be a matter for curiosity and goodwill comment rather than execration, at least in educated circles.[50]

Occasionally, however, insults towards the young wives of Chinese men warranted hearings by the bench. These insults could come from either side. In 1865, for example, Anna Thue, wife of a Gayndah Chinese businessman, charged another Gayndahite with making use of abusive and threatening language.[51] Her own witness did not attend the court but the defendant's did and swore that no bad language was used. Consequently, a disgruntled Anna Thue was charged court costs and expenses for the defendant's witness. At the South Brisbane races in early 1859, however, when Elizabeth Juwang took offence at indecent and insulting language used towards her by "a Chinaman," the defendant said he was drunk and had no memory of the incident. On that occasion, the bench ordered that his memory be refreshed with a fine and costs.[52] These court reports were generally written in a lightly mocking tone that suggested these young wives were quite capable of defending themselves and that it was ultimately the "celestial spouse" who deserved the reader's sympathy.

District newspapers occasionally carried items from the southern presses that must have affected public opinion concerning local Chinese residents and created fear around some disturbing incidents that occurred in their own community. These reports usually concerned the alleged sexual abuse of young European women, sometimes girl children, by Chinese men.[53] After 1875, stories of moral depravity among the Chinese in Victoria and New South Wales would become genuinely racist and hysterical, but before all that there were two incidents, one in Maryborough in 1863 and the other in Gayndah in 1870 that were strangely prescient and their investigations remained unexplained and unresolved.

In September 1863, the chief constable at Maryborough was charged with unlawfully celebrating the marriage of an underage girl to a Chinese man named Samuel Sue.[54] The girl, aged thirteen, had made a false declaration about her age before the district registrar, and, in the very careful wording of the press report, it appears that she had been introduced to Sue by another Chinese man and his European wife. It is possible that this disturbing case was settled out of court because although it was set down for hearing at the Assizes early the following year, none of the parties appeared in court on that occasion and no further reference was made to it. The second incident occurred in Gayndah in 1870 at the boarding house for Chinese men run by Anna Thue and her husband.[55] The alleged crime was the rape of a ten-year old nursemaid and the accused was George Sin/Sing who had lived in Gayndah for seventeen or eighteen years and had no previous offence; he pleaded not guilty and was undefended in court. The jury at his trial found him guilty of the lesser charge of attempted rape with a recommendation for mercy. Between the end of the trial and the judgement, however, the crown prosecutor declared that certain circumstances had come to his knowledge that threw grave doubts on the reliability of the evidence produced in court. An additional circumstance, that the prisoner was a man of good character, had emerged since the conclusion of the trial but because the prisoner had been undefended, this had not been elicited by evidence. In view of all this, the accused man who had already spent two months in detention was released. The editor of the *Maryborough Chronicle* expressed relief at the decision of the court but he was highly critical of the prosecution "so loosely conducted, and resulting in a conviction so unwarranted by the evidence."[56] He referred to a similar case where an indigenous man, Jacky Whitton, was found guilty of rape "on evidence very similar, and in the opinion of many persons, quite as little to be trusted, as that given in Sing's case," he noted. In that instance, the condemned man was hanged, leading the editor to regret, "We are sorry to have to suggest the odious hypothesis that the colour of Jacky Whitton's skin may have had something to do with stifling that tender regard for the interests of a criminal which was so conspicuously visible in George Sing's case." It is remarkable, in light of the anti-Chinese hysteria that gripped Australia later in the century, that the colour of George Sing's skin was either disregarded or overlooked in that carefully reasoned editorial.

By 1880, the shepherds from Amoy, who had arrived in the Wide Bay and Burnett districts simply as items of cheap pastoral labour thirty years before, had thoroughly adapted to colonial life in rural Queensland. They were then permanent members of a society that they had helped to create. Having been brought to the frontier districts to work for the first pioneers, they had become pioneers themselves. Throughout the early difficult years of indenture, they had displayed courage and tenacity at work, and defiance when treated unjustly. They also proved willing to learn and master strange new skills and habits. These were qualities that were appreciated by the receiving society. This appreciation was expressed by the leaders of those societies, and the other community members, for the most part, followed suit. Some of the Amoy men eventually ranked among the most prosperous and influential citizens of the district townships. Overall, theirs was a story of successful immigration.

After 1880, Australia changed radically. This was not simply the socio-economic change of population movements from bush to coast, or of the shift to agricultural settlement at the expense of the pastoral life. The change was overwhelmingly political and attitudinal, and as the voices of vested interests clamoured for attention, the shrillest cries were all about race. Life would prove to be more difficult for the children of the Amoy men than it had been for their fathers. Australian-born but relegated socially by degrees of racial "purity," they would suffer the indignity of witnessing their father's name placed on an index of aliens resident in White Australia and their own exclusion from areas of life in which their fathers had freely participated.

For indigenous Australians, of course, the consequences of a national policy of racial discrimination were infinitely more painful and destructive but within their own families and communities too, Chinese ancestry was a well-kept and shameful secret. As Guy Ramsay observed in his conversations with contemporary descendants of Aboriginal and Chinese unions, what he terms the "reassertion of White dominion" came at great cost, as one of his respondents explained:

> Dad never spoke about nothing… We're all born with all this long hair and Asian look about us, all of us in the family, and we're trying to figure where it came from. We all look at each other and think there's got to be something there… I don't know why he never spoke of it or told us about it. I couldn't question that either… I did ask my grandmother but I suppose you're to be seen and not heard in some things… I

      probably'll have questions on my lips for the rest of my life
      until I find out.[57]

    The shame and the loss resulting from the politically motivated policies of racial subjugation would haunt Australians for generations and leave an indelible stain on the nation's reputation.

Notes

Chapter 1

[1] Karl Polanyi, *The Great Transformation: The Political and Economic Origins of Our Time* (Beacon Hill: Beacon Press, 1957 [1944]), p. 159.

[2] Jack Gratus, *The Great White Lie: Slavery, Emancipation, and Changing Racial Attitudes* (New York: Monthly Review Press, 1973), p. 249.

[3] David Northrup, *Indentured Labor in the Age of Imperialism, 1834-1922* (New York: Cambridge University Press, 1995), p. 4.

[4] Douglas Hay and Paul Craven, eds, *Masters, Servants, and Magistrates in Britain & the Empire, 1562-1955* (Chapel Hill and London: The University of North Carolina Press, 2004), p. 4.

[5] Strictly speaking, indentured labourers did not replace either slaves or convicts as, in many places, they worked alongside freed slaves and ex-convicts. It is more accurate to say that they filled the labour gap that resulted from the almost simultaneous cessation of both slavery and transportation.

[6] Stanley L. Engerman, "Servants to Slaves to Servants: contract labour and European expansion", in P. C. Emmer, ed., *Colonialism and Migration: Indentured Labour Before and After Slavery*. Comparative Studies in Overseas History (Dordecht: Martinus Nijhoff Publisher, 1986), p. 267.

[7] In French Indochina, Tonkinese indentured labourers worked on the rubber plantations of Cochinchina and Cambodia that were developed there at the turn of the twentieth century. Tonkinese also laboured on copra plantations and tin mines in French possessions in the South Pacific up to the end of the Second World War. See Margaret Slocomb, *Colons and Coolies: the Development of Cambodia's Rubber Plantations* (Bangkok: White Lotus, 2007) and Miriam Meyerhoff, "A vanishing act: Tonkinese migrant labour in Vanuatu in the early 20th century", *The Journal of Pacific History*, v. 37, no. 1, June 2002, pp. 45-56.

8   Hay and Craven, eds, *Masters, Servants, and Magistrates...*, p. 25.

9   *Ibid.*, p. 4.

10   *Ibid.*, p. 26.

11   *Ibid.*, fn. 2, p. 4.

12   *Ibid.*, p. 32.

13   *Ibid.*, p. 33.

14   *Ibid.*, p. 32.

15   Peter Corris, *Passage Port and Plantation: A History of Solomon Islands Labour Migration 1870-1914* (Sydney: Melbourne University Press, 1973), p. 2.

16   *Ibid.*, p. 43.

17   "Exeter Hall" was a shorthand reference to evangelical and reformist groups in England such as the Anti-Slavery Society, the Aborigines Protection Society and the London Missionary Society.

18   Engerman, "Servants to Slaves to Servants...", p. 272.

19   *Ibid.*, p. 270.

20   *Ibid.*, p. 272.

21   Northrup, *Indentured Labour...*, Appendix, Table A.1 "Decadal exports of indentured migrants by origins, showing intended destinations, 1831-1920".

22   See graph in Northrup, *Indentured Labor...*, p. 107.

23   Paul Bailey, "Recruitment of Workers for Britain and France" in Lynn Pan, general editor, *The Encyclopedia of the Chinese Overseas*, second edition (Singapore: Editions Didier Millet, 2006), pp. 64-65. For a detailed study of Chinese indentured labour for war purposes, see Xu Guoqi, *Strangers on the Western Front: Chinese Workers in the Great War* (Cambridge, Mass.: Harvard University Press, 2011).

24   Northrup, *Indentured Labor...*, pp. 65-67. His figures for Indian external migrants for the period 1838 to 1924 add up to 6,574,800, including 5,239,00 involved in "regional migration" to Burma, Ceylon and Malaya. He terms the remaining 1,335,800 as "intercontinental indentured".

25   E. Van Den Boogaart and P. C. Emmer, "Colonialism and migration: an overview", in P. C. Emmer, ed., *Colonialism and Migration...*, p. 12.

26   *Ibid.*, p. 13.

27   Zhu Guohong, in Lynn Pan, gen. ed., *The Encyclopedia of the Chinese Overseas*, p. 62. Wang Singwu estimates the number of Chinese emigrating abroad between 1840 and 1900 at close to 2.35 million, 1.54 million of them to Southeast Asian destinations. See Wang Singwu, *The Organization of Chinese Emigration 1848-1888: With Special Reference to Chinese Emigration to Australia* (San Francisco: Chinese Materials Center, Inc., 1978), p. 9.

28   Northrup, *Indentured Labor...*, p. 61.

29   *Moreton Bay Courier* (MBC), 26 February 1848.

30 Alan Dwight, "The Use of Indian Labourers in New South Wales", *Journal of the Royal Australian Historical Society* (JRAHS), September 1976, pp. 114-35.

31 MBC, 19 December 1846.

32 Dwight, "The Use of Indian Labourers in New South Wales", p. 133.

33 Indian Labourers Protection Act, 26 Vic., No. 5, 1862.

34 Alan Dwight, "South Sea Islanders in New South Wales," *JRAHS*, March 1983, pp. 273-91.

35 Article 15, An Act to amend an Act, Intituled "An Act to amend and consolidate the Laws between Masters and Servants in New South Wales", 11 Vic., No. 9, 1847.

36 Dwight, "South Sea Islanders...", p. 286.

37 Clive Moore, ed., *The Forgotten People: a history of the Australian South Sea Island community* (Sydney: The Australian Broadcasting Commission, 1979), p. 7.

38 Corris, *Passage Port and Plantation...*, p. 1. The figures for Melanesian indentured labour, more generally called the Polynesian Labour Trade in the literature of the time, vary a little according to source. Engerman, p. 272, gives 61,200 to Australia and about 40,000 to other Pacific destinations; Northrup, p. 38, has 62,475 to Australia, 27,072 to Fiji, and 6,444 to Hawaii and the French Pacific. Clive Moore, Jacqueline Leckie and Doug Munro include around 1,100 who were shipped to Guatemala, and 4,634 to Peru. See *Labour in the South Pacific* (Townsville: James Cook University, 1990), p. xlix.

39 The 1871 figure is from Kay Saunders, *Workers in Bondage: the origins and bases of unfree labour in Queensland 1824-1916* (St Lucia: University of Queensland Press, 1982), p. 95. The other figure is from Gavin Souter, *Lion and Kangaroo: the initiation of Australia* (Melbourne: Text Publishing Co., 1976), p. 97. Peter Corris, *Passage Port and Plantation...*, p. 46, says there were 9,428 Melanesians in Queensland in 1891, of whom only 826 were females.

40 *Ibid.*, p. 131.

41 *Ibid.*

42 Refer to C. Y. Choi, *Chinese Migration and Settlement in Australia* (Sydney: Sydney University Press, 1975), p. 35.

43 "Index to Coloured Labour Asiatic Aliens in Queensland 1913", Queensland State Archives, Item ID 862496, also available on-line.

44 Lord Olivier, *White Capital and Coloured Labour* (London: The Hogarth Press, 1929), p. 100.

45 Engerman, "Servants to Slaves to Servants...", p. 266.

46 *Ibid.*, p. 282.

47 *Ibid.*, p. 284.

48 *Ibid.*, p. 266.

49 Northrup, *Indentured Labour...*, p. 126.

50 *Ibid.*, p. 129.

51   *Ibid.*, p. 119.
52   Lord Olivier, *White Capital and Coloured Labour*, pp. 10-11.
53   *Ibid.*, p. 102.

Chapter 2

1   Zhu Guohong, *The Encyclopedia of the Chinese Overseas*, p. 62.

2   "Hakka" means stranger or newcomer and the origins of these people is probably northern China, near present-day Shandong province. By the mid-nineteenth century, they were most numerous in Guangdong province where the prefecture of Jiaying, for example, was populated entirely by Hakka, and they were also numerous in the provinces of Guangxi, Fujian and Zhejiang. Of lowly status in the Chinese hierarchy, they generally settled in upland areas, leaving the more fertile plains to the Punti (*bendi*) as the older Chinese inhabitants are termed. The women never adopted the practice of foot-binding. Hakka people led the Taiping rebellion.

3   Guangdong province supplied the world's largest number of overseas Chinese, or 68 per cent of the total number of Chinese emigrants estimated at 8.2 million in 1957. In that year, Chinese of Guangdong origin accounted for 99 per cent of Chinese settled in the Americas. See *The Encyclopedia of the Chinese Overseas*, p. 36.

4   Canton and Amoy were the place names that the British used with reference to the cities now known in standard Chinese as Guangzhou and Xiamen. For historical reasons, the former names will be used in this study. Other place names are given *pinyin* spelling.

5   Wang Gungwu, Introduction, *The Encyclopedia of the Chinese Overseas*. Figures for China are from there and from Jean Chesneaux, *Peasant Revolts in China 1840-1949* (London: Thames and Hudson, 1973), p. 12.

6   *The Travels of Marco Polo the Venetian* (New York: Everyman's Library, Alfred A. Knopf, 2008), p. 230.

7   Edgar Wickberg, *The Encyclopedia of the Chinese Overseas*, p. 187.

8   Robert Nield, *The China Coast: Trade and the First Treaty Ports* (Hong Kong: Joint Publishing [H. K.] Co. Ltd., 2010), p. 41. According to Spence and Keay, the distance was respectively "20 miles" or "50 kilometres (30 miles)". Given the narrowness of the coastal belt, I have favoured the shorter distance given by Nield.

9   Jonathan D. Spence, *The Search for Modern China*, second edition (New York: W. W. Norton & Company, 1999), p. 44.

10   John Keay, *China: A History* (London: HarperPress, 2008), p. 434.

11   *Ibid.*, p. 455.

12   Spence, *The Search for Modern China*, pp. 57-58.

13 *Ibid.*, p. 129.

14 Robert Nield, *The China Coast*, p. 77. Spence gives the number of addicts as one million, but I believe this is a typographical error.

15 The dollar value stated here is the Mexican (Spanish) dollar which had wide currency in the East, including the young British colony of New South Wales.

16 Robert B. Forbes, "Personal Reminiscences", 1876, in Michael Wise, *Travellers' Tales of the South China Coast: Hong Kong, Canton, Macao* (Singapore: Marshall Cavendish Editions, 2008), p. 37.

17 John Keay, *Empire's End: a history of the Far East from high colonialism to Hong Kong* (New York: Scriber, 1997), p. 67.

18 *The Encyclopedia of Chinese Overseas*, p. 74.

19 *Ibid.*, p. 46.

20 *Ibid.*, p. 24.

21 *Ibid.*, p. 75.

22 Spence, *The Search for Modern China*, p. 77.

23 Chesneaux, *Peasant Revolts...*, p. 11.

24 Eric R. Wolf, *Peasants* (Englewood Cliffs: Prentice Hall, 1966), p. 52.

25 Jonathan Spence, *God's Chinese Son: The Taiping Heavenly Kingdom of Hong Xiuquan* (London: Harper Collins, 1996), p.28.

26 Chesneaux, *Peasant Revolts...*, p. 14.

27 Veneration of an "Eternal Venerable Mother" goddess was part of a tradition of underground or sectarian White Lotus folk-Buddhism that was based on a millenarian view of catastrophe on earth. According to Spence, it reached back to at least the thirteenth century. See *The Search for Modern China*, p. 112.

28 Nield, *The China Coast*, p. 103.

29 "Chinese Affairs", reprinted in *Sydney Morning Herald* (SMH), 23 March 1854.

30 *Ibid.*

31 British historian and scholar of Chinese literature, Julia Lovell, downplays the external causes of violence. She argues that current Chinese scholarship which regards the Opium War as the start of modern Chinese history subscribes to a thoroughly Western-centric view of the country's past. See *The Opium War: Drugs, Dreams and the Making of China* (Basingstoke: Picador, 2011).

32 *The Encyclopedia of the Chinese Overseas*, p. 27. Nanjing fell to the rebels on 20 March 1853.

33 Spence, *God's Chinese Son*, p. xxiv.

34 *Ibid.*, p. xxii.

35 "Protestant Missions in China" from the *Patriot*, reprinted in SMH, 24 December 1853.

36 "Chinese Christianity", SMH, 9 January 1854.

37 Chesneaux, *Peasant Revolts...*, p. 38.

38 Spence, *God's Chinese Son*, p. xxv.

39 *The Encyclopedia of the Chinese Overseas*, p. 56.

Chapter 3

1   In 1840, the colony of New South Wales was divided into three separate land districts for ease of administration: the Middle District, around the original settled area, the Southern or Port Phillip District, and the Northern Districts generally referred to as Moreton Bay.

2   In the Burnett District, an average run covered around 20,000 acres, but the term "run" was also used synonymously with stations consisting of several contiguous runs. For example, Philip Freill's lease for Burrandowan, gazetted in July 1851, was for eight runs totalling 184,280 acres with a capacity for 32,000 sheep. See *Supplement to the New South Wales Government Gazette* of 25 July 1851.

3   "The Northern Country", MBC, 14 November 1846.

4   The Pentonville exiles had served about two years in English prisons and were granted a conditional pardon to transfer to New South Wales and Van Diemen's Land where they were nominally free, although unable to return to England until their sentence had expired. The first among them arrived in Port Phillip in 1844 and 1,727 had arrived by 1849.

5   "Rivers Burnett and Mary", extracted from *Supplement to the Government Gazette*, SMH, 10 September 1847.

6   Area reported in Queensland 1871 Census.

7   Charles O'Connell had represented Port Phillip in the Legislative Council from August 1845 to June 1848, prior to his appointment in the Burnett. In 1846, he was embroiled in a scandal over the appointment of two local magistrates accused in the media of being "amenable" to the wishes of Ben Boyd in relation to provisions of the Masters and Servants Act. It was alleged that O'Connell had been saved from bankruptcy by Boyd money. See Marion Diamond, *The Seahorse and the Wanderer: Ben Boyd in Australia* (Brunswick: Melbourne University Press, 1988), p. 108.

8   "Crown Lands beyond the Settled Districts", from a supplement to the *Government Gazette*, MBC, 8 July 1850.

9   Burnett Correspondent, MBC, 27 October 1848.

10 Duncan B. Waterson, *Squatter, Selector, and Storekeeper: A History of the Darling Downs, 1859-93* (Sydney University Press, 1968), pp. 9-12.

11 "Wide Bay, The Burnett District", SMH, 11 May 1853.

12 *Ibid.*

13 Gov. G. F. Bowen to Bulwer Lytton, 6 March 1860 in S. Lane-Poole, ed., *Thirty Years of Colonial Government*, 2 vols. London, 1889, 1, pp. 110-11, in Kay Cohen

and Kenneth Wiltshire, eds., *People, Places and Policies: Aspects of Queensland Government Administration 1859-1920* (St Lucia: University of Queensland Press, 1995), p. 395.

14 Nehemiah Bartley, *Australian Pioneers and Reminiscences 1849-1894* (Sydney: John Ferguson in association with the Royal Australian Historical Society, 1978), p. 205.

15 Sylvia Morrissey, "The Pastoral Economy, 1821-1850", in James Griffin, gen. ed., *Essays in Economic History of Australia* (Milton: The Jacaranda Press, 1967), p. 72.

16 T. A. Coghlan, *Labour and Industry in Australia*, vol. I (Melbourne: Macmillan, 1969), p. 505.

17 James Boyce, *1835: The Founding of Melbourne & the Conquest of Australia* (Collingwood: Black Inc., 2011), p. 202.

18 Bill Metcalffe, *The Gayndah Communes* (Rockhampton: Central Queensland University Press, 1998), p. 5.

19 Michael Roe, "1830-50", in Frank Crowley, ed., *A New History of Australia* (Melbourne: William Heinemann, 1974), p. 101.

20 Quote from B. Penton, *Landtakers* (Sydney, 1934), in Duncan B. Waterson, *Squatter, Selector, and Storekeeper*, p. 3.

21 Russel Ward, *The Australian Legend* (Melbourne: Oxford University Press, 1978), p. 94.

22 Supplement to the New South Wales *Government Gazette*, 7 November 1851. Indigenous Australians were not counted in the Australian census until after 1967.

23 "News from the Interior - Gayndah", SMH, 17 October 1850.

24 "Original Correspondence - Gayndah", SMH, 24 April 1851.

25 *Government Gazette*, 17 June 1851.

26 B. J. Bertelsen, "Wide Bay", Letter to the Editor, MBC, 15 December 1847.

27 T. Archer/M. Wales, *Recollections of a Rambling Life* (Brisbane: Boolarong Publications, 1988), p. 160.

28 MBC, 23 February 1850.

29 "Squatters in the Northern Districts", MBC, 12 June 1852.

30 *Moreton Bay Free Press* (MBFP), 4 January 1853.

31 J. E. Murphy and E. W. Easton, *Wilderness to Wealth: Being a History of the Shires of Nanango, Kingaroy, Wondai, Murgon, Kilkivan and the Upper Yarraman Portion of the Rosalie Shire* (Brisbane: W. R. Smith & Paterson Pty. Ltd., 1950), p. 250. The authors also record the death in 1850 of Bertelsen's one-year old son, Neil Louis who, they say, may have been the first white child born in the South Burnett. *Ibid.*, p. 251.

32 John S. Ferriter, "The Blacks in the Burnett District", Letter to the Editor, MBC, 23 December 1850.

33   Original Correspondence, SMH, 4 September 1851.
34   "Domestic Intelligence, Burnett District", MBC, 25 September 1852.
35   *Ibid.*
36   "Chinese Labour", MBC, 23 October 1852.
37   Details of the Wakka people are derived from Jill Slack, *Then and Now: an Aboriginal history of Gayndah* (Gayndah: Gayndah Orange Festival Committee Inc., 1997).
38   *Ibid.*, p. 7. In 1897, Arthur Meston, in his official role as Protector of Aborigines, reported to the Home Secretary on the condition of the "blacks" in the Gayndah district. He noted that there were about 120 in all, that most of the men were employed on stations temporarily or permanently and that "they appear to be less urgently in need of assistance than any blacks I had seen in the settled districts". Those in urgent need of early attention, he argued, were "the women and children who are the result of cross-breeding that has removed them so far from the aboriginal as to require absolute separation". See the *Brisbane Courier*, 15 November 1897.
39   Reported in MBC, 14 August 1847.
40   B. J. Bertelsen, correspondence, SMH, 15 December 1847.
41   "The Blacks in the Burnett District", MBC, 8 September 1849.
42   *Ibid.*
43   "The New Parliament: William Forster", MBC, 17 May 1856, describes Forster as "maternally the grandson of the late Gregory Blaxland, Esq.".
44   Don Dignan, *The Story of Kolan* (Brisbane: W. R. Smith & Paterson, undated), p. 7. At the end of 1850, Richard Jones, MLC, was severely reprimanded by the Colonial Secretary for complaining to the governor on behalf of his constituents about the failure of the government to protect them from Aboriginal attacks. Jones was reminded that "some of the parties who have suffered had located themselves *beyond* the protection of the Government". This surely refers to Blaxland and his servants and accounts for the fact that their deaths were not included in the list of victims tabled in the New South Wales Parliament in 1853. See "Editorial - Outrages by the Northern Blacks", SMH, 26 December 1850.
45   Tony Matthews, *This Dawning Land* (Spring Hill: Boolarong Publications, 1986), p. 34.
46   *Ibid.*, p. 36.
47   Don Dignan, *The Story of Kolan*, p. 10.
48   Betty Bull, Fiona Drews, Margaret van Hennekeler, *Summer Memories through Winter Eyes* (Bundaberg, 1987), p. 87.
49   "Council Papers – Murder by Aborigines in the Northern Districts", SMH, 18 May 1853.
50   "News from the Interior", dated 31 March, SMH, 26 April 1852.

51 "Burnett District", MBC, 17 April 1852. Rawbelle was sold in Sydney on 23 September 1852, along with 17,100 sheep at 6s. 10d. per head. See MBFP, 5 October 1852.

52 New South Wales Legislative Assembly Votes and Proceedings 1858, p. 877.

53 Eric Rolls, *A Million Wild Acres* (Camberwell: Penguin Books Australia, 1984), pp. 54-55.

54 Correspondence with *Fiat Justitia*, MBC, 17 July 1852.

55 "Brisbane Circuit Court, 17-19 May", MBFP, 27 May 1853.

56 *Ibid.*

57 MBC, 2 April 1853.

58 "Wide Bay, The Burnett District", SMH, 11 May 1853.

59 James Boyce, *1835*, p. 156.

Chapter 4

1 "News from the Interior - Moreton Bay", SMH, 13 May 1850.

2 *Ibid.*

3 T. A. Coghlan, *Labour and Industry in Australia,* vol. I, p. 33.

4 Babette Smith, *Australia's Birthstain: the startling legacy of the convict era* (Crows Nest: Allen & Unwin, 2008), p. 144.

5 Coghlan, p. 333.

6 *Ibid.*, p. 429.

7 Figures derived from Coghlan, p. 438.

8 Editorial, "Our Want of Labour", SMH, 8 October 1846.

9 Editorials, "Debate on the Transportation Committee" and "Population of New South Wales", SMH, 16 October and 16 December 1846, respectively.

10 Editorial, SMH, 13 January 1847.

11 Correspondence, T. A. Murray, SMH, 19 January 1847.

12 Editorial, MBC, 31 October 1846.

13 Motion of Charles Cowper, MLC, reported in Editorial, "The Transportation Report Repudiated", SMH, 17 September 1847.

14 J. J. Knight, "In the Early Days. - XLI. The Birth and Growth of Brisbane and Environs", *The Queenslander*, 24 September 1892.

15 Editorial, "Glorious News", SMH, 11 April 1850.

16 N. G. Butlin, *Forming a Colonial Economy: Australia 1810-1850* (Melbourne: Cambridge University Press, 1994), p. 27.

17 Arthur Redford, *Labour Migration in England, 1800-1850* (Manchester University Press, 1926), p. 95. Pages displayed by permission of MUP on website http://books.google,com.au/books?id+_hMNAQAAIAAJ&, accessed on 6 August 2011.

18 *Ibid.*, p. 102.

19 *Ibid.*, p. 108.

20 Figures given by N. G. Butlin, *Forming a Colonial Economy*, pp. 28 and 362-68, derived from R. Madgwick, *Immigration into Eastern Australia, 1788-1851* (London: Longmans, 1937), p. 233.

21 Editorial, "The Immigration Evidence", SMH, 22 September 1847.

22 *Ibid.*

23 *Ibid.*

24 "Council Papers. Emigration. Despatch from the Right Honourable the Secretary of State to his Excellency Governor Sir Charles A. FitzRoy (No. 212), 30 August 1847", SMH, 27 March 1848.

25 Editorial, "Report from the Immigration Agent", SMH, 29 August 1849.

26 J. J. Knight, "In the Early Days, XXVI", *The Queenslander*, 20 August 1892.

27 *Ibid.*, XXIV, 28 May 1892.

28 *Ibid.*, XXXVIII, 20 August 1892.

29 "News from the Interior - Moreton Bay, Meeting at Ipswich", SMH, 23 January 1850.

30 "News from the Interior - Wide Bay", SMH, 12 September 1850.

31 "Legislative Council. Notices of Motion and Orders of the Day", SMH, 20 September 1847.

32 Alan Dwight, "The Use of Indian Labourers in New South Wales", p.114.

33 *Ibid.*

34 *Ibid.*, pp. 130-31.

35 Editorials, MBC, 19 and 26 December 1846. Alan Dwight confuses Tent Hill with a settlement near Glen Innes. The *Moreton Bay Courier* locates Friell's station on the Stuart River, a tributary of the Boyne and close to Burrandowan which he bought in 1848 and which was taken over by Gordon Sandeman, probably as manager, following Friell's death at the end of 1853.

36 "The Coolies", MBC, 19 December 1846.

37 *Ibid.*

38 Dwight, "The Use of Indian Labourers...", quoting Philip Friell, "The Advantages of Indian Labour", published Sydney, 1846.

39 "Minutes of Evidence", 29 August 1854, from "Report from the Select Committee on Asiatic Labor", Legislative Council of New South Wales Votes and Proceedings, 27 November 1854, vol. 2 (papers).

40 "Despatch respecting Asiatic Labor", dated 26 April 1861, Queensland Legislative Council, printed 16 July 1861.

41 Refer to Marion Diamond, *The Sea Horse and the Wanderer*. Boyd had 800 permanently engaged workers by October 1847 according to Alan Dwight, "South Sea Islanders...".

42 Marion Diamond, p.128.

43 *Ibid.*, p. 129.

44 Dwight, "South Sea Islanders…", p. 286.
45 Editorial, "Immigration from the South Sea Islands", MBC, 15 May 1847.
46 Diamond, p. 130.
47 Clause III, An Act to amend an Act, Intituled 'An Act to amend and consolidate the laws between Masters and Servants in New South Wales', 11 Vic., No. 9, 1847, assented to, 16 August 1847. Published in Supplement to the *Government Gazette*, 20 August 1847.
48 Diamond, p. 131.
49 Dwight, "South Sea Islanders…", p. 288.
50 Corris, *Passage Port and Plantation*, p. 1.
51 For figures, see introduction to Clive Moore, et al., *Labour in the South Pacific*.
52 A. T. Yarwood, "Attitudes towards non-European Migrants" in F. S. Stevens, ed., *Racism: the Australian experience, Volume 1 prejudice and xenophobia*, second edition (Brookvale: Australia & New Zealand Book Co. Pty Ltd, 1974), p. 173.

Chapter 5

1 Lord Olivier, *White Capital and Coloured Labour*, p. 102
2 "Immigration from China", SMH, 23 March 1847.
3 Eric Rolls argues that the term "Celestials" came from an ancient name for China, *tian chao*, the Heavenly Dynasty, and the belief that heaven covered only the land under the sphere of the Emperor. See *Sojourners: the epic story of China's centuries-old relationship with Australia* (St Lucia: University of Queensland Press, 1992), p. 34.
4 "Such a Reputation, c. 1906", in *Travellers' Tales of the South China Coast*, compiled by Michael Wise, p. 174.
5 Robert Nield, *The China Coast: trade and the first treaty ports*, p. 106.
6 Wang Singwu, *The Organization of Chinese Emigration 1848-1888*, p. 121.
7 Eric Rolls, *Sojourners*, pp. 32-33.
8 *Ibid.*, p. 34.
9 Wang Singwu, pp. 125, 128.
10 Rolls, p. 46.
11 Wang Singwu, p. 265.
12 *Ibid.*, p. 120.
13 *Ibid.*, Appendix VI, 1, *List of Ships*.
14 Maxine Darnell, "Responses and Reactions to the Importation of Indentured Chinese Labourers", Working Paper Series in Economic History, No. 99-2, University of New England, November 1999. Website, http://www.une.edu.au/febl/EconStud/wps.htm
15 *Ibid.*, fn. 5, p. 4.

16 Wang Singwu, Appendix VI, 1. In his evidence to the 1854 Select Committee on Asiatic Labor, Towns referred to his role as agent for the importation of fifty-four or fifty-five Chinese for the Colonial Gold Company.

17 F. D. Syme to A. Bogue, Esq, Amoy, 27 December 1846, reprinted in SMH, 23 March 1847.

18 "Report from the Select Committee on Asiatic Labor", Legislative Council of New South Wales Votes and Proceedings, vol. 2 (papers), 27 November 1854. References in this chapter are from "Minutes of Evidence ..." commencing on p. 927.

19 Wang Singwu, p.271.

20 Shortrede was proprietor and editor of the *China Mail* in Shanghai. His evidence before the select committee was based on the findings of the official investigation into the 1852 riots in Amoy. It was his opinion that "there is nothing worse in the slave trade" than some of the practices employed in the labour trade in Amoy.

21 Between February and April 1852, the SMH published six lengthy articles on "Chinese Immigration" by Paul Pax, the pseudonym of a lobbyist with detailed and intimate knowledge of the Amoy trade in indentured labour. This quote is from "Chinese Immigration No. VI (Conclusion)", SMH 3 April 1852. Hereafter referred to as Paul Pax VI, etc.

22 Kathryn Cronin, *Colonial Casualties: Chinese in Early Victoria* (Melbourne: Melbourne University Press, 1982), p. 11.

23 F. D. Syme to A. Bogue, Esq., Amoy, 27 December 1846, reprinted in SMH, 19 January 1847.

24 "Chinese Immigration", MBC, 10 April 1847.

25 *Ibid.*

26 "Minutes of Evidence before the Select Committee on Asiatic Labor", 29 August 1854.

27 Wang Singwu, p. 56.

28 Paul Pax III, SMH, 13 March 1852.

29 Minutes of Evidence ..., 27 November 1854.

30 Wang Singwu, p. 52.

31 Paul Pax III, SMH, 13 March 1852.

32 *Ibid.*

33 *Ibid.*

34 Paul Pax IV, SMH, 20 March 1852

35 Paul Pax III, SMH, 13 March 1852.

36 Wang Singwu, p. 42.

37 Paul Pax VI (Conclusion), SMH, 3 April 1852.

38 Hutchinson Hothersall Browne, "Minutes of Evidence ...", 27 November 1854.

39 Paul Pax VI (Conclusion), SMH, 3 April 1852

40 As recorded by Sydney authorities in 1852, according to Wang Singwu, p. 196.

41   "An Act for the regulation of Chinese passenger ships", 18 &19 Vict., c. 104, passed 14 August 1855, in force 25 January 1856. Website http://www.hklii.org/hk/other/ord/historical/1912/89.pdf accessed 31 August 2011.

42   Paul Pax II, SMH, 6 March 1852.

43   See Wang Singwu, p. 212 and evidence presented by H. H. Browne before the 1854 select committee.

44   Wang Singwu, p. 432, quoting from Enc. 16 in No. 14, Copy of Survey held on Three Vessels loading with Coolies at Amoy, 18 December 1852, Corresp. with the Superintendent of British Trade in China upon the subject of emigration from that country, 1853, GB *Commons Papers*, 1852-53, V68, p. 82.

45   *Ibid.*, p. 248.

46   Alan Shortrede, "Minutes of Evidence…", 29 August 1854.

47   Paul Pax IV, SMH, 20 March 1852.

48   *Ibid.*

49   Wang Singwu, p. 191.

50   Paul Pax IV, SMH, 20 March 1852.

51   Kathryn Cronin, *Colonial Casualties,* pp. 4-5.

52   Paul Pax IV, SMH, 20 March 1852.

53   Editorial, "Emigration", *People's Advocate and New South Wales Vindicator*, 17 February 1849.

54   Editorial, "Paul Pax and the Pagans", *Empire*, 11 March 1852.

55   SMH, 19 November 1851.

56   "Chinese Immigration - the *Douglass Bill* (Friday, 18 November)", SMH, 24 November 1851.

57   Editorial, "Immigration from China", SMH, 26 November 1851.

58   *Ibid.*

Chapter 6

1   This figure includes the *Eleanor Lancaster*, with 255 men on board, that departed from Namao, an island offshore from Shantou, for Newcastle on 19 November 1852, along with the fifteen shiploads listed by Wang Singwu in Table 1 in the previous chapter. Unless otherwise stated, information in this paragraph is taken from Appendix 5, Table 2 "Listing of Ships Carrying Chinese Labourers to Sydney and Moreton Bay 1847-1853" in Maxine Darnell, "The Chinese Labour Trade to New South Wales 1783-1853: an exposition of motives and outcomes", thesis submitted for the degree of Doctor of Philosophy of the University of New England, January 1997.

2   The figures supplied by Maxine Darnell are corroborated by independent, unpublished research undertaken by Ray Poon. The discrepancy in the figures for Wide Bay are acknowledged by both researchers. The first voyage of the

Duke of Roxburgh that left Amoy on 8 November 1850 with 242 labourers on board was destined for Moreton Bay but bad weather forced it to make landfall in Sydney. In March 1851, it was reported that 180 had arrived in Brisbane. A further unknown number (Darnell suggests twenty-two) went by two schooners to Wide Bay, but their presence on board was not listed in the manifest of either ship. There had been twenty deaths on the voyage, but these calculations still leave twenty labourers unaccounted for.

[3]   Maxine Darnell, Table 8b, "Chinese Labouring Population", *The Chinese Labour Trade to New South Wales 1783-1853...*, p. 207.

[4]   In the Wide Bay, according to government figures, the economic contribution of the Chinese was even more significant, accounting for 86 per cent of all shepherds in the district in 1851 and 43 per cent in 1856. These figures are unreliable, as Darnell points out, because sheep numbers reportedly doubled in the intervening years, making no sense of the halving of Chinese participation in the industry. *Ibid.*

[5]   SMH, 23 October 1848.

[6]   Darnell, p. 105.

[7]   Some of the clients of the trade played a direct role. According to Maurice French, the youngest of the Leslie brothers, the pioneering squatters of the Darling Downs, lived in China from 1848 to 1857 and arranged the hiring and transport of many Chinese "who proved excellent shepherds and servants". See *A Pastoral Romance: the tribulation and triumph of squatterdom* (USQ Press: Toowoomba, 1990), p. 51.

[8]   Darnell, p. 112.

[9]   "Chin-Ring in a Difficulty", MBC, 13 January 1849.

[10] "Moreton Bay News", SMH, 17 November 1851.

[11] Darnell, p. 119.

[12] *Ibid.*, p. 126.

[13] Towns to A. Trevethan, 31 January 1852, *Robert Towns Correspondence*, Mitchell Library, MSS 307/117, quoted by Darnell, p. 121.

[14] "Our Traffic with China", MBC, 22 November 1851.

[15] "Chinese Labour – its cost to the public", MBC, 11 October 1851.

[16] MBC, 3 July 1852 and 10 January 1853. Names are Ki Poot/Poon, Tam Lai/Tan Li.

[17] MBC, 17 February 1851.

[18] MBC, 8 January 1853.

[19] MBC, Supplement, 24 May 1851. Names are Soo, Ong Awk, Toe Tong, Tan Pong, Kim, Hong Li.

[20] MBC, 18 December 1852.

[21] MBFP, 29 November 1853.

22   MBFP, 27 May 1852, and Maxine Darnell, "Indentured Chinese Labourers and Employers Identified, New South Wales, 1828-1856" (website: www.chaf.lib. latrobe.edu.au/pdf/indentured.pdf), fn. 32.

23   Maxine Darnell, "Indentured Chinese Labourers ...", fn. 50.

24   MBFP, 27 May 1852.

25   Darnell, p. 194.

26   *Ibid.*

27   *Ibid.*, p. 195.

28   See J. E. Murphy and E. W. Easton, *Wilderness to* Wealth, and Roy Connolly, *Southern Saga* (Sydney: Dymock's Book Arcade Ltd, 1945 [1940]). This latter soundly researched although fictionalised history of the Burnett was written by a direct descendant of the legendary Gayndah pioneer and merchant, John Connolly, of the Union Wharf and Store at South Brisbane.

29   Russel Ward, *The Australian Legend*, p. 103.

30   *Ibid.*, p. 104.

31   Jan Walker, *Jondaryan Station: the relationship between pastoral capital and pastoral labour 1840-1890* (St Lucia: UQP, 1988), p. 77.

32   *Ibid.*

33   T. A. Coghlan, *Labour and Industry in Australia,* vol. I., p. 434.

34   *Ibid.*

35   Gayndah Bench, 2 April 1855, *Record Book of the Court of Petty Sessions Gayndah 30 October 1850 to 19 October 1859.* Queensland State Archives, A/4870.

36   Roy Connolly, *Southern Saga*, p. 329.

37   In the 1860s, Boondooma station also employed at least eleven indentured South Sea Islanders who all absconded. See advertisement in BA, 1 August 1868.

38   To James King, Burrandowan, 18 September 1853. *Boondooma Station Correspondence Record*, John Oxley Library, OM 66-7/F2 (Box 8614).

39   To C. Potts, Esq., 18 May 1853. *Ibid.*

40   To Messrs Gilchrist, Watt and Co, Sydney, 21 February 1854. *Ibid.*

41   To Messrs Gilchrist, Watt and Co, Sydney, 22 September 1854. *Ibid.*

42   To Messrs Gilchrist, Watt and Co, Sydney, 4 December 1854. *Ibid.*

43   To T. G. Rusden, Esq., 20 June 1855. *Ibid.*

44   Ng Hwat and Goe Chea served prison time for attempting to rescue prisoners from Native Police escort at Boondooma in January 1854. Only two broke their contracts: Gui Luing absconded in 1854, and O'Ping was paid up and went to Sydney in 1853. *Boondooma Station Wages Book.* John Oxley Library, OM66-7 (Box 8614).

45   Booubyjan Station, *Wages Book,1854-60, 1865-69.* John Oxley Library, OM76-6B, Box 8953.

46   Connolly, p. 328.

47   *Mount Perry Mail* (MPM*),* 24 October 1872, from the *Illustrated Sydney News* (no date given).

48   MBFP, 9 August 1853.

49   Ward, p. 104.

50   Maxine Darnell, "Indentured Chinese Labourers and Employers Identified…".

51   T. Archer/M. Wales. *Recollections of a Rambling Life* (Brisbane: Boolarong Publications, 1988 [1897]), pp. 158-59. Leases for St John's, Coonambula, The Flats, Eidsvold, and Telemark, totalling 71,160 acres were granted by the Crown Lands Office, Sydney, on 19 June 1850. See MBC, 8 July 1850. Leases for adjacent runs, Geumga, Malmoe and Mundowran covering a further 56,000 acres were gazetted in July 1851. See New South Wales *Government Gazette*, Friday, 25 July 1851.

52   *Ibid.*, p. 295.

53   "Minutes of Evidence taken before the Select Committee on Asiatic Labor", 29 August 1854.

54   *Ibid.* The Moreton Bay district generally referred to the Burnett, Wide Bay, and Darling Downs districts and the Stanley Boroughs around Brisbane.

55   The drawings were described at length in "Ingenious Defence of the Chinaman Charged with Murder", MBC, 26 October 1850. Note that Ang was incorrectly reported as "Au" in this article.

56   Shirley Fitzgerald, *Red Tape, Gold Scissors: the story of Sydney's Chinese* (Sydney: State Library of New South Wales Press, 2000), p. 64.

57   *Ibid.*

58   Gayndah Bench, 25 May 1854, and MBC, 8 July 1854.

59   Correspondence from E. Ross, *Brisbane Courier*, 9 June 1870.

Chapter 7

1   Darnell, p. 208, quoting Evidence of John Dobie, 9 July, 1852, "Report from the Select Committee on Immigration", New South Wales Legislative Council Votes and Proceedings 1852, vol. 2, p. 58. and "The Late Meeting at Brisbane", MBFP, 27 May 1852.

2   T. Archer, *Recollections of a Rambling Life*, p. 90.

3   Paul Pax, "Chinese Immigration III", SMH, 13 March 1852.

4   Paul Pax, "Chinese Immigration I", SMH, 28 February 1852.

5   "Domestic Intelligence – Ipswich", MBC, 8 May 1852.

6   H. H. McArthur, Letter to the Editor, MBC, 12 June 1852.

7   Lim Poh was no sooner released from gaol than he absconded again. R. and H. Watson posted a notice in the MBFP, 12 October 1852 that three men, No Tang/Taw, Hang and Lim Poh had absconded. Lim Poh was described as "short, thickset, fat, marked with smallpox, with yellow complexion and surly look."

8   *"Audi Alteram Partem"*, MBC, 5 June 1852.

9   Jan Walker, *Jondaryan Station*, p. 39.

10 Darnell, Table 7a "Comparison of Contracts", p. 163.

11 T. A. Coghlan. *Labour and Industry in Australia,* vol. I, p. 204.

12 *Ibid.*

13 *Ibid.*

14 *Ibid*, p. 438.

15 Darnell, Table 11a, "Shepherd and Labourer Wages Compared, 1849-1855", p. 291.

16 Latter figure reported in MBC, 2 October 1860.

17 MBC, 20 October 1860.

18 Ward, pp. 131-32.

19 Memo preceding first page of *Boondooma Station Wages Book.*

20 Connolly, pp. 180-81.

21 J. J. Auchmuty, in Frank Crowley, ed. *A New History of Australia*, p. 67.

22 Act 7 Geo. IV., No. 3., "An Act to repeal an Act intituled, 'An Act to make Promissory Notes and Bills of Exchange payable in Spanish dollars available, as if such Notes and bills had been drawn payable in Sterling Money of the Realm,' and to promote the circulation of Sterling Money of Great Britain in NSW (12 July 1826)", reproduced in Editorial, "The Local Currency", MBC, 25 May 1850.

23 Connolly, p. 81.

24 S. J. Butlin, *Foundations of the Australian Monetary System 1788-1851* (Sydney: Sydney University Press, 1953), p. 5.

25 *Ibid.*, p. 375.

26 Editorial, "The Local Currency", MBC, 25 May 1850. Article 5 of the law imposed a fine of between £5 and £20 for every note or order issued for a sum less than twenty shillings sterling. The judge and the attorney-general were in Brisbane for the first Circuit Court when they made public their opinion that was confirmed by a judicial decision in Sydney in July. See S. J. Butlin, *Foundations of the Australian Monetary System*, p. 377.

27 Editorial, MBC, 25 May 1850.

28 From the contract of Eat with Matthew Marsh of Maryland station, signed 7 May 1850. Darnell, appendix.

29 Butlin, p. 377.

30 Connolly, p. 182.

31 Coghlan, pp. 430-31.

32 "Breach of Masters' and Servants' Act", MBC, 9 August 1851.

33 Gayndah Bench, January 1853.

34 *Ibid*. This may be James Loy who was naturalized on 8 April 1864 and was then a labourer in Dalby. Alfred C. Thomas was a Burnett squatter. An amateur meteorologist, he wrote to the *Burnett Argus* on 10 November 1862 with careful details of the rainfall record he had kept on his run between 1851 and 1859 (inclusive). According to his weather analysis, October was the best month for lambing.

35 MBFP, 10 January 1854.

36 Gayndah Bench, 25 July 1856. From June that year, there was a police magistrate in Gayndah, Arthur Halloran, and his presence helped to ameliorate the rulings from the bench.

37 MBFP, 27 May 1852.

38 MBC, 29 May 1852.

39 *Ibid*.

40 MBC, 20 May 1854.

41 Refer to entry for Wienholt, Edward by D. B. Waterson in *Australian Dictionary of Biography*, http://adb.anu.edu.au/biography/wienholt-edward-4956. See also Maurice French, *A Pastoral Romance*, p. 219, where he quotes a friend of the brothers who regarded them as belonging "to the old Darling Downs set which is synonymous for high character and good faith, not less than for every kind of enterprise and improvement in the culture of livestock."

42 Michael Roe, in Frank Crowley, ed., *A New History of Australia*. p. 122.

43 "Burnett District", MBC, 31 March and 17 April 1852. At the time of the incident, the Native Police had no mandate to engage in this sort of policing. In August, however, the Colonial Secretary stated that he had issued instructions to the commandant of the Native Police to "detach a portion of his force to the assistance of the general police" in the Moreton Bay district. See "The Moreton Bay Police", MBFP, 10 August 1852.

44 Gayndah Bench, 30 March 1852.

45 "Burnett District", MBC, 10 and 23 October 1852.

46 This is surely journalistic licence. Presumably the author is referring to the First Opium War, 1839-42, but how or when a Fujian peasant would have encountered, let alone later recognized a serving British soldier during that conflict is beyond imagining.

47 Gayndah Bench, 9 November 1852.

48 MBFP, 21 December 1852.

49 Gayndah Bench, 18 January 1853.

50 MBFP, 1 February 1853.

51 Gayndah Bench, 25 April 1855.

52 *Ibid*., 31 January 1855.

53 *Ibid*., 16 June 1856. Pang was committed to trial at Brisbane Circuit Court on 15 September 1856, a year and a half after the original misdemeanour occurred.

His committal appears on "Return of Committals for Trial…" prepared by the Crown Law Offices, Sydney, 6 September 1858 that was ordered by Dr Douglass, MLC, to support the Chinese Immigration Bill. See *Journal of New South Wales Legislative Council*, vol. 3, 1868.

54 Gayndah Bench, 4 June 1855.
55 *Ibid.*
56 French, p. 51.
57 Darnell, p. 136.
58 Coghlan, p. 521.
59 *Ibid.*, p. 520.
60 "Wide Bay, The Burnett District", SMH, 11 May 1853.
61 *Ibid.*
62 Editorial, "Chinese Labour", MBC, 23 October 1852.
63 Ipswich correspondent, MBFP, 10 August 1852.
64 "Report from the Select Committee on Asiatic Labor".

Chapter 8

1 Letter to the Editor, MBC, 2 February 1850, and MBFP, 21 December 1852.
2 "New South Wales – Colonial Secretary: Letters Relating to Moreton Bay and Queensland Received 1822-1860", State Library of Queensland, (website http://www.slq.qld.gov.au). O'Connell started out in bad odour with the colonial secretary by arriving many months late at his post. See QSL Reel A2.18, pp. 440-43.
3 "An Act to restrain the unauthorized occupation of Crown Lands", 7 Will. IV, No. 4.
4 "Department of the Chief Commissioner of Crown Lands", SMH, 7 November 1851.
5 "An Act further to restrain the unauthorized Occupation of Crown Lands and to provide the means of defraying the Expense of a Border Police", 2 Vic., No. 27, Cl. 10.
6 John Hirst, *Sense and Nonsense in Australian History* (Melbourne: Black Inc. Agenda, 2009), pp. 35-36.
7 *Ibid.*, p. 36.
8 Gayndah Bench, 2 November 1854. The name of the Burnett run, unfortunately, is illegible. The reference to runs in the Port Curtis district is given by the *Australian Dictionary of Biography*, online edition, http://adbonline.anu.edu.au/biogs/A050400b.htm
9 As explained in Clause 2 of "An Act for taking an account of the population of New South Wales", 14 Vic., No. 18 of 19 September 1850, in preparation for the 1851 census.

10 "Archives in Brief 20 – Police service records", http://www.records.nsw.gov.au/
    state-archives/guides-and-finding-aids/…, p. 1. Act 14 Vic. No. 38, 1850.
11 Doreen O'Sullivan notes the appointment of Bartholomew Bannister that
    year. See *Gayndah on the Burnett* (Toowoomba: self-publisher, 1995). The
    constabulary was established in 1850 by the Act (14 Vic. No. 38) and placed
    under an Inspector-General of Police in Sydney. This did not, however, bring the
    police force of New South Wales as a unit under one control. See Commander
    Norman S. Pixley, M.B.E., V.R.D., R.A.N.R., "An Outline of the History of the
    Queensland Police Force 1860-1949" read at a meeting of the Historical Society
    of Queensland, Inc., on July 27th, 1950. http://espace.library.uq.edu.au/eserv/
    UQ:212738/s18378366_1
12 *Ibid.*, p. 59.
13 "New South Wales – Colonial Secretary: Letters Relating to Moreton Bay and
    Queensland Received 1822-1860", State Library of Queensland, (http://www.
    slq.qld.gov.au). QSL Reel A2.18, p. 461.
14 Bruce Kercher, *An Unruly Child: a History of Law in Australia* (St Leonards:
    Allen & Unwin Pty Ltd, 1995), p. 26.
15 "Illegal Warrants", MBC, 5 February 1853.
16 "Magisterial Wisdom", MBC, 8 July 1854. The Sydney Police Act (4 Will.
    IV, No. 7) of 1833 indemnified New South Wales justices for acts done in the
    execution of their office.
17 *Maryborough Chronicle* (MC), 3 October 1861.
18 *Burnett Argus* (BA), 14 August 1862.
19 In fact, Haynes was sent to Taroom in neighbouring Leichhardt district where
    he was the clerk of petty sessions. See BA Editorial, 11 January 1864.
20 Editorial, BA, 11 January 1864.
21 "The Tim Shea Tragedy", MC, 2 March 1867.
22 Editorial, BA, 27 March 1869.
23 Editorial, BA, 22 May 1869.
24 Lesley McGregor, in Kay Cohen and Kenneth Wiltshire, eds. *People, Places
    and Policies*, p. 59. As McGregor notes, "The link between the police and
    the judiciary placed a great deal of power in the hands of the judiciary; e.g. a
    magistrate, as officer in charge of police, could issue instructions to charge a
    person with an offence and then, as magistrate, adjudicate on the case."
25 "Opening of the First Circuit Court at Brisbane", MBC, 18 May 1850.
26 "Criminal Statistics", MBC, 28 February 1857.
27 Raymond Evans, *A History of Queensland* (Cambridge: CUP, 2007), p. 68.
28 "An Act to provide for the better Administration of Justice in the District of
    Moreton Bay. [Assented to, 11th March, 1857]", or the Moreton Bay District
    Court Act, 20 Vic., No. 25, 1857.
29 "District Court of Moreton Bay", MBFP, 3 July 1855.

30   BA, 17 February 1866.

31   BA, 27 March 1869.

32   "An Act to Consolidate and Amend the Laws relating to the Police Force. (Assented to 21st September, 1863)", or Police Act, 27 Vic., No. 11.

33   These native mounted police were organized according to a statute of New South Wales but they were never recognized in Queensland law and were frequently criticized by their detractors as an "illegal body". For a history of the Native Police Force in the Burnett District, see Margaret Slocomb, "The Harris Case: the Murder of an Aboriginal man by the Native Police in the Burnett District, 1863", *Journal of Australian Colonial History*, vol. 13, 2011, pp. 85-105.

34   As reported in MC, 3 September 1863.

35   In particular, see Douglas Hay and Paul Craven, eds., *Masters, Servants, and Magistrates....*

36   Master and servant legislation was repealed by the Ryan government in Queensland in 1916, but it remained on the statute books of the other Australian states for much longer. For example, a bill to repeal the very harsh Act of 1856 did not come before the Tasmanian House of Assembly until 1976. See A. P. Davidson, "A Skeleton in the Cupboard; Master and Servant Legislation and the Industrial Torts in Tasmania", *University of Tasmania Law Review*, (http://www.austlii.edu.au/au/journals/UtasLawRw/1976/2.pdf)

37   Hay and Craven, *Masters, Servants, and Magistrates...*, p. 55-56.

38   *Ibid.*, p. 21.

39   Michael Quinlan, "Australia, 1788-1902: A Workingman's Paradise?", in Hay and Craven, eds., Chapter Six.

40   *Ibid.*, p. 235.

41   From A. Merritt, "The Development and Application of Masters and Servants Legislation in New South Wales - 1845-1930", Ph.D. diss., Australian National University, 1981, in Michael Quinlan, "A Workingman's Paradise?", p. 239.

42   Queensland's population according to the census taken on 8 April 1861 was only 30,115 plus an estimated 15,000 Aborigines. Queensland Legislative Council, 1862.

43   See Quinlan, p. 240.

44   *Record Book of the Court of Petty Sessions Gayndah 30 October 1850 to 19 October 1859.* A/4870, Queensland State Archives. Unless otherwise noted, the following incidents are also taken from the record book of the Gayndah Bench.

45   Gayndah Bench, 2 April 1855; MBFP, 20 November 1855; MBC, 24 November 1855.

46   Darnell thesis, p. 287.

47   "Chinese Labour, its cost to the public", MBC, 11 October 1851.

48   *Ibid.*

49   "The Gaol", MBC, 3 April 1852.

50 Jan Walker, *Jondaryan*, p. 41.
51 These demonstrations were timed for periods of peak labour activity on the runs. On 23 January 1853, for example, eighteen Chinese labourers "absconded" from Yandilla station on the Darling Downs in the middle of shearing. See MBFP, 1 February 1853.
52 Editorial, *The Courier*, 16 July 1861.
53 Date and figure from Kay Saunders, "Racial Responses towards Melanesians in Colonial Queensland" in Raymond Evans et al., *Race Relations in Colonial Queensland: a history of exclusion, exploitation and extermination* (St Lucia: University of Queensland Press, 1988), p. 149.
54 *Ibid.*, p. 170 and Clause 2 of the Act.
55 Editorial, BA, 31 October 1868.
56 Editorial, BA, 1 August 1868.
57 Editorial, MC, 24 May 1877.
58 Editorial, BA, 31 October 1868.

Chapter 9

1 Shirley Fitzgerald, *Red Tape, Gold Scissors*, p. 66.
2 "Interesting Colloquy", MBC, 10 March 1849.
3 See, for instance, letter from A Subscriber, dated 29 January 1850, in MBC, 2 February 1850.
4 "Chinese labour", MBC, 22 February 1851.
5 This was the case, discussed later, where the man charged, Angee, was condemned and executed. Refer also to "Judgement on the Holbert Case", Brisbane Assize, 23 November 1851, in SMH, 2 December 1851.
6 Editorial, MBFP, 19 October 1852.
7 Vagrancy Acts: 6 Wm. IV, No. 6, 1835; 13 Vic., No. 46, 1849; 15 Vic., No. 4, 1851.
8 Refer to: MBC, 16 October 1852; Gayndah Bench records, 7 December 1852; MBC, 8 January 1853; and MBFP, 11 January 1853.
9 MBC, 6 June 1857.
10 MBC, 17 October 1857.
11 MBC, 19 January 1860.
12 MBFP, 25 March 1857.
13 MBFP, 29 July 1857.
14 MBFP, 15 April 1857.
15 MBC, 16 May 1857.
16 MBC, 6 June 1857.
17 MBC, 21 February 1857.
18 MBC, 30 May 1857.

19 MBC, 1 May 1858 and MBFP, 4 May 1858. In a terrible postscript to the whole affair, Charles Owen was murdered in 1864 in a revenge attack by a former European servant whom Owen had charged under the Masters and Servants Act. This man, Andrew Ritchie, was executed.

20 MBC, 30 June 1860.

21 MBC, 21 August 1860.

22 Refer to the list of selected names of those admitted between the 1860s and the 1890s on the website, http://www.judywebster.gil.com.au/casebooks-a.html

23 MBC, 28 June 1860

24 Reported in MBC, 11 August 1860.

25 See website, http://www.judywebster.gil.com.au/casebooks-a.html

26 MC, 29 May 1873.

27 Reported in MBC, 19 January 1860.

28 "Assize Intelligence - Moreton Bay", SMH, 5 June 1851.

29 "Escape of a Prisoner" and "Suicide", MBC 16 October and 20 November 1852.

30 MBFP, 20 November 1855 and MBC, 24 November 1855. This assault occurred in May, just one month after Lim Hein, and another named Toan, were sentenced to three months in Sydney Gaol plus a hefty fine for throwing stones at McLean and his horse. McLean seems to have been at war with the Chinese employed on Burrandowan.

31 Alan Dwight, "The Chinese in New South Wales Lawcourts 1848-1854", *Journal of the Royal Australian Historical Society*, V73/2, Oct. 1987, p. 80.

32 MBC, 16 November 1850. For details of Eu's incarceration on Cockatoo Island, see Shirley Fitzgerald, pp. 64-65.

33 See also Ian Barker QC, "Sorely tried: Democracy and trial by jury in New South Wales", inaugural Francis Forbes Lecture, Sydney, 2002 at website: http://www.forbessociety.org.au/documents/trial_jury.pdf

34 Leonie Gane, *The Hungry Ghosts of Boggo Road*, second edition (Boggo Road Gaol Historical Society, 2008), p. 19.

35 This was the second case involving the Chinese labourers from the first *Nimrod* consignment on Ideraway station. In October 1850, Ang (aka Au/Ong) appeared before the Ipswich Bench accused of shooting dead another Chinese shepherd there. See Chapter Six for details.

36 James Halbert, the overseer at Ideraway, had acted as interpreter at the trial of Ang in 1850. In the Brisbane Circuit Court, the judge ruled that Halbert was neither competent nor necessarily impartial and another interpreter was brought from Sydney to replace him. See Shirley Fitzgerald, p. 64.

37 SMH, 2 December 1851.

38 In chronological order, reports on the case appear as follows in 1852: MBFP, 22 July; MBC, 25 September; MBC, 23 October; MBFP, 16 November; MBC, 20 November; MBFP, 30 November.

39   Editorial, "British Justice and Chinese Interpretation", MBFP, 23 November 1852.

40   Editorial, "Chinese Crime and British Punishment", MBC, 27 November 1852.

41   From the *Maitland Mercury*, 22 December 1852 and reprinted in MBC, 8 January 1853.

42   MBFP, 20 November 1855.

43   Appearing in 1861: MC, 18 July; MBC, 26 July; MBC, 5 August; MBC, 17 September; MBC, 20 November.

44   *The Courier*, 22 November 1861.

45   "Trial of Deong for Murder", MC, 5 December 1861.

Chapter 10

1   Wang Gungwu, *The Encyclopedia of the Chinese Overseas*, Introduction.

2   C. Y. Choi, *Chinese Migration...*, p. 19 and fn. 9.

3   James Jupp, ed., *The Australian people: an encyclopedia of the nation, its people and their origins* (Cambridge: CUP, 2001), p. 210.

4   Hector Holthouse, *Gympie Gold* (Sydney: HarperCollinsPublishers, 1973), p. 34.

5   *Ibid.*, p. 21.

6   MC, 23 June 1869.

7   Chinese Immigrants Regulation Act, 41 Vic., No. 8, 1877 required each ship's captain to pay ten pounds for every Chinese arriving in Queensland, refundable on departure, subject to certain conditions.

8   MC, 3 June 1869.

9   Hector Holthouse, *Gympie Gold*, p. 107.

10   *Ibid.*, p. 163.

11   Choi, p. 21.

12   Eric Rolls, *Sojourners*, p. 211.

13   James Jupp ed., *The Australian people...*, p. 199.

14   *Ibid.*, p. 294.

15   MBC, 6 December 1851.

16   MBC, 8 May 1852 reported that the first ship of German immigrants was expected to arrive in June or July. It noted, "Messrs. Walter Gray & Co. of Ipswich have undertaken to receive orders for German immigrants, including skilled vinedressers, who, by the Government regulations, will be allowed free passages."

17   Peter Corris, *Passage Port and Plantation*, p. 75.

18   Robert Tooth returned to England in 1875. See MC, 26 January 1875.

19   The death-rate in Queensland for 1880 between the ages of 15 and 35, exclusive of "Polynesians", was 13.3/1000 and that of South Sea Islanders for the same

year was 62.89/1000, although this was only the reported number of deaths and the actual figure may have been higher. According to Myra Willard, "In not one case of the 443 deaths which occurred during the five years beginning 1875 on ten plantations in the Maryborough district, was a medical certificate of death forwarded to the Registrar, nor had this ever been done in the whole district unless the labourer had died in the local hospital." Myra Willard, *History of the White Australia Policy to 1920* (Carlton: Melbourne University Press, 1923), p. 166.

20 *Ibid.*, p. 76.
21 Rolls, *Sojourners*, p. 232.
22 *Ibid.* Rolls says there were thirty-five men, but the court report states there were thirty-nine.
23 MC, 30 April, 2 May, 5 September, 10 September, and 8 October 1874.
24 R. V. Jackson, *Australian economic development in the nineteenth century* (Canberra: Australian National University Press, 1977), p. 11.
25 *Ibid.*, p. 13.
26 Roger McGhee, "The Long Boom, 1860-1890" in James Griffin, gen. ed., *Essays in Economic History of Australia,* p. 141.
27 R. V. Jackson, *Australian economic development...*, p. 62.
28 McGhee, "The Long Boom, 1860-1890", p. 145.
29 G. L. Buxton, Chapter 5 "1870-90" in Frank Crowley, ed., *A New History of Australia,* p. 181.
30 "Depression of the Pastoral Interests", MC, 9 May 1871, reprinted from the *Darling Downs Gazette.*
31 Figures according to the Queensland census taken on 7 April 1861. Female farm-house servants earned £25.
32 MBC, 20 October 1860.
33 By 1863, assisted immigrants were starting to arrive in Maryborough in considerable numbers and wage rates were falling. The *Burnett Argus* reported that domestic servants could claim between £18 and £25 per annum, and shepherds £30-£40, but that many of the new arrivals remained "unoccupied" because they were demanding too much in wages. They were also reluctant to travel inland to the Burnett district. See BA, 20 July 1863.
34 Duncan B. Waterson, *Squatter, Selector, and Storekeeper*, p. 12.
35 "Travesty – Meeting at Gayndah", MBFP, 17 January 1854. Forster refused to accept the authority of a Brisbane-based government, and returned to New South Wales after Separation where he resumed his political career.
36 Bruce Knox, ed., *The Queensland Years of Robert Herbert, Premier: letters and papers* (St Lucia: University of Queensland Press, 1977), p. 19.
37 Kay Cohen, "Public Service Boards" in Kay Cohen and Kenneth Wiltshire, eds, *People, Places and Policies,* p. 97.

38 Editorial, MC, 21 July 1866.

39 *Ibid.*

40 MC, 4 July 1866.

41 "To the Working Men of Maryborough", MC, 15 September 1866.

42 MC, 7 April 1866, reprinted from the *Darling Downs Gazette.*

43 Editorial, MC, 4 July 1866.

44 "The Statistical Register", MC, 15 November 1870.

45 Editorial (Summary of 1870), MC, 3 January 1871.

46 "Depression of the Pastoral Interests", MC, 9 May 1871, reprinted from the *Darling Downs Gazette.*

47 *Ibid.*

48 "The New Queensland Land Act", *Brisbane Courier*, 6 February 1868.

49 *Ibid.*

50 "The Statistical Register", MC, 15 November 1870.

51 BA, 3 October 1868

52 MC, 10 March 1870.

53 MPM, 4 March 1875.

54 MC, 22 September 1877.

55 Buxton, in Crowley, ed., p. 181.

56 *Ibid.*, p. 181.

57 John Rorke, "White Australia – Origins", *Current Affairs Bulletin*, vol. 20, pp. 170-74, September 1957 in A. T. Yarwood, *Attitudes to Non-European Immigration* (Stanmore: Cassell Australia Limited, 1968), p. 22.

58 "Report from the Select Committee on Asiatic Labor", Legislative Council of New South Wales, 27 November 1854. See SMH, 2 December 1854.

59 "Chinese Immigration Bill", *Journal of New South Wales Legislative Council*, vol. 3, 1868.

60 *Ibid.*

61 See "Riot at Lambing Flat", SMH, 20 July 1861, p. 8.

62 *Ibid.* Editorial, p. 4.

63 *Ibid.*

64 This Act was repealed in 1867.

65 Shirley Fitzgerald notes that the first Chinese naturalisations occurred in 1857, when three men acquired certificates, so James Chiam, whose name was the first entry on the register for 1858, was a very early applicant. See *Red Tape, Gold Scissors*, p. 189.

66 MBC, 5 March 1859. All three names are incorrect: "Leong" was David Deong and "Drian" was John Deian. Pangsee's name was given in error for that of Thomas Ashney. Deian and Ashney are discussed in the following chapter.

67 The memorials are dated 16 October, 25 August and 18 October, respectively. State Archives, Queensland, Col/A9-60/2105, Col/A6-60/1497 and Col/A9-60/2104, Colonial Secretary's Office.

Chapter 11

1   Cathie May, *Topsawyers: the Chinese in Cairns 1870 to 1920*. Studies in North Queensland History No. 6 (Townsville: James Cook University, 1984); Barry McGowan, "Adaptation and Organization: The History and Heritage of the Chinese in Western New South Wales, Australia", 2007, website: http:// goliath.ecnext.com/coms2/gi_0199_6406890/Adaptation-and-organization-the-history.html; Royal Commission into Alleged Chinese Gambling and Immorality, New South Wales Legislative Assembly Votes and Proceedings 1891-92, vol. 8; J. Dundas Crawford, "Notes by Mr. Crawford on Chinese Immigration in the Australian Colonies", 1877, Great Britain Foreign Office Confidential Prints, F. O. 3742, available on website http://www.chaf.lib. latrobe.edu.au/education/history.htm

2   Shirley Fitzgerald, *Red Tape, Gold Scissors*, p. 84.

3   MC, 1 April 1869.

4   *Boondooma Station Wages Book and Correspondence Record, Booubyjan Station Wages Book, 1854-60, 1865-69*, OM66-7 and OM76-6B, respectively, both held at John Oxley Library, and *Yarrol Station Ledger, 1869-1883*, personal collection.

5   The *Nimrod* docked in Sydney on 2 October 1848 and according to Ray Poon, six men were transferred to the *Clarissa* which landed them in Moreton Bay on 28 October. The other fifty-six arrived one month later.

6   *Boondooma Station Wages Book*. This station had not hired men from the *Nimrod*, so Gue Lack completed his indenture somewhere else, perhaps at nearby Mondure station where Richard Jones had purchased sixteen men out of this first consignment of labourers from Amoy. James Blair Reid of Ideraway also engaged men from the *Nimrod*.

7   MBFP, 1 November 1853.

8   Gayndah Bench, 28 May 1855.

9   *Ibid.*, 11 February 1856. According to this date, Teang, would have arrived among the first of two consignments of Amoy labourers on the *Duke of Roxburgh*.

10 According to Duncan Waterson, 17,360 German migrants arrived in Queensland between 1861 and 1879. In *Squatter, Selector, and Storekeeper*, p. 126.

11 "Conditions in the Pastoral Industry of the Lower Murrumbidgee, 1860c.", reprinted from SMH, 30 November 1858 in C. M. H. Clark, *Select Documents in Australian History 1851-1900* (Sydney: Angus & Robertson Publishers, 1955), p. 187.

12 Waterson, p. 50.

13 MBC, 2 October 1860. The ration cost of £25 is similar to that calculated by Jan Walker at the inflated station store prices on Jondaryan station.

14 Enc. in H. Parks and W. B. Dalley to the Secretary for Lands, 25 September 1861, NSW Legislative Assembly Votes and Proceedings 1861-62, vol. 2, in C. M. H. Clark, *Select Documents...* p, 243.
15 Editorial, BA, 18 March 1865.
16 Waterson, p. 50, fn. 24.
17 *Ibid.*, p. 55.
18 Jan Walker, *Jondaryan Station*, p. 161.
19 *Ibid.*, pp. 97-98.
20 Table created from figures in *Booubyjan Station Wages Book, 1854-60, 1865-69.*
21 T. A. Coghlan, *Labour and Industry in Australia*, vol. II (Melbourne: Macmillan of Australia, 1969), pp. 787-91.
22 *Ibid.*, p. 1103.
23 *Ibid.*
24 Jan Walker, *Jondaryan*, p. 89.
25 The Yarrol run was tendered and first rent paid in 1854, too late for the lessees to have purchased indentured Chinese labour, although Ridler and Thorne had previously leased Durah, a run on the southern side of Burrandowan where there may have been Amoy men. Tan Chan's name appears in various forms in station books, newspaper accounts and official records, even in the Wade-Giles form of Tshan Shan, which suggests that he was studying the English language and experimenting with an equivalent transliteration of his name. In the Yarrol ledger, his name was entered as Channa. Eventually his name was formally recorded as Dan Channer. Archival details courtesy of Carole Channer.
26 T. A. Coghlan devotes a chapter to "The Crisis in Queensland During 1866" in *Labour and Industry in Australia*, vol. II, pp. 1168-85.
27 Walker, p. 105.
28 *Ibid.*, p. 106 and p. 161.
29 C. Y. Choi, *Chinese Migration and Settlement in Australia*, p. 30.
30 Walker, p. 89.
31 BA, 23 November 1863.
32 BA, 6 April 1866, from correspondent's report dated 29 March.
33 MC, 26 March 1868 and *Brisbane Courier*, 21 February 1871.
34 MC, 26 March 1868, from special correspondent's report dated 21 March 1868.
35 BA, 28 November 1868.
36 By 1867, Robert Ridler had the sole interest in Yarrol.
37 BA, 12 June 1869.
38 BA, 24 July 1869.
39 MC, 11 January 1870, and the *Brisbane Courier*, 11 February 1870, reprinted from the *Melbourne Argus*, 2 February 1870.
40 *Mount Perry Mail* (MPM), 30 October 1873.
41 MC, 18 June 1874, reprinted from the *Brisbane Courier*.

42 Tin Kat was fined in the Gayndah Police Court in 1863 for participating in a group assault on another Chinese man. See BA, 28 April 1863.

43 BA. 28 August 1869.

44 Mervyn Royle, *Perry's Past: A Centenary History of Perry Shire* (Mt Perry: Perry Shire Council, 1980).

45 *Ibid.*, p. 40

46 *Ibid.*, p. 23.

47 *Ibid.*, p. 40.

48 *Ibid.*, p. 41.

49 BA, 1 August 1868.

50 MC, 1 April 1869.

51 MC, 6 April 1869.

52 MPM, 31 July 1873.

53 *Ibid.*

54 Royal Commission into Alleged Chinese Gambling and Immorality, p. 28.

55 C. Y. Choi, p. 30.

56 Cathie May, *Topsawyers*, p. 112.

57 MPM, 25 June 1874.

58 *Ibid.*

59 Mervyn Royle, *Perry's Past*, p. 102.

60 MPM, 16 July 1874.

61 *Ibid.* At the same time, Ah Soy sold his interest in the garden near Martin's Sawmill to Mah Hing.

62 MPM, 7 October 1875 and MC, 7 March 1876.

63 BA, 26 September 1868.

64 Editorial, BA, 26 September 1868.

65 MPM, 29 July 1875.

66 MPM, 14 October 1875.

67 MPM, 11 November 1875.

Chapter 12

1 Apart from the already cited works, for historical patterns of Chinese migration see Wang Gungwu, *China and the Chinese Overseas* (Singapore: Times Academic Press, 1991).

2 J. Dundas Crawford, p. 3.

3 *Ibid.*, p. 5.

4 Dorothy Jones, *Hurricane Lamps and Blue Umbrellas: the story of Innisfail and the Shire of Johnstone North Queensland* (Cairns: G. K. Bolton Printers, 1973), and Barry McGowan, "Adaptation and Organization: The History and Heritage of the Chinese in Western New South Wales, Australia", 2007.

5   BA, 20 April 1867.
6   MPM, 29 July 1875.
7   MC, 10 January 1874.
8   J. Dundas Crawford, "Notes … on Chinese Immigration in the Australian Colonies", p. 3.
9   Details of Thomas Ashney's life are courtesy of the Gayndah Historical Society.
10   "Memorials or applications for certificate of naturalization", Col/A9-60/2105, Qld State Archives.
11   "Oath taken obtaining a Certificate of Naturalization", No. 46. Qld State Archives.
12   BA, 20 April 1867.
13   *Ibid.*
14   MC, 26 March 1868.
15   John Uhr/Ure was naturalized in Maryborough in 1863 and in his memorial he described himself as a shepherd, native of Amoy, aged 29. Maxine Darnell notes that in 1855, post-indenture, he worked for Murray Prior on Hawkwood station in the western Burnett. Prior had moved his flocks from Logan River, south of Brisbane to Hawkwood in late 1854, but it is not known whether Uhr had served his indenture with Prior or somewhere else.
16   MC, 12 June 1873.
17   MC, 13 July 1875.
18   Details of John Deian's life are courtesy of the Gayndah Historical Society
19   Following the death of Jemima Ashney not long after that of Ellen Deian, the child was cared for by John Chay, another successful Amoy man who was married to a European woman. He and Ashney applied for naturalisation on the same day. He took the oath of allegiance in Gayndah on 25 October 1861.
20   BA, 31 October 1868. There are no records for Ju Lock or Julop. He and Deian must have been very close for him to have lent Deian such large amounts of money, which suggests that they completed their indenture together on the same run and probably arrived in Australia together on the *Cadet.*
21   MPM, 18 September 1873. One of the executors of Deian's will was John Boyer, another Amoy man who was naturalized in Maryborough in December 1861.
22   Gayndah Bench, 25 May 1854 and MBC, 8 July 1854.
23   In the station wages book, Tan Chan is listed as Tan Chim and in the Store Account as Tan Jan.
24   MBFP, 27 January and 27 April 1858.
25   MC, 3 October 1861.
26   *Ibid.*
27   MC, 10 October 1861.

28 Phil Griffiths, "Containing Discontent: Anti-Chinese Racism in the Reinvention of Angus Cameron", *Labour History*, vol. 94, May 2008, www.historycooperative. org/journals/lab/94/griffithgs.html

29 "Report of the Royal Commission on Alleged Chinese Gambling and Immorality and Charges of Bribery against Members of the Police Force appointed August 20, 1891", New South Wales Legislative Assembly Votes and Proceedings 1891-92, vol. 8. See website: www.dictionaryofsydney.org

30 Crawford, p. 7.

31 Tan Chan appeared in court as John Jan and "took the oath as administered to Christians", according to MBFP, 27 April 1858. He did not marry until 1867, so his conversion was not for the purpose of having his children baptized.

32 Crawford, p. 8.

33 MBC, 17 February 1851. Hockings pushed Gan Som off the wharf into the Brisbane River in what he called "momentary irritation".

34 MBC, 17 April 1852.

35 The MBFP, 23 August 1859, referred to him as Charles Dean, and the MBC as Charles Keen/Keane, which was in error because at the trial of Kimboo in 1860, the MBC reported the name as Dean.

36 MBC, 24 August 1859.

37 *Ibid*. Mrs Sim ran another boarding house for Chinese men in South Brisbane. See MBC, 22 December 1859.

38 Crawford, p. 10.

39 Rev. John Gerardus Fagg, *Forty Years in South China: the life of Rev. John Van Next Talmage, D.D.,* on-line edition (New York: Anson D. F. Randolph & Company Inc., 1894), p. 137.

40 Cemetery records, Mount Perry, courtesy of Pat Smith.

41 Apart from John Deian, the Gayndah Shire Cemetery Burial Register lists the graves of Ah Ching (alias Old Peter) who died at the age of 80 in January 1898; Lim Ping who died in January 1903 aged 84; and Ah Sue who died in November 1888. At least two Amoy shepherds were buried in the Eidsvold station cemetery: Kee, who died in July 1860 and another simply remembered as "Chinaman" who was buried on 13 May 1861. See Eidsvold and District Burial Register, 1850-2001.

42 Crawford, Part II, p. 29.

43 Conversation with Buddy Thompson, Boondooma Homestead, 2012.

44 Barry McGowan, "Adaptation and organization ...", wrt Martin Brennan, "Chinese Camps", NSW Legislative Assembly Votes and Proceedings 1883-84, vol. 2.

45 Cathie May, *Topsawyers*, p. 48.

46 *Ibid*., p. 52.

47   The naturalisation records do not always state the location where the oath was taken, so it is impossible to give an accurate figure.

48   The Ration Shed Museum, Cherbourg, South Burnett.

49   Guy Ramsay, "Contentious Connections: Removals, Legislation and Indigenous-Chinese Contacts", *M-C Journal*, 4, 1, February 2001, at website: http://www.media-culture.org.au/0102/connect, accessed 17 August 2009.

50   See, for example, "South Sea Islanders Marrying", MC, 13 February 1872.

51   BA, 11 February 1865.

52   MBFP, 4 January 1859.

53   One item of this kind, "Chinese morality", was reprinted in the MC from the *Australasian* in the issue of 6 March 1869.

54   MC, 1 and 8 October 1863.

55   MC, 5 March, 23 April, 26 April 1870.

56   Editorial, MC, 26 April 1870.

57   Guy Ramsay, "Contentious Connections …".

Bibliography

Books and Articles

Archer, T. and M. Wales, *Recollections of a Rambling Life* (Brisbane: Boolarong Publications, 1988.)

Attwood, Bain and S. G. Foster, eds. *Frontier Conflict: The Australian Experience*. Canberra: National Museum of Australia, 2003.

Bartley, Nehemiah. *Australian Pioneers and Reminiscences 1849-1894*. Sydney: John Ferguson in association with the Royal Australian Historical Society, 1978.

Boyce, James. *1835: The Founding of Melbourne & the Conquest of Australia*. Collingwood: Black Inc., 2011.

Bull, B., Fiona Drews and Margaret van Hennekeler. *Summer Memories through Winter Eyes*. Bundaberg, 1987.

Burnett Country Development Council. *Burnett Country: 150 Years*. Mundubbera, 1999.

Butlin, N. G. *Forming a Colonial Economy: Australia 1810-1850*. Melbourne: Cambridge University Press, 1994.

Butlin, S. J. Foundations of the Australian Monetary System 1788-1851. Sydney: Sydney University Press, 1953.

Chesneaux, Jean. Peasant Revolts in China 1840-1949. London: Thames and Hudson, 1973.

Choi, C. Y. Chinese Migration and Settlement in Australia. Sydney: Sydney University Press, 1975.

Clark, C. M. H. *Select Documents in Australian History 1851-1900*. Sydney: Angus & Robertson Publishers, 1955.

Coghlan, T. A. *Labour and Industry in Australia, vols. I and II*. Melbourne: Macmillan, 1969.

Cohen, Kay and Kenneth Wiltshire, eds. *People, Places and Policies: aspects of Queensland Government Administration 1859-1920*. St Lucia: University of Queensland Press, 1995.

Connolly, Roy. *Southern Saga*. Sydney: Dymock's Book Arcade Ltd, 1945 [1940].

Corris, Peter. *Passage Port and Plantation: A History of Solomon Islands Labour Migration 1870-1914*. Sydney: Melbourne University Press, 1973.

Crawford, J. Dundas. "Notes by Mr. Crawford on Chinese Immigration in the Australian Colonies", 1877, Great Britain Foreign Office Confidential Prints, F. O. 3742. Website: http://www.chaf.lib.latrobe.edu.au/education/history.htm

Cronin, Kathryn. *Colonial Casualties: Chinese in Early Victoria*. Melbourne: Melbourne University Press, 1982.

Crowley, Frank, ed. *A New History of Australia*. Melbourne: William Heinemann, 1974.

Darnell, Maxine. "The Chinese Labour Trade to New South Wales 1783-1853: an exposition of motives and outcomes", thesis submitted for the degree of Doctor of Philosophy of the University of New England, January 1997.

Darnell, Maxine. "Responses and Reactions to the Importation of Indentured Chinese Labourers", Working Paper Series in Economic History, University of New England, School of Economic Studies, No. 99-2, November 1999.

Darnell, Maxine. "Indentured Chinese Labourers and Employers Identified, New South Wales, 1828-1856". Website: http://www.chaf.lib.latrobe.edu.au/pdf/indentured.pdf

Diamond, Marion. *The Seahorse and the Wanderer: Ben Boyd in Australia*. Brunswick: Melbourne University Press, 1988.

Dignan, Don. *The Story of Kolan*. Brisbane: W.R. Smith & Paterson, undated.

Dorset, Shaunnagh and Ian Hunter, eds. *Law and Politics in British Colonial Thought: Transpositions of Empire*. New York: Palgrave Macmillan, 2010.

Dwight, Alan. "The Use of Indian Labourers in New South Wales," *Journal of the Royal Australian Historical Society*, September 1976.

Dwight, Alan. "South Sea Islanders in New South Wales," *Journal of the Royal Australian Historical Society*, March 1983.

Dwight, Alan. "The Chinese in New South Wales Lawcourts 1848-1854", *Journal of the Royal Australian Historical Society*, October 1987.

Emmer, P. C., ed. *Colonialism and Migration: Indentured Labour Before and After Slavery.* Comparative Studies in Overseas History. Dordecht: Martinus Nijhoff Publisher, 1986.

Evans, Raymond. *A History of Queensland.* Cambridge: Cambridge University Press, 2007.

Evans, Raymond. *Fighting Words: Writing about Race.* St Lucia: University of Queensland Press, 1999.

Evans, Raymond, Kay Saunders, Kathryn Cronin. *Race Relations in Colonial Queensland: a history of exclusion, exploitation and extermination.* St Lucia: University of Queensland Press, 1988.

Fitzgerald, John. *Big White Lie: Chinese Australians in White Australia.* Sydney: University of New South Wales Press Ltd, 2007.

Fitzgerald, Shirley. *Red Tape, Gold Scissors: the story of Sydney's Chinese.* Sydney: State Library of New South Wales Press, 2000.

French, Maurice. *A Pastoral Romance: the tribulation and triumph of squatterdom.* Toowoomba: USQ Press, 1990.

French, Maurice. *Travellers in a Landscape: Visitors' Impressions of the Darling Downs 1827-1954.* Toowoomba: USQ Press, 1994.

Gane, Leonie. *The Hungry Ghosts of Boggo Road*, second edition. Boggo Road Gaol Historical Society, 2008.

Gittins, Jean. *The Diggers from China: the story of the Chinese on the goldfields.* Melbourne: Quartet Books, 1981.

Gollan, Robin. *Radical and Working Class Politics: A Study of Eastern Australia 1850-1910.* Carlton: Melbourne University Press, 1960.

Gratus, Jack. *The Great White Lie: Slavery, Emancipation, and Changing Racial Attitudes.* New York: Monthly Review Press, 1973.

Griffin, James, gen. ed. *Essays in Economic History of Australia.* Milton: The Jacaranda Press, 1967.

Hay, Douglas and Paul Craven, eds. *Masters, Servants, and Magistrates in Britain & the Empire, 1562-1955.* Chapel Hill and London: The University of North Carolina Press, 2004.

Hill, W.R.O. "Forty-five years experience in North Queensland," 1907.

Hirst, John. *Sense and Nonsense in Australian History.* Melbourne: Black Inc. Agenda, 2009.

Holthouse, Hector. *Gympie Gold.* Sydney: Harper Collins Publishers, 1973.

Johnston, W. Ross. *A Documentary History of Queensland: from reminiscences, diaries, parliamentary papers, newspapers, letters and photographs.* St Lucia: University of Queensland Press, 1988.

Jones, Dorothy. *Hurricane Lamps and Blue Umbrellas: the story of Innisfail and the Shire of Johnstone North Queensland*. Cairns: G. K. Bolton Printers, 1973.

Jupp, James, ed. *The Australian people: an encyclopedia of the nation, its people and their origins*. Cambridge: Cambridge University Press, 2001.

Keay, John. *China: A History*. London: HarperPress, 2008.

Keay, John. *Empire's End: a history of the Far East from high colonialism to Hong Kong*. New York: Scriber, 1997.

Kercher, Bruce. *An Unruly Child: A History of Law in Australia*. St Leonards: Allen & Unwin Pty Ltd, 1995.

Knox, Bruce, ed. *The Queensland Years of Robert Herbert, Premier: letters and papers*. St Lucia: University of Queensland Press, 1977.

Lippmann, Lorna. *Words or Blows: Racial Attitudes in Australia*. Harmondsworth: Penguin, 1973.

Loos, Noel. *Invasion and Resistance: Aboriginal-European Relations on the North Queensland Frontier 1861-1897*. Canberra: Australian National University Press, 1982.

Lord Olivier. *White Capital and Coloured Labour*. London: The Hogarth Press, 1929.

Lorwin, Lewis L. *Labour and Internationalism*. London: George Allen & Unwin Ltd, 1929.

Lovell, Julia. *The Opium War: Drugs, Dreams and the Making of China*. Basingstoke: Picador, 2011.

Markus, Andrew. *Fear and Hatred: purifying Australia and California 1850-1901*. Sydney: Hale and Iremonger, 1979.

Matthews, Tony. *This Dawning Land*. Spring Hill: Boolarong Publications, 1986.

May, Cathie. *Topsawyers: the Chinese in Cairns 1870 to 1920*. Studies in North Queensland History No. 6. Townsville: James Cook University, 1984.

McGowan, Barry. "Adaptation and Organization: The History and Heritage of the Chinese in Western New South Wales, Australia", 2007. Website:http://goliath.ecnext.com/coms2/gi_0199_6406890/Adaptation-and-organization-the-history.html

Metcalf, Bill. *The Gayndah Communes*. Rockhampton: Central Queensland University Press, 1998.

Moore, Barrington Jr. *Social Origins of Dictatorship and Democracy: Lord and Peasant in the Making of the Modern World*. Harmondsworth: Peregrine Books, 1977.

Moore, Clive, ed. *The Forgotten People: a history of the Australian South Sea Island community.* Sydney: The Australian Broadcasting Commission, 1979.

Moore, Clive, Jacqueline Leckie and Doug Munro. *Labour in the South Pacific.* Townsville: James Cook University, 1990.

Moses, A. Dirk, ed. *Genocide and Settler Society: frontier violence and stolen indigenous children in Australian History.* New York: Berghahn Books, 2004.

Murphy, J. E. and Easton, E. W. *Wilderness to Wealth: Being a History of the Shires of Nanango, Kingaroy, Wondai, Murgon, Kilkivan and the Upper Yarraman Portion of the Rosalie Shire.* Brisbane: W.R. Smith & Paterson Pty Ltd, 1950.

Nield, Robert. *The China Coast: Trade and the First Treat Ports.* Hong Kong: Joint Publishing [H. K.] Co. Ltd., 2010.

Northrup, David. *Indentured Labor in the Age of Imperialism, 1834-1922.* New York: Cambridge University Press, 1995. O'Sullivan, Doreen. *Gayndah on the Burnett.* Toowoomba: self-publisher, 1995.

Pan, Lynn, gen. ed. *The Encyclopedia of the Chinese Overseas*, second edition. Singapore: Editions Didier Millet, 2006.

Petrie, Constance Campbell. *Tom Petrie's Reminiscences of Early Queensland.* Hawthorn, Australia: Lloyd O'Neil Pty Ltd, 1975.

Polanyi, Karl. *The Great Transformation: The Political and Economic Origins of Our Time.* Beacon Hill: Beacon Press, 1957 [1944].

Redford, Arthur. *Labour Migration in England, 1800-1850.* Manchester University Press, 1926.

Reece, R. H. W. *Aborigines and Colonial Society in New South Wales in the 1830s and 1840s.* Sydney: Sydney University Press, 1974.

Reid, Gordon. *'That unhappy race': Queensland and the Aboriginal Problem 1838-1901.* Melbourne: Australian Scholarly Publishing, 2006.

Reynolds, Henry. *Frontier: Reports from the edge of white settlement.* St Leonards: Allen & Unwin Pty Ltd, 1987.

Reynolds, Henry. *The Other Side of the Frontier: Aboriginal resistance to the European invasion of Australia.* Ringwood: Penguin, 1982.

Reynolds, Henry. *The Law of the Land.* Ringwood: Penguin Books Australia, 1987.

Reynolds, Henry, ed. *Race Relations in North Queensland.* Townsville: James Cook University, 1978.

Rolls, Eric. *Sojourners: the epic story of China's centuries-old relationship with Australia*. St Lucia: University of Queensland Press, 1992.

Rolls, Eric. *A Million Wild Acres*. Camberwell: Penguin Books Australia, 1984.

Rosser, Bill. *Up Rode the Troopers: the black police in Queensland*. St Lucia: University of Queensland Press, 1990.

Rowley, C. D. *The Destruction of Aboriginal Society*. Harmondsworth: Penguin, 1972.

Royle, Mervyn. *Perry's Past: a centenary history of Perry Shire*. Mt Perry: Perry Shire Council, 1980.

Said, Edward W. *Culture & Imperialism*. London: Chatto & Windus, 1993.

Saunders, Kay. *Workers in Bondage: the origins and bases of unfree labour in Queensland 1824-1916*. St Lucia: University of Queensland Press, 1982.

Skinner, L. E. *Police of the Pastoral Frontier*. St Lucia: University of Queensland Press, 1975.

Slack, Jill. *Then and Now: an Aboriginal history of Gayndah*. Gayndah: Gayndah Orange Festival Committee Inc., 1997.

Slocomb, Margaret. "The Harris Case: the Murder of an Aboriginal man by the Native Police in the Burnett District, 1863", *Journal of Australian Colonial History*, vol. 13, 2011.

Smith, Babette. *Australia's Birthstain: the startling legacy of the convict era*. Crows Nest: Allen & Unwin, 2008.

Souter, Gavin. *Lion and Kangaroo: the initiation of Australia*. Melbourne: Text Publishing Co., 1976.

Spence, Jonathan D. *The Search for Modern China*, second edition. New York: W. W. Norton & Company, 1999.

Spence, Jonathan. *God's Chinese Son: The Taiping Heavenly Kingdom of Hong Xiuquan*. London: Harper Collins, 1996.

Spence, Jonathan. *To Change China: Western Advisers in China 1620-1960*. Harmondsworth: Penguin, 1980.

Stanner, W. E. H. *The Dreaming & Other Essays*. Melbourne: Black Inc. Agenda, 2009.

Stevens, F. S. ed. *Racism: the Australian experience, vol. 1 prejudice and xenophobia*, second edition. Brookvale: Australia & New Zealand Book Co. Pty Ltd, 1974.

Tavan, Gwenda. *The long, slow death of White Australia*. Melbourne: Scribe Publications, 2005.

Walker, Jan. *Jondaryan Station: the relationship between pastoral capital and pastoral labour 1840-1890*. St Lucia: University of Queensland Press, 1988.

Wang Gungwu. *China and the Chinese Overseas*. Singapore: Times Media Private Limited, 1991.

Wang Singwu. *The Organization of Chinese Emigration 1848-1888: With Special Reference to Chinese Emigration to Australia*. San Francisco: Chinese Materials Center, Inc., 1978.

Ward, Russel. *The Australian Legend*. Melbourne: Oxford University Press, 1978.

Wawn, William T. *The South Sea Islanders and the Queensland Labour Trade*. Canberra: Australian National University Press, 1973. Pacific History Series No. 5, edited by Peter Corris.

Waterson, D. B. *Squatter, Selector, and Storekeeper: A History of the Darling Downs 1859-93*. Sydney: Sydney University Press, 1968.

Willard, Myra. *History of the White Australia Policy to 1920*. Melbourne: Melbourne University Press, 1923.

Wise, Michael. *Travellers' Tales of the South China Coast: Hong Kong, Canton, Macao*. Singapore: Marshall Cavendish Editions, 2008.

Wolf, Eric R. *Europe and the people without history*. Berkeley: University of California Press, 1982.

Wolf, Eric R. *Peasants*. Englewood Cliffs: Prentice Hall, 1966.

Xu Guoqi. *Strangers on the Western Front: Chinese Workers in the Great War*. Cambridge, Mass.: Harvard University Press, 2011.

Yarwood, A. T. *Attitudes to Non-European Immigration*. Stanmore: Cassell Australia Limited, 1968.

Yen Ching-Hwang. *Coolies and Mandarins: China's Protection of Overseas Chinese during the Late Ch'ing Period (1851-1911)*. National University of Singapore: Singapore University Press, 1985.

Newspapers and Periodicals

Burnett Argus
Empire
Maryborough Chronicle
Mount Perry Mail
Moreton Bay Free Press
Moreton Bay Courier (Courier, Brisbane Courier)

New South Wales Government Gazette
People's Advocate and New South Wales Vindicator

Parliamentary Papers

"Report from the Select Committee on Asiatic Labor", New South Wales Legislative Council *Votes and Proceedings* 1854, vol. 2.

"Report from the Select Committee on Murders by the Aborigines on the Dawson River together with the Proceedings of the Committee, Minutes of Evidence and appendix", New South Wales Legislative Assembly *Votes and Proceedings* 1858, pp. 843-909.

"Chinese Immigration Bill" tabled 1 September 1858, *Journal of New South Wales Legislative Council* 1868, vol. 3.

"Report from the Select Committee on the Native Police Force and the condition of the Aborigines generally", Queensland Legislative Assembly *Votes and Proceedings* 1861, pp. 389-564.

"Despatch respecting Asiatic Labor", Queensland Legislative Council, 1861.

"Report of the Select Committee on the General Question of Polynesian Labor", Queensland Legislative Assembly, 1876.

"Report of the Royal Commission on Alleged Chinese Gambling and Immorality and Charges of Bribery against Members of the Police Force appointed August 20, 1891", Sydney 1892. Website: http://www.dictionaryofsydney.org

Archival Sources

Boondooma Station Correspondence Record, John Oxley Library, OM66-7/F2 (Box 8614)

Boondooma Station Wages Book, John Oxley Library, OM66-7 (Box 8614)

Booubyjan Station Wages Book, 1854-60, 1865-69, John Oxley Library, OM76-6B (Box 8953)

"Index to Coloured Labour Asiatic Aliens in Queensland 1913", Queensland State Archives, Item ID 862496 (also online)

Record Book of the Court of Petty Sessions Gayndah 30 October 1850 to 19 October 1859, Queensland State Archives, A/487

Index